LIVING IN INTERESTING TIMES:

A MEMOIR

Gabriele Neuhäuser Scott

ISBN: 978-1-63490-879-5

Published by BookLocker.com, Inc., Bradenton, Florida.

Printed on acid-free paper.

BookLocker.com, Inc.
2015

First Edition

TABLE OF CONTENTS

LIST OF ILLUSTRATIONS

GRUMACH FAMILY

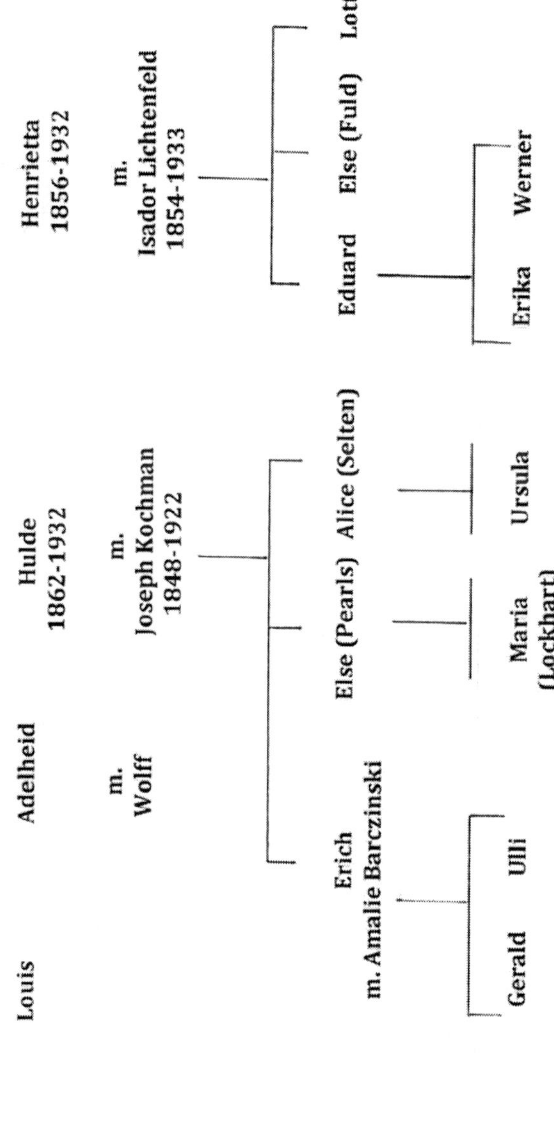

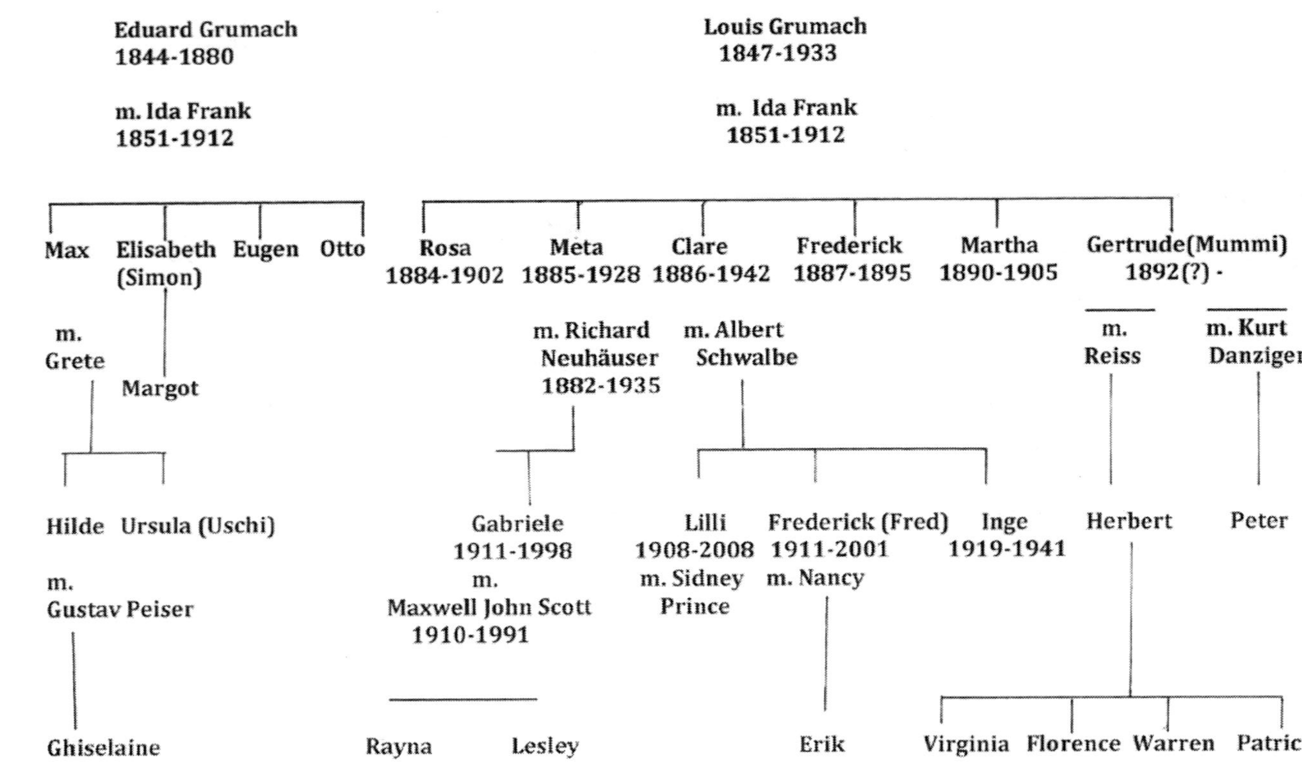
Grumachs : Eduard and Louis
Eduard Grumach
1844-1880
m. Ida Frank
1851-1912
Louis Grumach
1847-1933
m. Ida Frank
1851-1912
Max
Elisabeth
(Simon)
Eugen
Otto
Rosa
1884-1902
Meta
1885-1928
Clare
1886-1942
Frederick
1887-1895
Martha
1890-1905
Gertrude(Mummi)
1892(?) -
m.
Grete
Margot
m. Richard
Neuhäuser
1882-1935
m. Albert
Schwalbe
m.
Reiss
m. Kurt
Danziger
Hilde
Ursula (Uschi)
m.
Gustav Peiser
Gabriele
1911-1998
m.
Maxwell John Scott
1910-1991
Lilli
1908-2008
m. Sidney
Prince
Frederick (Fred)
1911-2001
m. Nancy
Inge
1919-1941
Herbert
Peter
Ghiselaine
Rayna
Lesley
Erik
Virginia
Florence
Warren
Patricia

INTRODUCTION

"May you live in interesting times."
Apocryphal Chinese curse.

While working on the manuscript of Gabriele Neuhäuser Scott, my goal throughout has been to retain her voice, but since she typed as ideas came to her, I have divided some sentences in two, or modified punctuation. Sometimes she wrote of the same occurrence or recollection twice, and in these cases I kept the one that seemed the best fit for a particular section. I have made minor grammatical changes and corrected some spellings. My own interpolations are indicated in square brackets and italics.

Memory is a slippery business. Gabriele had an extraordinary recall of names and places, even places that she had visited briefly perhaps sixty years or more earlier. However, impressions, feelings, and interpretations, are subjective. This is her story, so I didn't rewrite it even when my sister or I remember things differently. I did omit a few recollections, because not everything needs to be remembered. Where her memories of people seem less than complimentary, I have mostly left what she wrote. Here she was not always right and later she would realise this, as for example, surviving cousins became good friends in later years.

Towards the end of her remarkable life, Gabriele had many friends who valued her intelligence, her generosity, and her ability to remember their stories. She said once to me, "I used to be neurotic, but I'm not any more. I'm never bored, and I'm never lonely." She contemplated death without fear, and was an active participant in life until the day she died.

Rayna Patton, 2015

CHILDHOOD

I was born in my parents' flat, not in my mother's bedroom, as her bed was far too wide, but in the next room, which later became my room. At that time the walls were papered with white paper, alternate matt and shiny stripes, and my aunt Mummi had sent along a huge arrangement of branches of flowering almonds. My mother had a difficult instrument birth and said the things she always connected with my birth were the pink of the almond blossoms, the blue sky, and the strains of Sinding's *Rustle of Spring*, which was being played in the restaurant on the ground floor of our building.

My mother could not feed me and I took badly to feeding with cow's milk, so I ended up with what was then fairly common, a wet nurse. These were women who had either lost their own babies, or weaned them early to earn the money. They acted as nannies as well as breastfeeding their charges. There was a region east of Berlin of swampy country inhabited by a Slavic minority called Wends, and they were supposed to make the best wet nurses (Spreewälder Ammen). However, mine wasn't one of these.

Our flat was probably at least twice the size, if not more, of an Australian house. The front door opened into a hall, which itself was quite a good-sized room. It had a screen dividing the entrance part and on this and the walls were lots of pictures my parents had bought. I don't think they were very good at guessing which would be of permanent value; actually I can't remember one that was terribly good. My mother's artist friends did some, and I remember a terrible portrait of my mother in which her complexion was a sickly shade of green. This painter, Erich Waske, later became involved with a pseudo Eastern religious sect called Masdasnan, and my mother got quite interested in this as well, and once took me to a country place they had. The diet consisted of raw vegetables and nuts; there were grinders on several walls where one could grind up hazelnuts, which I rather enjoyed. This Waske ended up in a mental home suffering from religious mania, and I often wondered whether he went mad through belonging to that sect, or whether he joined it because he was already unbalanced.

The hall had a door to the left as one came in from the front door that opened into my day nursery, and that had a balcony overlooking the small

Bayerischer Platz 1 in Schöneberg
The building was destroyed during the war.

park (Bayerischer Platz). Another door opened into the music room, and this was in line with a library, and then a dining room. All these rooms were enormous, the music room fairly bare of furniture, with some sofas and easy chairs covered in black velvet along the walls, a small music cupboard, and a Steinway concert grand piano. The floor of all the main rooms was parquetry, which used to be waxed with a very heavy kind of polisher, and in the music room there was just one bearskin on the otherwise bare floor.

The library had wall-to-wall carpeting with Persian rugs here and there, and enough bookcases round the wall to keep my parents' library of about 5000 books. The walls were heavily paneled with carved wood and lead-lighted windows and the furniture consisted of three genuine old leather covered easy chairs, a huge Caucasian walnut desk with dozens of drawers (even a secret drawer) and a small coffee table. There were the usual leather covered sets of complete works of all the classics, including Shakespeare, which in its wonderful translation has become part of German literary heritage. There was also a large Bible from early in the 17th century, leather covered, with metal edges and with a metal hinge which could be locked.

The next room was the dining room, in contrast furnished in modern style with table and chairs also of Caucasian walnut, with highly patterned root wood put into panels at the backrest. Also there was a huge sideboard which contained the good china, the main dinner set being a set for twenty-four people of the traditional Limoges with a wide deep blue stripe and a narrow one of inlaid gold, in this case a continuous wreath of leaves. Silver too (not silver-plated, of course) for twenty-four people, all with my father's initials engraved on the handles, and with such interesting things as gadgets for opening oysters and for getting the meat out of crayfish legs. The china included such things as soup tureens and sauceboats, and there were several sets of crystal plates for sweets as well as other items of more valuable china, some hanging on the wall. Several drawers in the sideboard were taken up with lace and embroidery table centres, napkins, etc., and of course all the tablecloths were white damask, as were the table napkins. Plates were never put directly on the tablecloth, there was a plate at every seat, with a doily on it, and the plates for the food were put on this. What I liked best of all was a miniature silver tea set with teapot, milk and sugar containers, and cups, the whole on a tray only about 12" by 6”. There was also a glass cabinet on the other wall, with glasses for every kind of wine and liqueur. At a more advanced age I was taught just what glasses were used for which kind of wine, but when younger I used to enjoy my father taking one of the glasses and knocking it against others, playing various tunes.

These three main rooms were all separated by very wide sliding glass doors, and when my parents gave a party the doors were opened and the three rooms made into one enormous one. The carpet in the dining room was one of my favourites, a Tabriz with a soft grey blue ground colour. I much preferred this to the other Persian rugs that were predominately red.

The back entrance to the dining room was just an ordinary size door and not too far from the kitchen. This was particularly useful when Bombe Alaska was served. This was homemade ice cream made into an igloo shape and covered with a hot meringue, which was sprinkled with rum and set alight just before serving. I remember watching cook and the maid standing outside the dining room door and the maid lighting a match and putting it to the pudding just before taking it in. This was before I had started eating with my parents.

Meta and Richard

My mother's bedroom was furnished with genuine Louis 15th furniture made from lemonwood, which looked a light reddish colour and again had panels of patterned root wood and metal hinges. I was told that two of the pieces were modern replicas, but the rest were genuine. The bed was as wide as it was long, and there was a dressing table with hinged mirrors, five panels in all, so one could see one's sides and back when the maid did one's hair. There was also a bidet, which I enjoyed, but which was never used to my knowledge. I was allowed to come into my mother's bed for a while in the morning, but generally she was talking on the phone for ages, quite often to Hilde Grumach's mother, which I found boring, so I would pick up a book and start reading. This is how I came to read Van de Velde's *The Ideal Marriage*, which was all about the different positions for doing sexual intercourse, and really didn't interest me. When some years later the girls at my high school started giggling about this book I said: "That! I read that years ago and didn't think much of it."

My father's room was furnished in very dark wood, with darkish green walls. The most interesting thing in it for me was his collection of china dogs and other animals; I note that some, as the Royal Copenhagen polar bears, are still being made. There was also another stand with his Japanese collection, which he brought back from his sojourn in that country in the early days of the 20th century. I particularly liked some figures carved from ivory, one was a water carrier with two buckets hanging from a pole across his shoulder, the other a turtle seller, the basket had come open and some of the turtles were clambering out of it and one was on his arm.

Gabriele as a toddler

The main bathroom was next to this bedroom and had one door opening into it as well as another opening into the back hallway that divided the family's bedrooms from the smaller maids' rooms on the other side. The main bathroom had a set-in Roman bath and was all tiled, floor, bath, walls and all. One time when I was about ten my father let in the hot water before having a bath, with the result that the room steamed up and the tiles got very slippery. He fell in and badly scalded his legs, and I remember being sent for the doctor and running very hard to get there quickly. I got some praise for this, actually. There was a toilet in this bathroom, another bathroom and toilet, much plainer, for the maids, and another toilet that I normally used just at the front end of the front hallway, near the door to the entrance hall. There was a long narrow balcony also right along the side of the flat but nothing was ever done with this, whereas the front balcony had plant boxes which were filled with red geraniums or purple petunias in season by street sellers, who came up to take the old plants away and plant the new ones already big enough to flower. It was always my wish to do some gardening and much later I persuaded my mother to let me try with the window boxes. However, I picked completely unsuitable things like sweet peas, and had no luck at all. The kitchen was large with a long range sticking right out into the room. It was a gas stove, which was then very modern, though there was also still a coal range. I wasn't often allowed into the kitchen, as my mother said the cook didn't want to be bothered with me, and it was a special privilege when I was allowed to come and do something like chopping the parsley or shelling the peas. I do remember once when I was very young, sneaking into the kitchen, seeing a wooden board with rissoles all ready to cook and starting to play with the raw meat mixture, squeezing it between my fingers. The cook came in and caught me and smacked me hard on the hands; this must have made a great impression, as I was very young at the time.

When I graduated from the wet nurse my mother employed a nursemaid for me. She was a good-hearted woman and very fond of me, but spoiled me terribly. I remember being dressed up in frilly flounce muslin dresses which I hated, being taken for a walk and sitting down deliberately in the first muddy puddle I came to. She would just laugh and take me home to get changed. When I was nearly five my mother decided I must get a proper "Fräulein" (governess), she felt that not only was I being spoiled but also this woman had a very loud voice and laugh and my mother felt this was a bad influence on me. I am sure she was quite right, as even now I tend to talk too loudly, in spite of being told for most of my childhood that a lady never raises her voice.

My first Fräulein was a young girl in deep mourning who had just lost her mother and she must have been very poor, because I remember the servants saying that she never put her underclothes in the wash, and it turned out she only had the one lot and nothing to change into.

I taught myself to read from an illustrated ABC book when I was about four. This is much easier in German, because every consonant, vowel and diphthong has the same sound in every word in the language. I still remember the page with I, on the top a rooster sitting on a fence saying Kikiriki (this is what the German roosters say instead of cock-a-doodle-doo) and the bottom a hedgehog, which in German is Igel. The I of course sounds like the English ee.

I was a solitary child, being the only one. My mother became pregnant again when I was about three, but, though she went to several specialists, she was told that she and the child would die if she went ahead with the pregnancy, as she had contracted TB (almost certainly she was infected as a child) and this had flared up. So eventually she had to have an abortion. She then was sent to the balmy climate of Lago Maggiore to avoid the Northern winter and recuperate, and made a good recovery.

When I was quite young, about three, I went through a phase of walking up to smaller children in the park and pushing them over. Rather than sending me to a kindergarten to learn how to get on with others, my mother decided I was not safe to be among other children and kept me strictly isolated from them. Occasionally I was taken shopping with my mother. I did not much enjoy this. Often my mother would meet acquaintances, and after having dutifully curtsied I had to just stand and listen to uninteresting conversations. Then my mother would look at length in shops selling dresses, hats, and gloves, and pull me away when I wanted to stop and look at pet shops or florists. However, it always ended with a visit to a cafe, usually Kranzlers, and a treat of being given fresh bread-and-butter and two soft-boiled eggs in a glass. The glass was put into a stand of decorative metalwork, and I was allowed to dunk bits of the bread into the eggs.

From an early age I suffered from frequent attacks of tonsillitis with quite often very high temperatures. Once I must have been really sick (possibly when I had whooping cough) and had a night nurse, who was a

Catholic nun. In those days nuns used to shave their heads, and I woke up during the night and raised the house with my screams when I saw what seemed to be a man sitting by my bed; she had taken off her headdress. Again the ordeal ended with a treat. When I had recovered and just before I was allowed to get up, I was given a meal of squab (I could pick whether I wanted this braised with mashed potatoes and gravy or boiled with rice). My very first memory is lying in a cot with my arms tied to the top of it. My mother told me that this happened when I was less than a year old and had chicken pox, and it was done so I wouldn't scratch and scar my face.

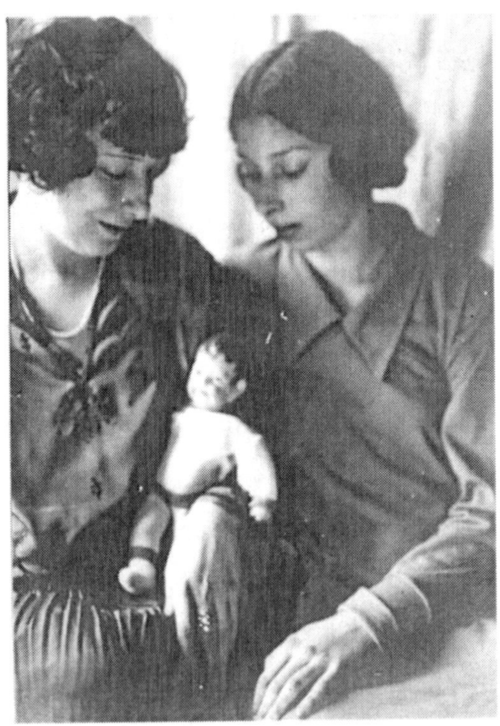

Meta and Gabriele

My mother was always very disappointed because I didn't care for dolls; she had loved them as a child. I was given lots of them, some very beautiful, but never had the imagination to play with them successfully. I was far more interested in living things, flowers or animals. I had a very nice Käthe Kruse doll. Probably this would be quite valuable as a collector's item these days. It had a stuffed cloth body with moveable arms and legs, and a head made from metal covered with cloth painted to look really lifelike. Mine was a boy doll called Luit Matten with lederhosen and all. My mother once told me that he had complained to her that I neglected him and never played with him. I rushed off and she thought she had made an impression. Within a minute I returned and said, "I just asked him and he said you told fibs and he never said any such thing." I don't remember this event, my mother told me about it.

I started school at five. Both my parents had very much disliked their conventional schools, so they picked for me an experimental school, the Berthold Otto School in Lichterfelde. Berthold Otto, whom I remember as a very old man with a little black cap on his white hair, had the theory that children have a natural wish to learn, which is killed by normal methods of teaching. In his school the children voted whether they wanted to have lessons or play, and unfortunately he had quite a few pupils who had come there from other schools and been already ruined for his ideas, as well as a few mentally retarded children and other misfits. So much of the time was spent in play, and with my uselessness at sport and general shyness and inability to mix with other children, I spent most of my time reading.

Berthold Otto himself was a scholar and he taught a couple of White Russians to prepare them for university entrance. There were only three divisions, beginners, juniors, and middle school. Though I hated the place I stayed there until I was thirteen. I never got out of the junior class, which was taught by Berthold Otto's daughter Irene. The middle school had a proper teacher, who had taught in conventional schools, and I believe they actually did learn things, but when I once applied for admission to this it was put to the vote of the pupils, and not being popular I was rejected. The school was a long way from my home. It entailed walking across the (Bayerischer Platz) park, waiting for one tram to go just two stops, then crossing a road and waiting for another tram which only went about every twenty minutes, and then a walk of twenty minutes to the school from the tram stop, a journey of over an hour each way.

When I first started school, my Fräulein used to take me, wait there and take me home. One day we were walking to the tram stop on the way home, when the tram approached. Fräulein promptly started to run for it, and I ran after her, and managed to get one arm and one foot onto the tram just as it moved off. A man standing on the platform pulled me up and actually took me home, where he told my mother what had happened, and the hapless Fräulein promptly got sacked. The next governess was a much older experienced woman, who, when she was in a good mood used to tell me about some of her previous charges. However, she used to hit me and tell me that I would get much worse if I dared to tell my mother. I don't know how my mother came to guess, but eventually she questioned me till I admitted it, and another governess bit the dust. In fact I never saw her again after that talk with my mother. She rather heaped coals of fire on my head by sending me *Heidi of the Alps* as a goodbye present, which I loved and which remained my favourite for quite a while. This was just the first volume that ends with Heidi being sent back to her grandfather from Frankfurt, and I was thrilled when a couple of years later I finally got the second volume that showed how it all ended.

There were very few children's books in my childhood days. Apart from *Heidi* there was a very poor translation of *Alice in Wonderland, Pinocchio,* a French classic called *Nobody's Boy* by Hector Malot, *The Wonderful Journey of Nils* by Selma Lagerlöf, children's editions of *Robinson Crusoe* and *Gulliver's Travels,* and numerous books of fairy tales and myths and legends.

There existed also at that time children's annuals and little moral tales like Uncle Arthur's bed-time tales, as well as some lighter reading, which however my mother didn't really approve of. I remember Hilde Grumach lending me volumes of a long series called *Nesthäkchen,* starting off with *Baumeister's Rangen,* with roughly translates as the Builder's rascals and dealt with a family of two boys and a small girl, the baby of the family, who got into various not very serious bits of strife. This went on and on with her growing up, having children, and later grandchildren of her own. Her grandchildren were girls, brought up in the Argentine, and one was dark with blue eyes, the other blond with brown eyes, which I thought very romantic, and for years I planned to have daughters with that colouring myself. Another book I liked was called the *Family Fläffling,* about a music teacher with seven children. It started off with all the children going about the district trying to find a rented place where the owner wouldn't object to all the children. Eventually they found a place and nearly lost it, because the two eldest boys camped in the backyard to watch a meteor stream that was expected that night, the landlord thought they had been out with bad company but relented when he found the truth of the matter. There was one boy, Frieder, who was a musical genius and kept getting into trouble for forgetting to do things when he played the violin, so eventually his father confiscated it for a year and taught him piano instead. Sadly he never achieved very much, not having the right personality for a concert player. This too had various sequels as the children grew up. Somewhat later I came across Felix Dahn's *The Fight for Rome*, all about the Goths, who were highly romanticized, starting with the death of Theodoric the Great, and ending with the Goths being finally defeated by the general of Justinian of the Eastern Roman Empire based in Constantinople. The book ended with the remnants of the Goths gathered on the crater of Mt. Vesuvius and just in the nick of time being rescued by a boat arriving from Iceland (Thule), but the hero leader and his girlfriend jumped into the crater. I loved this so much that I practically knew all three fat volumes by heart. Another book I remember was all about the adventures of an Easter bunny, who was made into a little boy by magic and sent into the human world to learn how to make more attractive Easter eggs, and so preserve the life of the clan. He had innumerable adventures and eventually returned safely just ahead of the wicked fairy that kept trying to stop him, and showed how chocolate eggs were made.

Being a voracious and very fast reader, I once tried to slow myself down by reading books upside down, but found after a few weeks that I could read just as quickly that way. I also raided my parents' library, reading most of the classics (often only until the heroes grew up.) For example the only Dickens I read right through was *Oliver Twist*, the others I threw away when the heroes grew up and fell in love. I read forty volumes of an unexpurgated *Arabian Nights*, and loved the stories as fantasy, the sexual parts passed right over my head at that age. There were public libraries in Berlin at that time, but even when older I was not allowed to go there, as my mother was afraid I would pick up fleas.

To return for a moment to earlier childhood, I remember the weekly markets held on the market place in front of the Schöneberg Rathaus (apparently still going). Most of the stall holders came in from the country with produce, live poultry, and so on and I felt sorry for the chickens, which were tied together by the legs in bundles of six or so. There were also stalls with fish, which sold live crayfish and oysters, and of course flowers. At Christmas time there were Christmas markets along some of the streets with stalls of various Christmassy things, wooden carved angels, Christmas tree decorations, Christmas bakeries and sweets, novelties and inexpensive toys for Christmas stockings, and always at one end Christmas trees for sale – these were cut fir trees ranging in size from tiny to enormous, and I loved going with my mother and some servants to pick our tree for the year. The salesman would open up the tree and shake it out and turn it slowly so we could see it was even and had no holes in the frame of branches. The servants then carried home the tree, which was kept in the unheated cellar until just before Christmas. Our block of apartments had two flats on each floor, with a lift, to which I was not allowed the key until I was about eleven, and a locked front door, to which I was given the key at about eight. Before that I had to ring the bell and wait for the janitor or his wife to open the door for me, which I hated doing, as they weren't exactly happy to be called out from their small ground floor flat behind the lift. We lived on the top (4th) floor, as my father said he didn't like having people walking about on his head, and though we lived there for seventeen years we never got to know any of the other tenants. The landlord had a flat on the second floor, and I used to annoy him by putting "eyes" of silver foil made into a ball into the hollows that served as eyes for the lion's head doorknocker in the middle of the front door. The people on the other fourth floor flat were minor nobility (von Kessler). He had some job in the foreign office, and they had twin daughters a few years older than I, who were always beautifully dressed in white embroidered linen dresses with pleated skirts and frilly petticoats. I remember one time when they came to my mother with some message and she asked them to sit down, one said: "We'd better not, we can't ask the servants to iron our dresses more than three times a day." After that they stopped being held up as good examples to me. The block of flats had a huge cellar right under the block, with every tenant having a small part as his private section. Ours was divided up by a kind of wooden batten fence and there were stored potatoes, apples and also my father's wines. Then there was the attic, also the size of the whole city block, which contained the laundry and was also used for drying clothes. This was reached by the back steps which opened from the kitchen, and neither the cellar nor the attic was heated, nor was the back staircase. I remember the milk (and fresh bread rolls) being left outside the kitchen door and in winter the milk quite often being completely frozen in the bottles. Washday was a big event. Each tenant had his own day, and as in Germany it was a status symbol to wash clothes as rarely as possible. Our washday was once a month. A washerwoman came in for the occasion, but all our servants were expected to help as well. As a result we always had a special washday dinner, so called Irish stew, which was a stew of mutton, potatoes, onions, cabbage, and flavoured with caraway seeds sewn in a linen rag that was fished out before service. During and just after the war, when fuel was hard to get, we had a straw box. This was a wooden box with the inside, lid and all, being thickly padded with hay or straw. The stew was brought to boil on the stove, and then while it was still boiling the pot was transferred to the box, where it kept simmering for hours without any further heat being applied. We had a special ironing room and another woman who came to do the ironing every month. There was also a sewing machine in that room, and a sewing woman came also once a month, I think, to do mending and alterations. I remember well my mother deciding that I was getting too old for my very short dresses, and asking this woman to lengthen them all. I hated the thought of that and kept wearing the ones that had not been done. Then the following month the woman arrived with the latest Vogue magazine, and pointed out to my mother that the latest fashion was for very short dresses, so I escaped ever having to wear long ones. This must have been when I was about eleven. The only thing I really remember of the First World War is another very early memory. I know we were on holidays somewhere, and a troop of light cavalry went past off to the war, with my father at the head. People were cheering and throwing flowers at the soldiers, and I felt very proud because my father was getting more flowers than the other soldiers. I can have been only three then. Actually my father did his war service at the Eastern Front, but in office work not actual fighting, I think because he had had rheumatic fever he was reclassified.

Our holidays were mostly spent at the seaside on the Baltic Sea. The Germans have strange customs on the seaside. On arrival they hire a beach chair type of thing that looks a bit like an old-fashioned bee-hive with an opening in the front, but roofed over, and usually two or three can sit inside. This is put somewhere on an empty place on the beach, and the temporary owner then makes a wall around it, a kind of castle, which when finished is decorated with either shells or little flags or similar. When I was very young, women still went bathing from bathing carts that were drawn by horses just into the water; one got in at a door on the beach side, changed inside, and then went down some steps on the seaside to do the actual bathing, reversing the process when getting out. This was so no one could see women actually shedding clothing. Bathing suits had half sleeves and legs below the knees, with the women's having a kind of skirt as well. I never cared much for the seaside, and spent much of my time walking about at the high tide mark looking among the seaweed for pretty shells or bits of amber. The local tourist shops were selling amber jewellery, and occasionally a piece with a fly or other insect was embedded in the amber, which is of course fossilized gum from drowned pine forests. I kept hoping I would find apiece good enough to make into something, but never did find more than little bits. At low tide I used to take my little bucket and go looking in the rock pools for anything alive the tide had left behind, small fish, sea stars or sea urchins, and on one occasion even a sea horse. There must have been lots of other children in those places, but I can't remember ever playing with any of them, for by that time I had become completely solitary and full of complexes. I do remember, I must have been five or six at the time, my nurse trying to get me to take part in a ring-a-ring-a roses game in the park and my hoping that the earth would open and allow me to get away underground and come out in our cellar, to get away from everyone. One of the problems was that Lichterfelde, where I went to school, was a very right wing and anti-Semitic part of Berlin and I had been abused on the way home from school, and even at school. Being so hopeless at sports didn't help. I still remember how awful it felt when the captains of two teams took turns at picking people for their side, and I was left till last and then they would say, "I had her last time, you have to take her this time." By this time I was of course shortsighted, and never could see the ball till it hit me. If I could get away with it, I would sneak off and look for field mushrooms on the edge of the playing field.

The good thing that I remember about the way home from school is that it went past one of Germany's largest cactus nurseries, where I spent many happy hours admiring the plants. There was also an empty house in a very old and overgrown garden into which I used to sneak at times, lie under a Philadelphia with my current book, and enjoy the peace and the beautiful smell of the mock orange.

At the age of five I started learning to play the piano. I was never much good or terribly interested, and had to be forced to practice, which is why I later decided not to have my children taught unless they really wanted to. Also, after my mother's first attack of TB, I was taken to a woman who made me do exercises and deep breathing. She kept threatening me with dire results if I breathed with my mouth open, and I had to spend hours trying to touch the floor with my fingers, which I never succeeded in doing. I sometimes wonder if my later back and hip troubles were in part caused by this exercise. My mother also tried to make me more graceful by sending me to a eurhythmic class, and seeing how much I was in terror of mixing with children my own age, tried to overcome this by having me join a class of young adult girls, who were really very nice to me and sort of made a pet of me. I remember one dance in which I was supposed to be a little fawn and the big girls nymphs chasing me, done to some Strauss waltz. Later on my mother tried to send me to dancing class, again I must have been ten or eleven. This was run for children of good middle class families, and the girls were told to sit on chairs along one long wall of the room, with the boys standing along the opposite wall. On a signal by the teacher the boys had to go over and ask the girls of their choice to dance. What happened of course was that the pretty and popular girls had swarms of boys descending on them, and in the end I and another girl who was very tall and had a bad case of acne were left, and two unfortunate little boys were stuck with us. Anyhow, I absolutely refused to go back after this first time. Then my mother tried a different idea and sent me to a working class dancing class, which was a bit better. In fact one young chap who was already working took a liking to me, and kept asking me to dance, leaving marks of his sweaty hands all over the back of my dress. One day he asked me if he could walk me home and I told him I was quite capable of walking home on my own, which was the end of a beautiful friendship. As with sport, I had absolutely no talent for dancing, and later always said, "I don't dance" whenever I had to go anywhere where people were dancing. (I was the one who minded the handbags).

During my childhood I nearly always had to play alone. I was terrible at sport and avoided team games, or indeed any play that required other children. There used to be seasons for certain games, for example skipping, marbles, and so on. I did some skipping on my own, also played with rubber balls, throwing them against a wall in complicated sequences, doing such things as turning round twice, or clapping my hands between throwing and catching the ball. I also had hoops, wooden rings about a meter high and a centimeter thick, painted in different colours, which were rolled along the road by hitting them with a little stick. Then there were tops, small cone shaped wooden ones with a nail at the bottom, which had to be started by winding the string of a 'whip' round them, anchoring them in a crack in the pavement and then pulling the whip quickly. They then spun along the road, and were kept going by hitting them with the whip. All these things could be used only because there was so little traffic on the roads then. I did have marbles, but as this was something usually played with other children I never got good at it, as it wasn't fun just to do on one's own. Only rarely could I find any adult who would give the time to play a game like snakes and ladders or checkers with me. I was told the way the chess pieces moved, but not having anyone to play with I didn't get any further. A bit later the scooter was invented and I tried out my cousin Hilde's one day when we visited the Grumachs. However the first thing I did was to go down a steep hill, when I promptly had a fall and skinned my knee badly.

After that my mother would never buy me one. I did have a yoyo, then a complete novelty, but never got up to doing the fancy things advanced players did. I loved blocks when I was little, both the ones covered with paper showing a different picture on each side, and the wooden ones with arches, etc., to make houses, but never did any good with the Meccano set I was given later. Another failure was a fretsaw set. I got as far as doing a very poor wooden dog I gave to my father, and which, poor man, he even put among his treasured collection for a little while, before burying it in a bottom drawer. One of my mother's friends had a son my age, very artistically gifted, who with a similar fretsaw set cut the most beautiful jewellery and ornaments out of ivory, which disheartened me even more. Another gift was a weaving kit with beads. I never used this for the purpose to which it was intended, but I did use the beads as I did the buttons from my mother's button box, pretending that they were people, the largest and most beautiful ones being, say, king and queen, small pretty ones children. I made up similar games with the beads and also marbles but buttons were definitely the best. *[A housemaid taught Gabriele to knit and to do lace knitting, which she did to the end of her life, creating amazingly intricate doilies and table centres with cotton thread of varying thickness, and very thin needles.]*

Another thing I used to like was to walk along our flat looking into a mirror held horizontally, so that one saw the ceiling. This was quite nerve-racking; even though I knew that the floor was completely level I found it hard to walk over what appeared in the mirror to be a high wall (the top of a doorway) or even worse, a long drop. This latter was in our front passage, which had an extra larder or store room under the ceiling, into which I never went, because one had to get up and down a ladder to get into it, and I had absolutely no head for heights. However, walking along the passage with a mirror and coming to the end of this hanging larder it looked just as if one had to step into a drop of six feet or so and it took a lot of willpower to do this.

I think my fear of heights went back to when I was about three and a housemaid took me to the Schöneberg Town hall, where she had an errand to do. This was on the first floor, and going down I had no handrail so I sat down and started to work myself down the long flight of stairs sitting. She told me if I didn't walk properly I would be put into jail and eventually I did, feeling terrified all the time. I do know where I got my phobia about cockroaches. Someone once gave me a drink of milk in an opaque glass, and when I got to nearly the bottom I found lots of small cockroaches drowned in it, some I swallowed and was terribly sick. I hated the things ever since, and later stayed away from a zoology lesson during which we were to dissect a cockroach.

At an early age my mother employed a young English woman to take me for walks on the afternoon and speak English to me. On wet days we just sat in the house and talked. She gave me *The Scarlet Pimpernel* to read, five pages for each time she came, but after reading about fifteen pages I got interested in the story and read it right through, ever after I could read English pretty fluently. This woman had learnt German in Saxony, which has a very peculiar accent (dialect) and spoke German with a mixture of English and Saxon accent. She told me once she was looking for a friend's flat on the board of tenants and couldn't find it. A man came by and she asked him in German if he knew where the friend lived and he answered her in English. She was very disappointed, having prided herself on speaking perfect German. My mother also tried a French woman, but I had been so indoctrinated against the French in the Berthold Otto School that I hated the language and just didn't want to learn it.

Even though we weren't Christians, Christmas was a big event in our annual calendar. It began with the Advent wreath, which was hung on the front door with four candles, a new one to be lit every Sunday before Christmas. My presents had to be something I had made myself, and I also remember making paper chains for decorations, and my mother reading aloud Dickens' *Christmas Carol*. Both my mother and father were artistically gifted, which made me resent my complete lack of talents all the more, and every year the tree and the presents were different and beautiful. I remember one year when my father had wrapped all my mother's presents in white tissue paper with a gold, red, or silver star, cut out by hand, pasted on each parcel. The tree was put in the music room and the doors to this kept strictly shut until the day. Presents were put on the sofas, which had been covered with sheets for the occasion, and each year the tree would be different, one year a natural look with small red apples and silver and gold painted walnuts, another an all white tree. There was always a fairy doll or angel right at the topmost branches, and of course real candles. We always had a goose stuffed with small apples for Christmas dinner, and on Christmas Eve we had the goose liver with onion rings, sauerkraut and mashed potatoes at lunchtime.

The actual present giving happened late in the afternoon of Christmas Eve. The sliding doors between the library, where we were all waiting, we being the domestic staff and me, would open and we would see the Christmas tree lit up in an otherwise dark room, with my mother on the piano playing and singing, "Still night, Holy Night", and us all joining in, after which we went in and looked at our presents.

I remember once when I was about six and had that rather nasty governess, she had kept on telling me that I had been so bad that when the doors opened I would not get any presents but just a large switch. So when the doors opened I started screaming, threw myself on the floor and refused to go into the room. Eventually my mother calmed me down and in fact I got a wonderful lot of presents that year, but I can still remember the terror I felt.

When I was about ten my father got rheumatic fever again and very badly. For the next two summers he and my mother went to a spa which they hoped would improve his stiff hip, and I was sent to a holiday camp for children, in the hinterland of the Baltic. The place was rather nice, with a beautiful big garden and nice countryside. I was about the oldest child there and was given a little room of my own, which was good, as we had to take a nap after lunch, and at least I could read there. The food was terrible. I particularly remember breakfast, which consisted of lumpy and often-burnt porridge, and bread and margarine. If one had one bowl of porridge one could have one slice of bread, if two bowls, two slices, and if three or more, as much bread as one wanted. We all got weighed every week and small prizes were given to the children who put on the most weight. I wanted to win this, but unfortunately always overate the day before weighing and had a bilious attack, so I had no luck. However, I did manage to win the large prize for gaining the most overall weight for the holidays, gaining five pounds. The prize for this was an excursion of the winner's choice either to an old tower on a little hill with commanding views, or to the pier at the nearest seaside resort. I was very keen to see the old tower, however the powers that be decided that the seaside trip would have more general appeal, so that's where we went, much to my disgust. Not even being bought a large seashell in which one could "hear the sea" made up for the disappointment.

I was sent to the same place again next year, and for the same reason. This time the owner, who during the rest of the year ran a farm, had a number of walnuts that still had the outer rind solidly attached to the nut instead of being dried up and easily pulled off. She asked the larger children to get this green rind off the nuts, but they all, except me, soon lost interest. As it exempted me from taking part in official games and activities, I kept on with it. I was not allowed a knife, in case I hurt myself, using some blunt biscuit cutters to do the job, which made it a lot harder. I was given three very large and completely unripe champagne pears as a reward, and told to keep them in a cool place till Christmas, when they would be delicious. My mother was far from thrilled when I returned home with my arms nearly up to the elbows stained a dark brown. In vain did she try to scrub the stain off, or bleach it with peroxide; it remained with me for ages. This is of course the stain that in folklore was used by the gypsies to disguise fair children they stole, and was quite indelible, though, as my mother had pointed out to me at an early age, why any gypsy would want to steal children, when they all had swarms of their own, didn't make sense. By the way, those three pears given to me ripened up as promised right on Christmas, but my mother suggested I give them to my father as a Christmas present. I did so rather reluctantly, and was allowed a bite of one, which was absolutely delicious.

For the second part of this holiday we went to Holland. We spent a few days in Amsterdam, where there was a special Rembrandt exhibition with paintings and drawings from all over the world lent for the occasion. I liked Rembrandt's *Man with the Gold Helmet*, also some of Frans Hals and those small interiors by Vermeer and others of his school, but after an hour or two I got tired of looking at pictures and went back out into the vestibule where I sat and did a Chinese puzzle my father had bought for me. One day my father took me to some relations who had a diamond cutting business and I was shown over the place. In the end we went back into the owner's office and he put a black velvet cloth on a table, took a small bag out of his safe and poured out dozens of large diamonds. He then asked me which one I liked best, and I said a bright yellow one, and he told me that this actually was quite an inferior one from Brazil, and that the blue-white ones from South Africa were far more valuable. I still thought the yellow one was the prettiest.

We then went on to Nordwyk, which is a few miles north of Scheveningen, but is much smaller. Each hotel, including ours, had fences running from the building down to the sea so that one could not walk along the beaches the way one could at resorts on the Baltic. There was no nice hinterland either, with woods and orchards, but just bare and uninteresting sand country. The sea itself was also disappointing, with no amber, few nice shells, and it only came to bathing height at high tide. At low tide there would be a huge stretch of wet sand going almost to the horizon. These shallow parts of the sea are of course what the Dutch have built in with dykes and made into dry land. Again I decided that I did not like seaside holidays.

The following year, again on a holiday, this time with my mother and a woman friend of hers, we were walking along an esplanade where some boys were playing soccer, and the ball flew up and hit my mother on the chest. That night she had a hemorrhage, possibly from the ball breaking up one of the old calcium encapsulated TB spots. This was the beginning of the end. I was twelve at the time, and after that my mother spent much of her time away at various sanitariums. The first winter she went to Switzerland, unfortunately during a very bad winter with blizzards and extreme cold, which didn't improve her at all. After that she went to milder places such as Lausanne above the Lake of Geneva, where I visited her at Easter time and saw the Castle of Chillon, also all the "crocodiles" of boarding school girls being marched along on walks. My mother would come home during the warmer months, and still keep up her piano playing, but could not sing. She used to say how ridiculous it was for Mimi in *La Traviata* and other opera heroines to sing long arias while dying of TB.

Eventually she went to a sanatorium in Baden-Baden, where she had a private nurse, a Grey Sister. This is a Catholic order of nurses who do not live in convents, but go out into the world. This woman occasionally took me for walks in the very beautiful parkland along the Os River, with masses of huge rhododendron bushes and lovely large trees. This was very well planned so one got different views every few steps, much use being made of trees with gold and red foliage as well as my favourites, silver birches and the European Mountain Ash. There was also a trout breeding establishment on the Os, which was quite a little river, and they had a restaurant with tanks holding the trout from tiny ones to large edible size ones. One could pick one, and it was netted out and cooked straight away, which is of course the only way to eat trout. This nurse also told me about a job she had as nurse to the small children in an American family. There she was called Miss Breimeyer, and she told me about one little boy of about four, who when she disciplined him in any way used to say "You are naughty, Miss

Meta towards the end of her life

Bee-I-myer, I don't like you."

My mother looked, if anything, more beautiful as she got worse, but unfortunately unlike most TB patients she had a good deal of pain from old adhesions. Eventually the doctors told my father that she could only live a few weeks at the most, and offered to give her an overdose of morphine, an offer he gratefully accepted. I was told about this, as I was in Berlin in school at the time. My mother died when I was nearly seventeen. She had a large funeral in the Jewish cemetery. She was never quite sure whether to believe in a hereafter or not, and told me that if it was possible to do so she would give me some sign after she died. During the service a small bird of some kind flew around the room several times, singing loudly. I remember wondering if I was wrong, that there was a hereafter, and this was the sign my mother had said she would give me, particularly as my Aunt Hulda, (Gerald's grandmother), who was a real ghoul and loved going to funerals, told me that in all her years of attending funerals she had never seen anything like it.

After my mother's death we moved to a smaller flat, *[Dahlmannstrasse 27 in Charlottenburg]* and the first cook-housekeeper having got married, we got another whose father owned a mill in a village and who had a sister just my age. She once took me home for a holiday, somehow the village school didn't have holidays at the same time, and I attended it for a couple of weeks, which was quite interesting. Come to think of it this must have been before my mother died, as village schools only took children to thirteen to fourteen. We spent quite a bit of time picking out ergot-infected seeds from the wheat (they were black and easy to see). These, if left in large numbers, would make the bread poisonous, and also brought a good price from chemists who used them as an abortifacient. I enjoyed my stay there and loved a small creek/swamp area with lots of different water lilies and water birds.

Being brought up during what in Germany was still the Edwardian age, manners played a great role in my childhood. I had to curtsey to adults, and when I started having meals with my parents had to stand with folded hands on the back of my chair, until my mother sat down. I was told at an early age how to use utensils and in which order they had to be on the table. I remember one occasion when I was perhaps seven and I dropped my table napkin from my lap onto the floor. I was about to duck under the table to pick it up, when my mother stopped me, rang her little bell, and when the housemaid came in said: "Miss Yella has dropped her napkin, will you please pick it up for her?" When I didn't behave well enough I was sent to eat with the servants as a punishment, but this backfired as I really enjoyed it. The conversation was so much more interesting and no one worried about my manners. I was not allowed to go to movie pictures, as my mother thought they were only fit for servant girls. This was in the early days of things like the *Perils of Pauline*. Later this rule was relaxed. The first picture I ever saw was *San Francisco*, later such as films as *Henry the Eighth* with Charles Laughton, and *Metropolis* by Karl Lang, which are now classics still occasionally appearing on late-night TV.

Just after the First World War there were street fights and communist riots in Berlin, and my father sent us to Munich to be out of danger. We went to a small guesthouse, and my mother's large cabin trunk with most of our clothes was lost and never turned up. My mother made friends with a couple of young Swedish music students, who told her later that everybody in the guest-house doubted the story of the lost trunk and thought we were just too poor to have many clothes. However, they said, one can see that they are a good family from the way that child behaves at table. Well, I am afraid in spite of that early promise my mother never succeeded in making a lady out of me. Munich I remember then as being cold and wet and dreary, and I never really liked it since, though there were some nice gardens by the Iser River. One of the Swedish girls was playing the witch in Humperdinck's *Hansel and Gretel* and I was taken to a performance. I must have been seven, as this was just after the war. I remember particularly the scene where the children go to sleep in the forest after their prayers, and the fourteen angels come down from heaven to protect them. In this performance they had seven pink angels on one side, and seven blue ones on the other, all graded from tallest to smallest. Later when the witch tried to eat Hansel a little girl next to me started screaming and I said to her, "Don't be silly, that is just my Aunt Thora dressed up."

I saw this opera again a few years later, and was quite disappointed to see all fourteen angels dressed in white with golden wings. Other operas I saw at an early age were *Mignon*, by Thomas, the story based on one told by Goethe in his novel *Wilhelm Meister* about an Italian count's daughter stolen by gypsies at an early age, whom the hero buys from the gypsies to save her, and how eventually she gets reunited with her old and blind father who has spent years looking for her. Very romantic, though the composer was French. Then *Der Freischütz* by Weber, the first German Romantic opera, all complete with demon, thunderstorm, and a happy ending. Then *Lohengrin* by Wagner, which was spoiled for me by Elsa being six feet tall and very fat, and Lohengrin about 5 foot high and equally fat. I still see these every time I hear the music, just as I always see the hippopotami dancing with the crocodiles when I hear the "Dance of the Hours." (*Fantasia*)

Grock. Photo by Lotte Jacobi

I was also taken to various plays deemed suitable for children, and to individual artists. I saw Pavlova dance the dying swan, heard Vladimir Pachmann on the piano, saw eccentric Rubinstein behaviour, Grock, the world's best clown, Pacelli, the world's greatest juggler and many more. I remember one variety concert that had a very clever comedy sketch by the German Jewish comedian Pallenberg, and a playlet based on the music by Hindemith, called *The Elopement.* This was extremely clever, one first saw the actual elopement, the young man bring a ladder, putting on the girl's window, climbing up, helping her down, and the father looking out and shaking his fist at them, then it gave the entire thing in reverse, with the music also being note by note reversed from the original. I must say I thought the reverse music sounded better.

Occasionally I was taken to the famous Circus Busch, which had a proper building in Berlin and not just tents in the open. However, I once saw a little boy killed in an act where his father balanced a long wooden pole on his head and the boy climbed up this and then stood on his head. I did not believe it when the Ringmaster came out and said he had not been badly hurt, and sure enough read in the paper next day that he had been killed. After that I refused to go to any more circus performances.

My father's taste in music wasn't as highbrow as my mother's and he liked all kinds of hit music of the twenties and thirties and had a very large record collection, which was kept in the best of condition. When I was about ten I was given permission to play his records; the gramophone and record cupboard were kept in the library, but each time had to sign a paper saying I promised to change the needle after every side played and would put records back into their envelopes and into the right place in the cupboard. My father was compulsively tidy. He used to say only dirty people had to do spring-cleaning, the others would have their places perfect all the time. He would be able to write from some business trip and ask for an item, saying it was on the left side three inches from the back in the second drawer on the left. I remember once being barred from the library for a month because I had not plumped up the cushion I had been sitting on when I left. I liked lots of my father's records, things like *Alexander's Ragtime Band*, the Comedy Harmonists, and lots of other German and American hits.

I used to spend many times walking to school making up stories about rescuing the fairy queen's baby and being granted either one wish, or three wishes in return. One wish was always to be beautiful and popular. Other than that there were such things as being able to speak and understand all languages on earth as if they were my own, and to go back in time to the Age of Reptiles and be able to come back with some specimens. I also had a lot of recurring dreams. In fact I got to be able to dream in installments, if I thought of last night's dream when going to bed I would go on dreaming from that point on. Even now I get the occasional recurrence of some of those childhood dreams. Once, when we were on holidays in the Riesengebirge we saw a rather strict man with two well-behaved children walking in front of us. For years I had dreams about these people, how he wanted to murder his children and odd things like that. Apart from the normal flying dreams, I had others which were proper stories and quite often more interesting than my day-life.

When I was about twelve my room was completely redecorated with all the old layers of wallpaper and paint stripped off. I found that over the original white satin striped wallpaper the room had been painted first pink and then blue. Now it became a room more in keeping with my advanced years, with a sofa, and desk as well as bed and wardrobe. I was always very untidy, and quite often when my dresses fell off a coat hanger I just left them on the bottom of the wardrobe. I remember my father coming in to check on me one day and saying, "Well, you don't seem to care for these clothes so they may as well go to the poor,'" bundling the lot up and taking them away, leaving me with only a few dresses that I didn't like or wear very much. He also cured me of leaving tidbits on my plate till last, by waiting till I was about to eat them, and then reaching over with his fork and saying, "I see you don't like this, so I'll take it."

Relatives played quite a large part in my childhood. For a start we had to go to my grandfather's place to dinner every second Sunday. I hated this very much. I was not allowed to take a book to read, and once the huge hot midday meal was eaten, with anything up to forty or fifty people present, all the adults went off into bedrooms for a nap, and the children had to go into one of the living rooms and keep quiet. There was absolutely nothing to do, except rocking on the huge rocking chairs; I don't think there was even one book in my grandfather's house. I quite liked some of my cousins separately, but hated these mass meetings, which were even worse when there was a special occasion, such as my grandfather's eightieth birthday. We had some distant relative who was good at making up occasional verses for such occasions, and I remember he and another relative gave a sketch in which they talked about how old Lilli was. This is Lilly Prince, now in Florida. [*She died in 2008.*] She was always very mature for her age and was constantly held up to me as good example, which didn't endear her to me. She was twelve at the time, which means I must have been about nine or ten, and they started off saying she must be at least eighteen and then coming down to the great surprise to find she was only twelve. Another cousin, Margot

Simon, who was a few years older still, was held up as a bad example to me. She was rather horrible, tall and awkward with a big bosom and long spidery arms, and when she met me in the street she would throw her arms around me, press me against her bosom, and shout loudly, "Yella, how lovely to see you," which made me feel like sinking into the ground. My mother never succeeded with "A lady never raises her voice," but she did instill into me "A lady never shows her feelings in public." I never got over this and even when quite old hurt my husband's feelings by pulling away if he wanted to walk hand in hand with me somewhere on the street. I am sure Margot had as much to do with this as my mother's teachings.

I had a second cousin, Erika Lichtenfeld, whom I admired as she was good-looking and popular. I had to go to her birthday party once and as usual hated being in a crowd of others; also I had to eat the then traditional chocolate pudding, which I detested. Then my mother decided that she would give such a birthday party for me, over my anguished protests. I completely disgraced myself by locking myself into a lavatory and refusing to come out until all the guests had gone home. As I had forgotten to take a book, I was rather bored, and spent most of the time in one of my favourite pursuits, looking out of the small window, which had a view of a dingy back courtyard with rubbish bins, and a screen of wire netting about seven feet from the ground to stop people from throwing things down. I imagined myself jumping down, wondering whether I would go through the netting in little pieces, or whether it would break under my weight. Methods of suicide were often in my mind, and a bit later I also quite often tried to think of ways of killing my father without being found out.

Louis Grumach

THE GRUMACH FAMILY

According to a doubtless apocryphal family legend, the first Grumach was a Scot who left his country in a small boat in the 18th century because of religious or political troubles. He landed near a small fishing village on the Eastern Baltic, married a local girl and "Germanized" his name from MacGrue to Grumach. This story came from my aunt Mummi via a relative in East Prussia, who apparently survived Hitler and whose hobby it was to keep a family tree of enormous proportions. It seems unlikely to me that there should have been a Jewish fishing community, or that a Scot who cared about religious or political issues should have become Jewish simply to marry, but there is now no way to find out. My cousin Lilli remembered nothing more except that she too was told that tale. However that maybe, there was a large clan of Grumachs in East Prussia, many of them poor.

The Grumach family came from the region of Allenstein, East Prussia (now Poland) rather like the people in *Fiddler on the Roof*, and presumably they had their share of pogroms and rapes to put up with, as quite a number of my relatives had the high cheekbones and grey or blue eyes and fair hair of the Slavs.

Sometime in the 19th century my grandfather Louis and his elder brother Eduard came to Berlin as young men, carrying packs on their backs, and for sometime worked as peddlers. However, Eduard apparently was a bit of a business genius as well as tall, blond, and blue eyed. With the help of his brother, Eduard built up in a few years a retail/wholesale textile business selling clothes, underwear, umbrellas and Manchester (household linen and cottons, such as sheets and towels), which became the family firm Gebrüder Grumach. In those days marriages were mostly arranged affairs, with love playing a negligible part. Men married for property or business expansion, or just for their wives' dowry. However, Eduard's marriage was a true love match. His wife, the good-looking, intelligent, and artistically gifted Ida Frank came from an old, established and well-off family, and she fell in love with him and visa versa. They had four children, Elisabeth, Max, Eugen and Otto. There is a story that when his daughter was born Eduard was so excited that when he went to register the birth he had forgotten the name his wife had chosen by the time he got there. He was shown a list of girls' names and picked one, but when he came home his wife was very upset and sent him back to change it. However, he was informed that once a name was registered it could not be changed. Ida said, "I don't care, I am still going to call her Elisabeth." By the time Elisabeth was getting married all the people concerned were dead, and no one remembered the incident. No Elisabeth Grumach was registered, and there was quite a bit of trouble until an older member of the family remembered and the marriage could proceed.

Unfortunately Eduard died of typhoid at the age of thirty-six, and according to then prevailing Jewish custom, his younger brother Louis had to marry his widow and be a father to her children. Louis was engaged to a very nice girl whom he loved, and he was not at all happy at having to annul the engagement and marry Ida; being a rather stupid and insensitive man he never quite forgave her. (The girl he had been engaged to married a man called Bonin and occasionally attended our extended family functions.) With perhaps the exception of Max, the eldest boy, he never cared for his brother's children either. Max was a conventional man who attended a university, joined a fraternity that did duelling, and was very proud of his dueling scars. He was very "German", changed his religion to Lutheran, and was a decorated officer in the First World War. He and his wife lived near us and had two daughters, Hilde and then Uschi (Ursula) about five years later. I saw more of them than my other relatives because my mother and Grete, Max's wife, got along very well. The marriage between Max and Grete was arranged, and when they met for the first time apparently both said about the other: "Isn't he (she) ugly?"

Hilde, Uschi, Grete and Lilli

Hilde was about three years younger than I, and I remember that her mother once told her that she and I should be friends and she said, "She is a relative, relatives can't be friends." I mentioned this to her when we met in Berlin in 1992, and she said that I used to tell her spooky stories and frighten her; I vaguely remember there was an old chess pawn behind a curtain in one of my grandfather's living rooms, and I used to make up stories about him being enchanted. There was a large gathering of the family every second Sunday at my grandfather's flat, with thirty to fifty people. There would be a huge hot meal, usually duck with very fatty gravy, and followed by the one thing I liked, a very nice lemon mousse. After this enormous meal all the adults found themselves somewhere to have a post prandial nap, and we children had to keep quiet in the enormous living room. I was not allowed to take a book, and I don't think there were any books in my grandfather's house, so there was nothing at all for me to do, which is probably why I grew up with a dislike of large functions and gatherings.

Hilde was sent to finish her schooling in France and studied pharmacy. She married a French student but was later divorced. Her daughter Ghiselaine went to University and is married with two children. I have a photo taken in 1961 that Lilli sent me of Hilde, Uschi, Grete, and her standing in Toulouse together. Hilde owned or managed a pharmacy there.

Elisabeth at the age of eighteen was married off to a man twice her age. At the wedding of her half sister, Clare is supposed to have said, " It's not too bad now when she is eighteen and he is thirty six, but think, when he is seventy two she will be only thirty six!"

The second son, Eugen, took after his father in looks and spirit of adventure. He went to South Africa and joined the S.W. Mounted Police. He was either killed in some action or died of a fever. The third son, Otto, was the black sheep and was sent to America as a remittance man. I remember him coming back with a rather vulgar wife and a son and daughter. Everyone said the daughter wasn't his, but I remember the boy was rather nice. Anyway he went back to America and disappeared. The male descendants of that boy, if there were any, would be the only Grumach male descendants.

Ida had six more children from Louis, as well as numerous miscarriages and stillbirths. The eldest girl Rosa (b. 1884) took after her mother in beauty, brains, and artistic gifts, and my mother loved her dearly. There were two more girls, Meta (my mother) and Clare, a boy called Frederick (Fritzchen) who was the apple of his father's eye, Martha, born two years later, and Gertrude, the youngest, who was always called Mummi. Fritz was apparently a very bright boy and one of those children everyone liked. Unfortunately when he was seven he, and also my mother, contracted diphtheria. Ida wanted to give her children the recently invented anti-diphtheria serum, but Louis consulted his doctor, an old fashioned man who did not believe in this new-fangled idea, so Louis refused permission despite all of Ida's pleas for a second opinion. Meta recovered, but Fritz died. This finally drove Ida over the edge. She had what was then called a mental breakdown and went into a mental home. I think she made a partial or total recovery, but could not bear to return to her previous life with my grandfather. She seems to have behaved quite normally most of the time, and the children visited her regularly, but when she saw my grandfather she wildly attacked him. She spent the rest of her life in that place, dying in 1912 at the age of sixty-one.

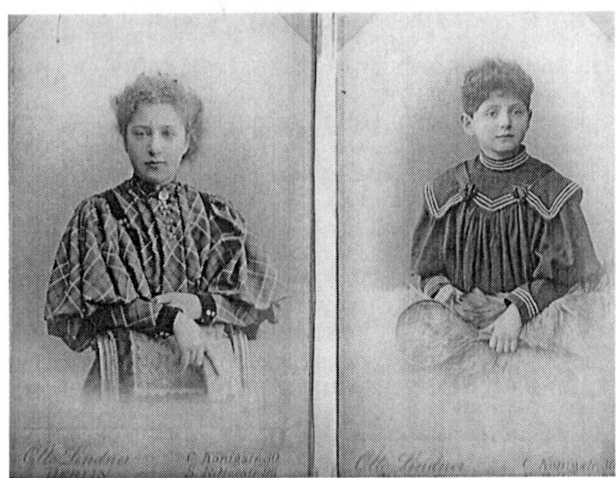

Rosa(?) and Meta, c. 1895

Rosa was sent to a Swiss finishing school at about the age of sixteen. This was in the days when girls were educated mainly in "accomplishments": French and Italian, drawing, singing, pokerwork, and playing the piano. They were then sent to balls and were expected to marry in short order. Rosa wrote heartbroken letters to her father asking to come home but without success. The headmistress of this small private school had tuberculosis and insisted on kissing each girl goodnight, and Rosa contracted the disease. Eventually she was sent home with an advanced case of TB, of which she died in at the age of eighteen. She infected in turn Martha, who died three years later at the age of fifteen, and Meta and Mummi, both of whom did not develop active forms of the disease until later.

As the surviving three Grumach girls grew up, my mother was regarded as the ugly duckling of the family. All the other girls had curly hair, brown eyes, and pink cheeks. She had straight, rather oily black hair, a pale skin and large blue-gray eyes, and both in my memory and in photographs was really very beautiful. However, her type of looks was not fashionable then and she was rather flat chested. When she went to a tailor to have a suit made he bemoaned the fact that she had no bosom. She said she couldn't help it, and he said, "Your cousin Miss Fuld hasn't anything either, but she arranges it so it looks like something." My mother hated the conventional parties and dances of her class. She studied music seriously, had a very good mezzo-soprano voice and could easily have become a concert singer, and she had a real talent on the piano as well. She could draw very funny sketches and caricatures and had a gift for telling jokes well, often in Berlin dialect. She early on made friends with artists and singers *[including the noted soprano Elisabeth Schumann]* and went to artist balls, often in fancy dress, rather than those of the Jewish middle class. She refused any attempt to arrange a marriage for her, and at the age of twenty-four was considered an old maid. It was a real surprise to everyone when she not only married, but married very well – my father not only didn't need her dowry, he had enough money to buy into the firm. She and Mummi had a double wedding. I was born in on May 11th 1911. During the war, when she was expecting her second child, my mother got 'Lungenspitzenkatarrh'. She consulted several specialists who told her she should have an abortion or both she and the child would die, and regretfully she did so.

Meta in the early 1920s

Clare tried to educate herself by learning the 24-volume encyclopedia by heart, never progressing past page four. She married

Alfred Schwalbe, the brother of the famous photographer, Lotte Jacobi, who died in America in her nineties. Lotte said that her brother was not a good person, and so did my mother. The family decided, probably after the fact, that he married Clare for her dowry. He bought a landed estate (Rittergut) and led the life of a feudal lord, complete with the right of the first night. I remember one holiday we spent at the estate when I was about nine. There was a very long wooden table with the top five feet or so laid with a white tablecloth and loaded with hams, roasts etc., and there he sat in solitary splendor at the end of the table. Then in descending order were my mother and I, his wife and children, and then all down the table the workers on the estate down to the lowest dairy maid, each of whom got a plate of gruel or stewed turnips and stewed plums to eat. Eventually he ran out of money and had to sell the farm. He and Clare had a rather messy divorce when Lilli was about fifteen. By that time Clare was rather neurotic, and while she got custody of the two younger children Fred and Inge, Lilli was allowed to choose and stayed

Clare and Inge

Fred, Lilli and Inge

with her father and his next wife, a nice woman who managed him much better than Clare.

There was a stepdaughter who ended up in Israel; she may have come from a previous marriage. Lilli was about three years older than I and was always held up to me as a good example: "Why can't you be more like Lilli?" which at the time did not make me like her very much. She was a child with perfect manners who always did and said the right thing. She and her brother Fred (Frederick) came to America before the war.

Clare and Inge both died in concentration camps during the Hitler regime. I hoped to sponsor them to come to Australia, but the war broke out before they could leave Germany. [*According to the Yad Vashem, based on transport records, they died in separate concentration camps, Clare in Riga Bisumuiza, Riga, Latvia in 1942, aged 55; Inge, was sent first to Sabac camp, and then to Zasavica Camp, Yugoslavia where she died in 1941, aged 22). The daughter of Inge's stepsister, Ora Maloul, also submitted records of their deaths.]*

Mummi was regarded as the beauty of the Grumach family, being small and dainty with curly brown hair and brown eyes, pink cheeks and charming manners. My mother sometimes suspected that she was not too sincere, but apparently she retained that sweetness of character right up to her death. My mother used to say that when she fainted she used to fall against things and hurt herself, but Mummi always fainted very gracefully, with her clothes neatly arranged and her legs crossed. Mummi married at sixteen. Actually it was a double wedding for her and my parents. At the wedding, Mummi's bridesmaids carried bouquets of pink rosebuds and forget-me-nots, and her bouquet was white roses and lily of the valley. (My mother carried white orchids, and her bridesmaids mauve orchids.) It always sounded very romantic to me.

Mummi's husband was a dashing army officer (Reiss) who gambled and womanized, and they were divorced before she was twenty. She remarried by twenty-one. Her second husband was Kurt Danziger, who was a real prototype of a cultured European gentleman, and whom everyone liked. They lived in a beautiful house in Heidelberg where we visited once or twice. They had a lovely house with a spiral staircase, and I was particularly impressed with the walk-in wardrobes. They had a lovely garden too, all ups and downs. We went to a performance of *A Midsummer Night's Dream* in the courtyard of the old ruined castle, and to another play, which ends with a castle burning, for which the ruins were lit up with red floodlights. I was told that at certain times the parks and the castle were to be avoided, because a sacked gardener had thrown about garlic seed, when the garlic flowered the whole place stank of it.

My mother told me that on marrying Kurt Danziger Mummi lamented that she would have to change all the monograms on her linens, and Kurt said, " I love you very much, but even for you I won't change my name to Ranziger." The son from the first marriage was Herbert Reiss, and from the second Peter, who was born with a birthmark on his face. He was treated with radiation to remove it and ended up with a badly scarred face. The family went from Germany first to Switzerland and then to the United States, where they had a difficult time getting admitted at Ellis Island because of Peter's disfigurement.

However, they had plenty of money and could hire a good lawyer who softened all hearts. They bought a kind of country estate in Mount Vernon I think. After Kurt died Mummi moved to New York, getting rather close to Lilli and her husband Sidney who also lived there. Herbert married and had four children, a boy and three girls. (Virginia, Patty, Warren and Florence.)

Perhaps after the death of Rosa, my grandfather took the girls on a "grand tour" of Europe, as far as Naples and Rome. My mother remembered that when they went by boat to the Isle of Capri to visit the Blue Grotto, even though the sea was calm my grandfather started to get seasick, and in vain called for the boat to return to land and let him off. She also remembered the young Italian boys who dived for coins for the entertainment of tourists, and who looked as if they were made of silver in the blue of the grotto. She was taken for an audience with the pope and allowed to kiss his foot. She didn't like Rome and said once you have seen a dozen churches and a dozen Roman remains you get tired of them. She brought back as a souvenir a crucifix which was supposed to have been blessed by the Pope, and years later gave it to one of our housemaids, who was a Catholic and thought it was just wonderful.

Early on the Grumach brothers brought their three sisters to Berlin, and married them off to business associates. Their old-fashioned names, Hulda, Henrietta, and Adelheid, set their births firmly in the mid-nineteenth century. Adelheid, the eldest, had no children and was widowed early. The family story went that when she had not become pregnant after being married for a time, she was persuaded to see a

The Grumach family c. 1914. Richard probably took the photo. L. to R. Back row: Hulde, Clare, Mummi, Grete, Max, Joseph Kochmann, Isador Lichtenfeld, Henrietta, Meta. Front row: Lilli, Louis Grumach, Fred.

doctor, who examined her and said in surprise, "But Mrs. Wolff, you are still a virgin." She did not even understand what he meant, but when she finally had it explained she said, "Well, when we were first married he did try to do some odd things, so I slapped him on the face and told him not to be so disgusting and he never tried again." With Ida out of action she came and kept house for my grandfather, and the other two sisters also contributed advice and interference. Henrietta was fat and good-natured, but Hulde could be rather nasty and my mother detested her.

Louis being a self-made man had great respect for educated people, and he engaged a well-qualified but rather horrible woman to be governess to his children. The girls went to a school just around the corner from where they lived, and the governess made them get up early to study, and study again for the rest of the day when they got home. Their only exercise was for an hour each week at school. She used to hit them all the time, except for Mummi, the youngest, who was the cook's pet. The first time the governess slapped Mummi she ran straight into the kitchen, smacked the cook on the face and said, " *That's* what she did to me!" The cook went into the classroom to do battle and after that Mummi was exempt from punishment.

I have an idea that Adelheid may have followed some orthodox Jewish food laws, but by the time I grew up nobody in our family seemed very religious, and the few times I was taken to the synagogue the one thing I remember was that women had to sit in a gallery behind thick carved wooden panels, so they could see out but nobody could see them. Even at a young age I resented this, particularly when someone told me that that only boys could pray for their dead fathers, which was why Jewish men so desperately wanted a son. The only time I went near a synagogue was when we had to go to a family funeral, and until I was about seven I didn't know I was Jewish.

The second sister, Henrietta had one son, Eduard, [*who later became a Director in the firm, along with Richard Neuhäuser*] and two daughters. Eduard had a son, Werner, and an older daughter, Erika, who was my age and a really nice girl, very good looking with light brown curly hair, large blue eyes, and a good complexion. She was also very bright and went to Freiburg University just after I left there. She later married an architect and I once visited them in an outer suburb of London. (You could see Eton College from their place.) [*Isador Lichtenfeld, Henrietta's husband, was a managing director in the firm along with Louis and Richard until he died, when Eduard took his place. Isador and Henrietta are both buried in the Jewish cemetery in Weissensee, Berlin. Henrietta died in August 1932, and Isador in April 1933, good timing for both.]*

The third sister Hulde married a man called Kochmann, who had a not very important job in the firm. [*They too are buried in Weissensee, in the Grumach family plot. Hulde died in November 1932, and her husband Joseph in 1922.*] They also had a son and two daughters, both of whom later divorced. The son Erich was infected with syphilis at an early age and when I knew him had that kind of semi-paralysis that people used to get in the late stages of the disease, possibly also with some brain damage. He was the father of Gerald and Ulli, both of whom were not stupid and both of whom had bright sons, so he probably would have been different from the way I remember him if he had not been sick. One of his sisters was Alice Selten, who lived in some European city (Paris?) and in 1993 at the time of this writing was 96, reportedly saying she did not need the handrail to get in and out of trams. She had a daughter who had a beautiful face but unfortunately was badly deformed and hunchbacked from having had polio when she was three years old, and who died before her mother. Else Kochmann, Erich's wife and the mother of Gerald and Ulli, lived for quite a long time in Australia. She was apparently a remarkable woman, building up a business painting china etc. after coming here without money and with limited English.

As you can see many of my cousins were really second cousins, their fathers and my mother were first cousins, but in Germany one didn't make such distinctions. I called all my second cousins' parents aunt and uncle, though they were really cousins once removed.

Great Aunt Hulde was a great-grandmother at fifty-four, having married at seventeen and produced her first daughter at eighteen. My mother disliked Hulde very much, partly because she took it upon herself to spank her brother's children after their mother disappeared into that home, and she was supposed to be rather spiteful. Actually my mother disliked most of her relatives, or at best tolerated them. As I have said, conventional life among the Jewish bourgeoisie bored her stiff, and she preferred to mix with the artists she had something in common with. She had picked up the anti-Semitic zeitgeist and said such things as, "The Jew are a small but nasty race," and when I wanted to know why I was penalized by the other children for being a Jew, quoted *Struwwelpeter* at me: "For if he tries with all his might he cannot change from black to white." Until I actually started to correspond with Lilli and Ulli, and to visit Gerald and Elizabeth in Melbourne, I always thought my mother's family were a pretty dumb and awful lot and was quite glad not to be saddled with a lot of family.

Richard Neuhäuser

NEUHÄUSER HISTORY

I don't have much information about the origins of the Neuhäuser family. My mother always said that they were Sephardim, that is, Jews who descended from those expelled from Spain in the late 15th century, as opposed to the Ashkenazi Jews who were from Russia and Poland, and most of those in Germany. I think this is apocryphal; my mother, as so many assimilated middle class German Jews, looked down on the Eastern Jews and thought the Sephardim were superior. However, I have since read that most of the Sephardim went round the southern part of the Mediterranean, though Algiers, Morocco and Egypt, and those now in Egypt are generally darker skinned and also more fundamentalist than the Ashkenazi.

My own knowledge only goes back to my great-grandmother, who must have been a remarkable woman. Her husband died when she was quite young, leaving her with three young sons. She continued to run the family farm, educated her children, and lived until she was 104, still in her own home and doing most of her own work, mentally alert to the last. I chiefly remember her for the saying, which I have used a lot, "What you haven't got in your head you have to have in your legs," whenever I forgot something and had to go back for it, as well as "Wenn du dennst du bist allein, mache diene Nägel rein" ("When you think you are alone, clean your nails.") All of the Neuhäusers were healthy and long lived; my great grandmother's sister lived until 102, and at that age was still housekeeping for two banker sons, with only a 15-year-old girl from an orphanage for the "rough". Another great-aunt was diagnosed with cancer in her eighties. The doctors operated and saw that the cancer was inoperable and widespread, so they sewed her up and sent her home to die. She spent some months in bed and then started to improve and lived for another six years, eventually dying of old age. Her doctor was so surprised that he requested an autopsy, and no sign of cancer was found. My mother always said that if she had been a Catholic and gone to Lourdes it would have been called a miracle instead of spontaneous remission. I remember a time when my father took me to visit his relatives in the Rhineland, and I saw all these people in their eighties, nineties and some over 100, including the 102-year-old great aunt. However, others were blind, deaf, paralyzed, senile, or all of these, and this is really when I first decided that I would do something about things if I ever reached that stage. Of course in those days cataracts were inoperable and the only hearing aids were ear trumpets.

My father's father became a "Kaufman," sort of halfway between a shop owner and a merchant, and married (doubtless in an arranged marriage) a girl called Doris Sahlmann who came from a prosperous merchant family in Frankfurt am Main. She was neither beautiful nor intelligent. As my other grandmother, Ida, was very beautiful and both my grandfathers quite handsome men, I always blamed my own looks on her.

My father's family came from Mannheim, which is an industrial town and fairly new by European standards, becoming a town about 1660. It is only a few miles from Heidelberg, and about 150 miles north of Freiburg, and about the same distance south of Bonn, which is not far from Cologne. My grandfather Sigmund Neuhäuser settled in Ludwigshafen, the twin city to Mannheim on the other side of the Rhine. (Just like Buda and Pest are on opposite sides of the Danube.) He ended up building a factory that produced equipment for breweries, and did very well until he invented stiff cardboard envelopes for packing beer bottles instead of using straw. Though they seemed successful in trials, once he had released them for general use they failed dismally. It took only one bottle to break and the beer from this would soften all the other envelopes so the whole crate was lost. I don't know whether he actually went bankrupt, but he did retire with comparatively little money. Clearly it was an idea before its time.

Richard Neuhäuser in 1884, aged about two.

My grandparents Sigmund and Doris had two children, my father Richard, and a daughter Elsa. I wonder if they were Wagner fans? My father must have been a difficult child. In spite of his intelligence he did badly at school, which he hated, so much so that he was warned that unless he improved he would not pass the "Einjähriche", an exam all German boys going past elementary school had to sit for at sixteen. In this time of compulsory military service, the normal period of enlistment was three years, but those who passed the exam only had to serve for one year, and emerged as non-commissioned officers. My father must have taken the warning to heart; he got his first attack of rheumatic fever at this time and lost quite a lot of school time, but on his next school report it said, "In spite of long illness, much improved," and he had no problems with the exam once he had made his mind to pass it. He turned out to be very good with horses, and was put in the Ulans, the Light Cavalry, ending up as something like a sergeant. In those days of course a Jew could not become an officer.

My grandfather wanted my father to go into the family business, but having an adventurous spirit and also the "wanderlust" that I inherited from him, he left Germany as soon as possible after finishing his military service, and went to America. He never told me much about this, but I got stories from my mother. Apparently he did all sorts of interesting things, like being an assistant to a seller of patent medicines and later assistant to a snake catcher. He also went to South America and was tutor to the sons of a German hacienda owner in Brazil, and no doubt did all sorts of other things I don't know about. He kept in touch with his parents, and eventually his father, who wanted him to come home, sent him a one-way ticket. However he had no desire to return as a failure, so he sold or swapped the ticket for one to Japan, where he went early in the 20th century. He was very impressed with the Japanese arts and crafts, somehow managed to learn Japanese quite quickly and well, and then went around selling for merchants such things as lacquer work, ivory sculptures, silk kimonos with gold and silver embroidery, and lots of other things which were at the time still produced for domestic consumption and not for export or tourists. Somehow he persuaded the merchants that if they trusted him with samples, he could get them big orders in America. Returning to America, he hired space in a hall for his exhibition. I have an idea that it was in St. Louis, possibly at that famous Fair in 1904, but I am not sure about this. However, he ended up getting lots of orders, and in a fairly short time developed a thriving business, perhaps being one of the first to popularize Japanese arts in the West. He finally sold the business for a lot of money, and once he was a success returned to Germany.

His father was thrilled, and sent him off on a trip around Germany to visit business friends. When he visited Louis Grumach, he was invited home for dinner and met my mother, who was then twenty-four and regarded as an old maid by her relatives. My father, who did not suffer fools gladly, had been meeting lots of young "higher daughters" who had the normal accomplishments but were giggly and silly, and he was delighted when my mother could talk intelligently about Japan and its arts. After a few more visits he asked her out on an excursion to the Grunewald, the forest area near Berlin. By this time the aunts were so keen to see her get married that they actually allowed her to go without a chaperone, and on that occasion they became engaged. He arranged to phone the next morning; the phone was in the hall, and having warned him that the aunts would be listening, my mother spoke to him in the most formal manner. My mother said she distinctly heard the sighs of disappointment from behind the door.

My aunt Elsa in Mannheim married a man called Alfred Mann in the Rhineland, and had two sons, Robert, and a much younger one whose name I don't remember. I detested Robert, who was fond of practical jokes like pulling a chair away from someone about to sit down, or sneaking up on someone and shouting "Boo!" He was however a gifted tennis player and played in competitions. I once played Ping-Pong with him and he beat me 21-0, which I didn't mind at all. The younger one I remember vaguely as being a nice little boy. I also met a cousin of my father's who also loved playing practical jokes and who had a houseful of gadgets made to look like something else. For example, you lifted the phone and found a bottle of brandy underneath.

When I knew my grandparents they were already retired and lived in a very pretty villa in Weisbaden. One of my earliest memories is their white painted villa covered with pink rambler roses, and a white picket fence with a bench outside it. I sat on the bench and had a view of a wide valley with meadows sloping down to a river, which might have been the Main or the Rhine, while a young Alsatian dog ran around trying to dig out moles from the numerous molehills on that meadow. I might have been about three at the time and certainly not shortsighted, as the picture is very clear and detailed. Later my grandparents lived in other places like Bad Nauheim, north of Frankfurt, and Bad Kissingen, a spa not far from Mannheim in another direction. Halfway between Mannheim and Freiburg is Baden-Baden, where I spent quite a bit of time during the holidays, as my mother was in a sanatorium there during the last three years of her life. After my grandfather died, my grandmother Doris went to live with Aunt Elsa. She got senile at an early age of 78 or so and my father, and later I, paid for her upkeep. Just before I left she wandered off and fell and broke her hip, dying shortly afterwards of pneumonia. This was a blessing as she was about to go into a home, and it was 1936.

My father found it hard to come to terms with the customs of the German middle class, and often embarrassed my mother. For example, it was the custom for people to arrive at least half an hour late for an social invitation, but he insisted on being on time, so if the invitation said 7:00 p.m. he would drag my mother there at that time exactly and often the hosts were not even dressed. On another occasion he insisted on giving one of my mother's cousins a large, perfectly plain crystal container full of priceless green tea as a wedding gift. She thanked him rather lukewarmly, and promptly sent it to the kitchen, only realising its worth when someone more knowledgeable asked what she had done with this treasure.

When I was growing up my father's favourite breakfast was Kellogg's cornflakes with light cream, and he was fond of American music, including Gershwin's *Rhapsody in Blue*.

BERLIN

Berlin is not a very old town as European cities go. Of course Germany is not an old country either. Apart from short periods when some strong ruler arose there really was no country called Germany, just a conglomeration of dozens of smaller units, from kingdoms like Bavaria or Saxony to principalities, Grand-duchies and Dukedoms, some only consisting of one town, a castle or palace, and a few acres of land. However all those rulers were counted as true royalty and one of their principal exports was eligible spouses for rulers of other countries. A few examples are Catherine the Great of Russia (Princess of Anhalt-Zerbst), Albert, Consort of Victoria (son of the Duke of Coburg Saxe-Gotha), and Queen Mary, wife of George V (daughter of the Duke of Teck).

The first reason for this disjointedness of the country was the obsession of the early rulers with being called rulers of the Holy Roman Empire, which led to constant squabbles with the popes, and gave local feudal lords powers that had long been curtailed in countries such as England and France.

In the settlement of Europe after the Napoleonic wars, Germany became a loose federation and national feelings began to rise, ending with the abortive revolution of 1848.

Prussia is a rather poor part of Germany, with flat country and very sandy soils, which was said to account for the hard-working humorless nature of the Prussians, compared to, say, the Rhinelanders. The rise of Prussia began with the father of Frederick the Great, who built a strong army, and was particularly fond of his "Lange Kerle", an elite regiment of very tall soldiers; any tall young man was likely to find himself press-ganged into this. His son, Frederick the Great, was a remarkable character. He started as a boy loving the arts and poetry and rebelling against his father's militarism. As a young man he tried to flee Prussia with a friend, but was captured, had to watch his friend executed and was himself imprisoned. After this he learned to conform and eventually as king fought Austria and defeated her on two occasions. He kept his love for music and literature, invited Voltaire to his palace, played the flute well, and composed for this instrument. He was also far-sighted enough to encourage the Huguenots from France, and the Jews to set up business and industries in Berlin.

The Hohenzollerns continued as kings of Prussia, though none was as capable as his ancestors. In fact my mother, whose history lessons at school consisted largely of dates and facts concerning the kings, told me that the only thing they learned about one of them was that his favourite meal was corn beef and cabbage. However, Bismarck, who became chancellor and the real ruler of Prussia after successful wars against Denmark, Austria, and France, unified Germany and in 1871 a German Empire was declared, with the King of Prussia becoming Emperor of Germany. It was this late start as a nation that led to excessive nationalism and eventually helped to bring about the Second World War.

Berlin had started life as a little fishing village and later became a town in the Hanseatic League, though not as important as, say, Hamburg or Bremen, but its real growth didn't start till the rise of Prussia in the eighteenth century. During my childhood the buildings were mainly Victorian in style and from the 19th century, though the palaces and some of the public buildings were from the 18th. Frederick the Great like his father lived in Potsdam, and he built there a smaller version of the Versailles Palace and gardens, which he called Sanssouci. In my days there were just a few streets of the old fishing village left in Berlin, with the Nicolai Kirche about the oldest building. My grandfather and the family business were in that area. The last Emperor, William II, came to the throne at age twenty-two. His grandfather had lived into his nineties and his son, who was married to one of Queen Victoria's daughters, was rather enlightened and planned a more democratic system for Germany. Unfortunately he died of throat cancer shortly after succeeding to the throne. William II was a stupid fellow, whose first act was to sack Bismarck and say he would make his own decisions. He hated the English; the reasons given for this when I was at school were that his mother didn't like him, because he had a withered left arm, or that Queen Victoria spanked him when he was visiting her as a small boy. It was he who had the Kaiser Wilhelm Gedächtnis Kirche built, and insisted on alterations that spoilt the already not very good design even more. The lack of natural resources had largely been offset by development of industry since the eighteenth century, so Berlin as seat of imperial Germany, and later of the German Republic, became a very large city. When I lived there it had five million inhabitants.

I remember from my early childhood the gaslights still on the streets, and the lamplighters coming around every evening with a flame on top of a long pole to light them, and returning in the mornings to extinguish them with a thimble-shaped thing on top of the pole. There was also a stand of horse-drawn cabs at the side of our little park (Bayerischer Platz) and I remember the drivers in winter being dressed in heavy coats with fur collars, gloves, and caps with earmuffs, standing by the horses and swinging their arms out and then round their bodies to keep themselves warm. The horses had nosebags with a mixture of straw and oats that were put on while they were standing.

Königstrasse, 1902. The future Grumach firm may have been in the triangular building on the corner.

They also had blinders to stop them from shying if anything went past at the side. These were just ordinary horses, but there were also lots of real carthorses similar to Clydesdales with long hair at the fetlocks. During snowy weather horses would often fall. Bags were put under their feet and sand strewn about and then the horses would be taken away to be made into horsemeat. People ate this during the First World War, and I am told had a rather sickly sweetish taste.

Before the 1920s women wore long skirts, sometimes with bustles, corsets, and large hats with flowers, artificial fruit, or ostrich and egret feathers decorating them. Men generally were bearded or had at least a moustache, and wore coats with tails, top hats, carried canes with gold or silver or ivory knobs (quite often sword canes), and wore pocket watches with a gold chain draped across their waistcoat.

All the same, even during my childhood Berlin was pretty modern. We had electric trams, the underground rail system was well established, and the town was sewered, all probably because of the newness of the city. Our place was quite new when my parents moved in, and had electric light, an elevator, and gas stoves. However, many places I visited even when I was at high school in the twenties and early thirties still had gaslights, or even kerosene mantle lamps and wood stoves. Refrigerators had been invented, but even my parents who were quite well off only had an ice chest. Practically everybody lived in rented flats. There was nothing equivalent to our modern units, and nobody would dream of buying a flat. Only the very rich owned houses, usually well out in outer suburbs. Playing golf was a rich man's game only, because all golf courses were deliberately built in places not accessible by public transport, so only people with their own carriages, or later cars, could belong. To allow for frustrated gardeners there were allotments. These were city blocks not yet built on, divided into strips about three or four meter wide by maybe thirty or forty meter long. They were rented to people fairly cheaply, and some built little garden houses and depending on individual taste grew vegetables, flowers, or sometimes even a small fruit tree or a few berry bushes. Generally the work was done on Sundays, as working hours were very long and six days a week, but of course in summer the days were long too. Daylight started about 3 a.m. and it was still light at 9:30 p.m. This meant that in winter it didn't get light till quite late in the day, and it was dark again about 2:30 p.m., so we had to sleep in broad sunlight in the summer, and in winter get up and work much of the time in the dark. Our climate was rather extreme, as Berlin was not near the sea.

The coldest winter I remember was in 1929, when the temperature went down to -29° Celsius and we were warned to wear gloves, woollen stockings and earmuffs, as otherwise we might lose our ears or fingers and severely damage our legs by frostbite. I remember in winter the beautiful "ice flowers" patterns of ice on the windows. We had double-glazing and central heating where we lived. I do remember once when I was riding on a tram I saw a little boy who had licked the glass of the window and his tongue had frozen onto it. The tram had to be stopped and some woman in a nearby house came out with a kettle of boiling water, and hot rags were put on the outside of the window to warm it enough for the boy to get his tongue off, but I presume he had to see a doctor later. The streets during snow were often sprinkled with sand to stop the horses from falling, and the snow on the footpaths was first shoveled into heaps on the side of the road, with each house owner being responsible for the part outside his building. Then the snow piles were sprinkled with coarse salt, which melted the rest of the snow. In parks or where this had not been done, children made slides, often quite long, on which one could glide with just ordinary boots on, and also we had small sleds to go down the hills. During very cold weather places like the Wannsee would be frozen solid enough for people to skate. There was a nice largish park where Hilde Grumach lived which had a couple of small lakes, and there were also artificial skating rinks with ice that had been produced by hosing water onto a tennis court or similar place. I had skates but I never got very good. I remember once Hilde's father took her and me skating. He had been a very good skater, but he was fifty-three at the time and had a fall and broke his arm, whereas we could fall constantly without hurting ourselves. I didn't like the cold weather much and used to be glad when I could go home again.

Berlin in the twenties was a very interesting place, changing very rapidly from the late Victorian style. The twenties were the age that the Americans named "flaming youth" and Berlin was probably the most corrupt place in the Western world. There were nightclubs for all kinds, not only male or female homosexuals, but also sadists and masochists, and so on. I remember my mother telling me how to pick a prostitute, and that those who wore high red heels and carried a small horsewhip were catering for masochists. There was also a lot of crime, though it wasn't publicized as it is now. My parents had steel panels attached to the inside of the front and back doors, and a bolt that went into the ceiling and floor, as well as safety chains. There was a little peephole, so one could check who was at the door, and I was warned never to put my eye close to this, as someone might stick a wire through my eye. I had a door key from a fairly early age, which I kept on a string around my neck for safety. One night when I had been to a show, I came home fairly late, about 11 p.m., to find that my father had forgotten or not known I was out and had bolted the door. I doubt that I could have made anyone hear even if I had run the bell, but in any case I was afraid to do so. For a while I sat on the steps, but soon got tired of that so I went out and decided to walk to the Markets, which were miles from where I lived. I got to the markets about 2:30 a.m. and walked about enjoying watching the wagons with produce come in and stalls being readied for trading, which began about 4 a.m. Some nice person offered me a bread roll and a cup of milk-coffee. After 3:30 a.m. I started walking home again and got there about six a.m. I sat on the stairs again, well out of sight of our door, and waited till my father went to work, and then I went into my room, got changed, and went to school. Having had no sleep at all, I don't suppose I did very well at school that day. I must have been about thirteen at the time, already at grammar school, but I never felt in any danger, being very plain. In fact it was one of my sorrows that I wasn't good-looking enough to be a prostitute, even if I had wanted to be one, though in fact I didn’t.

[In the early 1920s, when Gabriele was about ten, Germany began a three-year period of hyperinflation. She recalled in conversation seeing women congregating outside the factory gates to collect their husband's salary so they could run to the stores and buy supplies before the prices

went up. As the value of the currency continued to fall, they brought wheelbarrows to carry away large bundles of nearly worthless money. "From the middle of 1922 until the middle of 1923, prices increased by over 100 times. Measured by the price of food, prices were 135 times higher at the end of the period than they were at the beginning. Measured by how many marks it took to buy a dollar, prices were 222 times higher. Yet even this was mild compared to what happened from July to November of 1923, when prices increased by somewhere between a million and a billion times their previous level." Wikipedia. Six years later marked the start of the Great Depression. Her father would not permit Gabriele to work during this latter period, saying that others needed a job more than she did.]

The Berliners seem to be a different breed from the normal Prussians, something like the Cockneys of London. They spoke a very distinctive dialect that my mother was very good at imitating. She was one of those rare people who could tell jokes well, and lots of her jokes were Berliner jokes. German is of course a highly inflected language, with endings of nouns and pronouns differing depending on what part of the sentence they are, almost as in Latin they have four cases, not only subject and object, as in English pronouns, but also different endings for Possessive, Dative and Accusative. I think they are called near and far object in English, for example, "I gave him an apple," has apple in Accusative and him in Dative. The Berliners used constantly get these mixed up and say, for instance, "Ich liebe Dir," instead of "Ich liebe Dich," for I love you. There is a rhyme that goes "Ick liebe Dir, ick liebe Dich, wie's richtig ist, dass weiss ick nich, ick liebe Dir im dritten Fall, ick lieber Dir im vierten Fall, Ick liebe Dir in jedem Fall." In English this is, "I love you in the third case, I love you in the fourth case, I love you in any case." As I wrote it they also say "ick" instead of "ich" and in many words the long e sound instead of the ei sound. Berliners generally are quick-witted, friendly and have a sense of humor, again like the Cockneys. In my youth lots of the jokes were told about shoemakers' apprentices, and I remember my mother dressing up as one for a fancy dress ball. Only the working class Berliners generally spoke dialect, the educated ones spoke "Hochdeutsch," literally High German, which isn't really right. The northern part of Germany is generally flat and the Southern part mountainous, so the people in the North speak Platt (flat) German, which is more similar to Dutch, and the Southern ones quite differently. When Luther translated the Bible into German he made up a language from an amalgam more like that spoken in the middle of Germany, and this became Hochdeutsch, the language taught at school and spoken by educated people. However, unlike the English, even the most upper class people still had recognizable accents or at least inflections.

In my childhood there were lots of class distinctions. First the aristocracy, the high ones, such as counts and barons, then the people with just a "von" in front of their name, then the upper middle class, the middle middle class, the lower middle class, the upper working class, and so on. As Jews we could not be upper middle class, though we lived a similar lifestyle. Generally upper middle class were professional people, army officers, high public servants and wealthy merchants.

Nearly everybody except the very poor had at least one servant. My parents had a cook and two maids, augmented when they gave a party

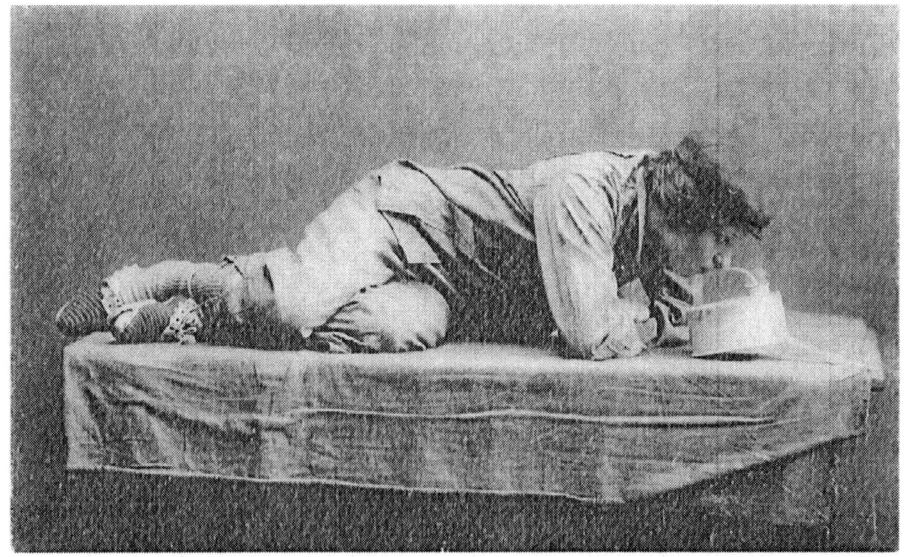

Meta dressed as a shoemaker's apprentice

by extra staff hired from an agency for the occasion, plus my nurse. However, even such people as the wife of a post office worker would have at least one maid of all work, in those cases the wife would do the cooking and the maid the "rough", scrubbing floors, black leading the stove, and things like that. These maids were often girls from orphanages, or girls from small farms. My parents paid somewhat more than normal and treated the servants well, so most stayed till they got married.

Another thing that differed in Germany from our customs was the form of address. If a man were a postmaster, or dentist, his wife would be Mrs. Postmaster Muller, or Mrs. Dentist Krause; if the husband had a doctorate the wife would be Mrs. Dr. Also unlike England, all children of a nobleman would inherit the title, so that a count could have ten children and they would all be counts or countesses. After the monarchy was abolished a law was brought in that such titles were to be just part of the name, and there was a joke about the illegitimate son of a countess having to be called countess and not count. There were lots of beggars in the streets when I was young. I am afraid I used this at times to get out of trouble. My father insisted that I kept book about my income (pocket money) and expenditure and examined the book every week. I generally forgot to write things down and did up the book at the last minute having forgotten some items, so when I was short I used to write "Beggar 10 Pfennig," or whatever. I don't think there were any really bad slums in Germany, though, or at least I never came across any or heard about them.

Sometimes my nurse or one of the maids would take me to a fair. I saw lots of sideshows, things that have long since been banned, such as the fattest man on earth, a bearded lady, groups of dwarfs, flea circuses in which the fleas pulled little carts or danced with tiny ballet skirts attached to them and were rewarded by being allowed to suck the blood of the trainer. Chemist shops still sold leeches, though these were going out of fashion, and medicines and pills were made on the premises, though we already had some, like aspirin, which were made in factories. Gothic print was still used more than Latin script and I remember reading in a book how a small child refused to go past a butcher shop because she read "Beef and Pork Butcher," in Germany "Rind und Schweineschlächter" as "Kind un Schweineschlächter", because in Gothic script the capital K and R are very similar, and "Kind" of course is "child."

(The butcher's wife would be addressed as Mrs. Rind und Schweineschlächter Schmidt.)

All over Berlin there were little beer restaurants called Aschinger. When I was broke as a student I used to go to one of them and order one small light beer. There always was a large bowl of fresh bread rolls in the middle of the table, and on these I would fill myself up while disposing of the beer. There were also lots of cafés that sold the decaffeinated Coffee Hag which tasted just as good as the real thing and made its inventor a millionaire. He could sell the coffee for a good price, and the caffeine to drug manufacturers. He came from Bremen and spent some of his money by buying up an old street in Bremen, restoring the houses and giving them rent free to people who promised to live the old lifestyle, with no running water, sewerage, or electricity, and trades done in the old pre-machine way. This became a tourist attraction and I enjoyed seeing it during one of our holidays.

The Kurfürstendamm was even then an area of lots of good hotels, expensive shops and restaurants and nightclubs. I enjoyed an occasional meal at Kampinski's, and my father on occasions took me to good Chinese restaurants. There was also a Norwegian restaurant that sold smoked reindeer meat, which I loved. The zoo was right at the end of the Kurfürstendamm and I often visited it. The various museums and theatres were much the same as they are now, and I believe the Botanic Garden I knew is still in Dahlem.

HIGH SCHOOL

At thirteen I finally told my mother, not how unhappy I had always been at the Berthold Otto school, but just that I was learning absolutely nothing and would never matriculate unless I went to a proper school, so I had private coaching from a young girl for nine months, and then was accepted by the progressive headmistress of a secondary school in East Berlin. I was given a test which must have been hilarious to grade. I remember that in the math test I put the algebra sums into the triangles drawn for a geometry problem, and I had forty-seven mistakes in one page of English dictation. However, the headmistress took a chance and accepted me more or less on trial.

In my first school I literally had learnt nothing except maybe the borders of Europe. My high school class mates had started French at eight, Latin at ten, English at 12 and were going to have a choice of either continuing with these three languages or dropping French and starting Greek the following year. I was excused French, which I had no chance of picking up, and I gradually caught up with the other two languages. English wasn't too bad as at least I could read it fluently, following the earlier time when my mother got a young English woman to come and speak the language with me two afternoons a week. We had about fourteen subjects, but the important ones were Latin and Greek, and some of the others we would only have for one period a fortnight. I never really got over the lack of solid early grounding, I think I could have been quite good at math, but never having learnt multiplication tables I was never quite sure whether 7x 8 was 54 or 56, and similarly with other subjects. Our matriculation consisted of written exams in the four main subjects, Latin, Greek, German and Math. All other subjects were judged on past class reports. If there were a great discrepancy between these and the written exams, the pupil would have an oral exam conducted by university staff to see what his real ability was. This eliminated cheats, and gave a chance to people who might have been sick or very nervous during the written exam. I emerged with an A for Greek and biology, a B for Latin, and C's for everything else, which considering my early school history wasn't too bad.

Our high school was, as I said, progressive for the times. We had children who were Catholics, Lutherans, or Jews, and nobody cared. Some of the girls, just a few, came from fairly well to do homes. One, a girl who experimented at an early age with marijuana and cocaine, was the daughter of a diplomat and a very docile mother, but many of the girls came from quite poor homes and some of those who did not take languages were real working class. At least two I remember were staunch communists.

Apart from my normal uselessness at all sports one of my troubles at school was my eyesight. My mother didn't believe in glasses. When she was a child she and her sisters were taken to an optometrist, who prescribed glasses for all of them. My aunts wore theirs and all grew up very shortsighted. My mother hated hers and kept on breaking them accidentally on purpose, and ended up with practically normal sight. I would say in hindsight that she probably just wasn't as shortsighted as the others, as I know what a wonderful feeling it is to see properly with glasses after having lived in a blur all of your remembered life. Anyhow my mother firmly believed that wearing glasses would make my eyes worse and even once sent me away to a quack doctor, a Count Wieser in a small town in Thuringia, who had a theory that one could strengthen shortsighted eyes by exercises and by giving people glasses intended for longsighted people which made them see even worse. I spent hours looking at a chart trying to read the letters. What happened was that in the end my eyes started to water and the tears acted as lens and made me see the letters, after which I was released for the day. I often wonder whether the strain on my eyes in that period could be responsible for my later getting glaucoma.

I boarded there with a decayed gentlewoman who had been a lady in waiting to the last Empress and was very proud of the fact. She told us once that another lady-in-waiting had become engaged and discovered that her intended was a rotter and broken her engagement. The Empress promptly dismissed her, saying it was nearly as bad as getting a divorce. My landlady was all in favor of this sentiment. Among Count Wieser's more interesting patients was the future king of Yugoslavia, also a brother and sister who were the offspring of a Dutch father and a Japanese mother. The boy looked completely Asiatic, but the girl was one of the most beautiful people I have ever seen, with practically European features, a white and pink complexion, very black hair and deep violet eyes, the only time I have seen eyes of that colour.

By the time I went to high school I had been to a few outstanding films with my parents. My father loved Charles Chaplin and I enjoyed all his early works, *Circus, Goldrush, The Kid,* etc., though they all had rather unhappy endings. I had always hated cruelty in any shape or form, and such things as the wicked stepmother being either torn apart by four wild horses, or rolled down a hill in a barrel studded with nails, and particularly the Prince in "Rapunzel" falling into the thorns and having his eyes pierced made me very upset and unhappy. Picture shows in those days were always the last part of the programme after several newsreels and one-reel cartoons. I used to hate most of these, even though of course they were just cartoon characters like Tom and Jerry, with pianos being dropped on the characters and a horrible one about two bears with the larger one repeating, "Bend over, Junior" and then kicking the smaller one, which made me burst into tears. I did like the very early Walt Disney cartoons, such as "Autumn", which was one of his earliest nature ones, and of course later *The Vanishing Prairie* and *The Living Desert,* but that was much later. It was not till I was twelve or so that I started going to movies on my own or with a schoolmate. I still remember the first such I saw, which was called *The Illegitimates,* and had three appealing child actors in it. At first they were boarded with what we used to call an Angelmaker who starved them. One died, and the eldest, a boy, changed the death certificate from "Heart failure" to "Starvation." An inquiry followed and the two survivors were found new and this time happy homes. The boy was with a woman who wanted to adopt him but when he turned twelve his father, a bargee, turned up and demanded him back, as he was now old enough to help on the barge.

Anyhow, it all ended happily with the boy restored to the nice lady. The second picture I saw was very famous at the time. It was called *Girls in Uniform* and was set in a school for orphans of army officers in Prussia that was run on severe militaristic lines. The new girl got into all kinds of trouble, and the only teacher who befriended her ended up getting sacked, while the girl committed suicide. I never really liked Potsdam after that; it always was a very right-wing area with lots of former army people living there.

I also saw the great German operettas of the time, with sets by Max Reinhardt, who later went to Hollywood. The main ones I remember were *Madame Pompadour*, by Leo Fall, *Madame Dubarry* by Millächer, *White Horse Inn*, and of course *The Threepenny Opera* in the original performance, though not the Premiere. Then came the film *The Blue Angel*, which I recently saw again on late night TV and still think was quite a good film, though very sad. This was, of course, the film that made Marlene Dietrich famous.

Once while I was in high school we went on a fortnight's trip to the Rhineland and beyond. Two teachers went with us; one was our Latin teacher but she had absolutely no idea of home management and did awful things about our food. I remember chiefly getting into trouble because I refused to eat bread and margarine with a slice of salami on it. Margarine then was made from whale oil and tasted horrible and in vain did I ask just to be given the bread and sausage without it. One meal which we all enjoyed, and which I kept in my repertoire later in life, was a cheap and simple one: boil the required amount of spaghetti in saltwater till cooked, drain, add some tinned corn beef and a tin or two of tomato soup, stir well, and reheat. This is particularly nice if a knob of butter (not margarine) is added on serving and melts into the dish. Our trip was mainly to see Roman remains in such places as Trier, Worms, and Cologne, but of course we also saw other sights and did a fair bit of hiking through nice countryside. We slept in youth hostels, which were very plain but clean.

At that time the Rhineland was still occupied by the French, and I remember us being told off by a local because we looked at and aped the French soldiers marching by. We were told that they had to be completely ignored. In one place a local doctor invited us to his house for an evening meal. As we were all starving we were very thrilled. Wine was served, and I, and a couple of others who didn't drink, asked for water, which however wasn't forthcoming. The doctor thought it a huge joke to make the girls drunk, and he and his two sons went round the table filling up any empty glasses. I enjoyed the food provided, which included such things as savory biscuits with smoked salmon and caviar. By the time we came back to the youth hostel at least three of the girls were very sick and spent the rest of the night vomiting. Next morning the manager of the hostel was furious and threatened to have our school blacklisted by the youth hostel association.

After leaving the Rhineland we went on along what is now called the Romantic Way, to medieval towns like Rothenburg and Dinkelsbühl, which I loved. We saw some beautiful old churches with some of Tilman Riemenschneider's famous hinged altarpieces. During the next long hike

I kept lagging behind and eventually confessed to a classmate that I was feeling sick. My temperature was taken and proved to be very high. The class was booked to go back to Berlin by train the next day, but I was obviously not in a fit state to travel so I was put into the public ward of the town's hospital and left there. This was in the days when public wards were long halls with maybe twenty beds along each side. The other patients were all adult women and somehow in great awe of the doctor, who came to visit the ward every day. The nurses checked that all the beds looked perfectly tidy and no one was allowed to move in case they wrinkled a sheet. I read my book, and the woman in the next bed was quite shocked about this, but when he came the doctor actually asked me what the book was and was perfectly human.

When I had recovered sufficiently my father sent some money and I was put on the train home. I must have been still pretty weak, as I slept all through the night and through most of the next day after I got home.

Though I was never wildly popular, I got on better at secondary school and even made a friend or two. One girl invited me home to an orthodox Jewish home, where I met kosher cooking for the first time, things like that glass tube they put on the front door with some Hebrew words in it, and the men eating with little caps on. Before that I had known that I was Jewish, but had known nothing at all about the religion except that the women were not allowed into the body of the synagogue but had to sit behind heavy wooden shutters on galleries, that daughters were not supposed to be able to pray for their fathers, and lots of other types of discrimination which I resented a lot, years before anyone ever thought of women's rights. I kept on wishing I could have been born not

Jewish, and preferably part of a large family, but as from an early age my mother often quoted to me from Struwwelpeter, "For if he tries with all his might, he cannot change from black to white."

At my friend's place I learnt to play Skat, a very good German card game similar to but better than bridge, played with three players. This is a thing I had always missed, neither of my parents would waste their time playing games and I never had anyone to play them with, so had to fall back on solitaire. I was rather amused at some of the foods rules of the orthodox Jews; they had to have two completely separate sets of china, cutlery and cooking utensils, one for meals with milk or milk products, and one for those with meat, because it says in the Bible, "Thou shalt not seethe the lamb in the milk of its mother." Then in theory they were supposed to have a third set for their holy week, but if they couldn't afford that they could get the rabbi to come and purify one of their normal sets. It all seemed silly to me.

INTERLUDE

I had wanted to be a zoologist ever since I was about six years old. Before that I wanted to be an orchid hunter in South America, but gave up that idea because I had no head for heights and couldn't see myself climbing trees. My constant and only requests for birthday and Christmas presents were for books on natural history. Among my favourite reading were the books by the Canadian wildlife writer Ernest Seton Thompson, the Danish Carl Ewald, Maeterlinck's *The life of the bee*, and even more *The life of the termites*, and a book which in fiction form told all about the marvels of ants. The heroine was an ant who for some odd reason travelled about and was invited into communities of various other kinds of ants, including the Australian sugarpot ant, the slavekeeping red ants, ants which lived in symbiosis with an Acacia tree, which provided hollow spines for them to live in, and "honeybread" for them to feed on, in return for protection from other insects which would eat its leaves. Our heroine, Atta, was a leaf-cutter ant and eventually started her own hive with a little bit of fungus she kept in a mouthpocket all through her travels, the fungus being fed with the decomposing bits of leaves and the fruiting bodies of the fungus feeding the colony. At the age of maybe eight I did not wonder how this ant managed to meet ants from all parts of the world, though I disliked *The Swiss Family Robinson* at the same age, not only because of the constant kneeling and praying but also because even then I knew it was impossible for things like kangaroos, tigers, and tapirs all to occur together on one small island. Of course, apart from fiction I also had proper zoology and botany books. Having so few books to read I kept re-reading the same ones time after time and knew most of them by heart. Many years later I obtained copies (in English) of Carl Ewald and Ernest Seton-Thompson for my children, and even then remembered every detail perfectly.

I was of course a city child and not allowed cats or dogs in our flat.

When I was about ten or eleven I was given my former day nursery, which was well away from the rest of the rooms, to have as my own, and I was allowed to keep birds and fish. After that all my pocket money went for either new animals, or containers and food for them. I had to keep the birds in cages, though I made them as large as I could, and always had a dream of enclosing the balcony that opened from this room and making an aviary out of it, just for the warmer months of course. However, I never got that far. The fish were kept in fairly large aquariums, large enough to breed, and I did in fact breed South American cichlids or mouthbreeders quite successfully. These were very aggressive fish, which had to be kept strictly one pair alone, and I had both the blue and the red cichlid, which were very beautiful and interesting to watch. They would make a foam nest of air bubbles coated with spit among the waterweeds and there lay the eggs and watch over them. When the young hatched they would keep them in their mouths until a certain size, and after that they would swim about, dad in front, babies behind, and mum last of all. At any hint of danger all the babies would rush back into the parents' mouths. This was quite different from the behaviour of fish such as guppies, swordfish, or Siamese fighting fish, which produced live offspring, but once having done so would eat their young as soon as look at them.

I was not very successful at breeding birds, chiefly because I could not give them sufficiently large cages. I liked the small finches, and had a wide variety of them, as well as some beautiful Peking robins and a few other insect eaters, which had to be supplied with mealworms and mashed hardboiled eggs. Strangely enough, though of course these were the days before air transport, Australian finches were extremely expensive. For years I wanted some zebra finches, but could never afford them. African finches and some Asian ones, butterfly and tiger finches, one could buy for a few pence, but a pair of zebras cost about 20 Mark. I discovered a very large wholesale and retail animal shop near the Alexanderplatz and spent many happy hours looking at the wares offered, which included a lot of exotic reptiles, frogs and salamanders from South America, including the axolotl, which remained normally in its larval form throughout life and produced its young in that state, but could be made to grow into the adult form with doses of iodine. Some of the frogs and lizards were extremely beautiful, and I haven't seen a better variety of these in any zoo I have visited.

Early on I discovered Hahn's cactus nursery, the second largest in Germany, which was in Lichterfelde on my way to that terrible experimental school I went to, and again I spent many hours there window-shopping, perhaps emerging with one small plant in a two inch pot. I had received permission to keep my cacti on two dumb waiter type of trays, provided that I didn't make a mess. The latter proviso meant that I could not repot anything, and the dry air in the centrally heated flat led to recurrent red spider infestation. I had a beautifully illustrated book on cacti, published by Haage, who had Germany's largest nursery in Erfurt, and it was always my ambition to get the things to flower; but I never succeeded until, many years later, I started another cactus collection in Mount Isa, and after that at King Street (in Clontarf).

After I finished high school, I found that it would be impossible to do what I wanted to do in Berlin, as half the lectures and labs were held at the University and the other half in Dahlem, nearly two hours away by public transport. So I decided to go to a small university to do my first three years, which had to be completed before one could start to think of post-graduate work. I chose Freiburg on Bresisgau at the southern end of the Black Forest, partly because it was nice country, partly because it had a good reputation for science subjects, and partly because it wasn't as anti-Semitic as many other universities.

I found myself student housing in a house which adjoined one owned by one of the student associations "fraternities" which practiced duelling and hard drinking, and I could hear much of what was going on through my bedroom wall. I started taking Botany, but dropped it very quickly as one had to be able to draw, and I was hopeless at that, so I took chemistry instead. Not wanting to sit the State examination I didn't need a third subject.

On the whole I enjoyed my time in Freiburg. It was a pretty town with nice surroundings, and I used to spend my holidays travelling, taking advantage of the very cheap airfares offered by Lufthansa to students. I would work out an itinerary each time, the only trouble being that I liked some of the places so much that I wanted to visit them a second time. One Easter holiday I spent going first to Munich, then to Heiligenblut near Salzburg, and when it started to rain there I took the train to Cortina in the Italian Dolomites. This was much too large a town, so I went on and up to Tres Croces, which was situated among glaciers and lakes of melted glacier water, light green and opaque in colour, and had Edelweiss and gentians growing right around the hotel. This was one of the few occasions when I stayed at a fairly expensive hotel, as this was the only place in Tres Croces. I then went on to the North Italian lakes, staying first at Locarno, which was still wintry with the first wildflowers showing among patches of snow, then going to Lake Como and Lago Maggiore, which was much more Mediterranean, with magnolias in flower.

Another time I went to Marseilles, where I had my only and very satisfying taste of the true bouillabaisse, the fish soup that is a specialty of the area. I walked all over the old harbor parts of Marseilles, but did not see any of the famous crime and nightlife. I enjoyed seeing Chateau D'If, the setting of the start of Dumas' Count of Monte Cristo, a book I had loved as a child and read many times with all its sequels.

From Marseilles I took a small steamer that was going to Algiers, as far as Palma de Majorca in the Balearic Islands. This was long before international tourists had discovered it. I was looking for the lizards which are some of the more spectacularly beautiful ones in Europe, and I would have liked to go to Ibiza where there is a lizard of the same species, but of totally different colouring.

One day I walked right across the central hills of the island to the place where Chopin lived with George Sand and composed the famous *Raindrop Prelude.* I got rather tired, and on the way home, having joined up with another German girl, we actually accepted a lift back to Majorca, though generally I didn't like hitchhiking. I had a very rough passage from Marseilles to Palma, traveling steerage of course. I shared a tiny cabin with eight other women, three tiers of bunks around three sides, leaving just room for the door on the fourth. The luggage was piled in the middle of the floor, and there was also an Alsatian dog. During the night it got very rough and I found myself standing on my head one moment, and on my feet the next. The luggage kept sliding across what floor space there was and the poor dog kept yelping as things hit it. Everybody except me was seasick and the smell became very unpleasant. At first sign of daylight I got up and went up on deck, standing right at the back of the boat and watching it go down one huge wave and up the next equally large one. There were only three of us at breakfast, which turned out a very good and plentiful meal. Leaving Palma I took a boat to Barcelona, the sea this time being quite calm. I had been living on bread and the beautiful Spanish oranges and not much else, and blamed the diarrhea I got on this diet, but I presume it was just one of those infections tourists get from the water.

I wasn't feeling very well when I arrived in Barcelona and rather reluctantly started looking for a German-speaking doctor, dragging myself along the wide and sunny streets of Barcelona without really appreciating anything. Eventually I found the doctor and told him I thought I had a temperature, which he took and found to be almost 41°C. So without much further examination he diagnosed pneumonia and told me to go to bed and stay there, which I did and made quite a quick recovery. However, after that I decided to return home.

While I was on Majorca I attended the Easter service at the cathedral, which started with a procession of magnificently dressed church dignitaries. I was surprised to find the person giving the sermon to be a small unimpressive man dressed all in black (a Jesuit?). However, he was a wonderful orator, and even though I hardly knew any Spanish I got quite carried away listening to him. Instead of "Amen" he ended with "Esso es", which means "And so it is".

Another time I went to Milan, then to Genoa and then right along the Rivieras, first the Italian, then the French. I liked the Italian Riviera much better, as it was more natural and unspoiled. The French Riviera, even then, was full of tourists and facilities for them. Mentone, where my mother had spent some time during her illness, was not too bad, and I was interested in the cactus gardens, designed and made by an eccentric Englishman *(in Mortola?)* on a very steep hillside, just a little less steep than a cliff. The cacti were chiefly types of prickly pear and large columnar cacti, really nothing very beautiful, particularly when compared to the lovely ones I later saw in Canberra and South Australia, but they were well laid out with narrow paths zigzagging about the hillside and beautiful views of the Mediterranean everywhere.

In Monte Carlo I was not allowed into the casino because my passport was marked "student." I was annoyed as I was really curious to see it, having read so much about it. I had no intention of gambling; I only wanted to see the place, but telling them that didn't help at all. From Cannes I did a trip by local bus to Grasse, the town of the perfume industry, which I really enjoyed. The hinterlands, the valleys behind the actual Riviera, are beautiful, with hills and valleys. Flowers are grown for miles around Grasse, and you see fields of violets, narcissus, roses, and so on. I was shown over the factory where the perfume is extracted from the flowers by various methods, and then blended into the commercial perfumes. I don't expect that this still exists, as nowadays perfumes would be made from artificial substances.

I found Nice the most disappointing place of all. It was quite a large town and the beaches even more artificial than in the other places, with concrete walks and palms in tubs everywhere. This was one area I certainly had no desire ever to see again.

I had frequent trips to Switzerland, both in summer and winter. I had early discovered that I much preferred mountains to the seaside and that in fact a couple of weeks in the high Alps would benefit your health more than six weeks on the seaside, possibly because the thinner air makes the body produce more red blood corpuscles. Again I preferred the very small places, going to Arosa in winter. I was never any good at any sport including skiing, and of course I was very shortsighted and not yet wearing glasses, so I frequently collided with trees and the like. However, I liked sledding down mountains, though it was a bit of a bother to have to drag your sled back up each time. Generally, I just went for walks, enjoying the sight of the snow laden fir trees with the red squirrels and various types of tits that let you come quite close to them. One also saw the occasional hares and roe deer, and once even a group of chamois. This part of Switzerland, particularly Davos, was full of sanitaria for TB patients (c.f. *The Magic Mountain* by Mann) and one frequently saw patches of blood on the ground, where some patient had spit them. Another place I loved in Switzerland and always wished to visit again was the Bluelake (Blausee) at Kandersteg, reached from the village by a narrow path, with the lake very deep but the water so clear that one could see the trout swimming twenty meters below the surface. I also spent one early spring at a small place above Lausanne, on the lake of Geneva, which was known for the number of boarding schools of the "finishing" type that existed there. One could see the castle of Chillon from there, and I also visited the castle itself and had a look at the dungeons, and setting for the poem *The Prisoner of Chillon* by Byron, I think.

Another memory I have is of a boat trip across the Bodensee (Lake Constance) in the evening, just as blue sky and sun were returning after a thunderstorm. After sunset the moon rose over the water and looked about ten times its normal size, shrinking as it rose, and the still-ruffled water with reflections of blue and black looked rather like the colours of a blue budgerigar.

One of my few sojourns in France took me from Avignon to Nimes and Arles in Provence, with the very striking Roman remains, including an aqueduct over a river which was still in good enough condition after 2000 years for cars to drive over, even though the Romans used no mortar but just fitted their stones so well together that they lasted practically forever. There is also a very well preserved amphitheatre in Arles, and this is where I saw my one and only bullfight. I only went because I was told that unlike Spain, in the Provence the bulls were not killed, and no horses were used, in fact there were no professional bullfighters. What happened was a test of skill between bull and man. The bull had a little rosette fixed between its horns, and local young men tried to remove this without getting hurt by the bull. The bull of course would chase them, and if they were in real danger they could vault across a six-foot fence to get away from him. On at least one occasion the bull, too, jumped the fence and ran around the arena, with all spectators sitting in the front rows hastily climbing further up.

I would have liked to go back to Sweden or Norway. My only stay in Sweden was just after the war, when my mother and I spent about six weeks in a pastor's house in Sweden, and I got the first taste that I remember of cream. I remember one night being wakened as there was a very severe thunderstorm, and everybody sat huddled in the dark in one room. I probably would have slept through it if I had been left alone. It was a bad storm; I remember the lightning going right round the room along the electric light wires, and also had my only sight of ball lightning. However, later on Sweden and the other Scandinavian countries were always too expensive for me, which was a pity, because I had loved the book by Selma Lagerlöf 's *The wonderful adventures of Nils,* which she of course wrote as a disguised geography lesson, and I would have loved to see a lot more of the country. However, one can't have everything. Among the potential trips I hoped to make one day was one to the Lena and Jenissei [*Yenisei*] rivers in Siberia (in summer of course), and this is another place I never actually got to. My atlas was marked in coloured inks all over the place with journeys I planned to make some day, and it is interesting that Australia was just about the only place I never had any desire to visit.

One of the last, and possibly the most interesting of my trips while I was a student, was to Yugoslavia. I started off in Venice, which I explored on foot, as I couldn't afford a gondola trip. I took a bus trip to the Lido, the famous beach, and found it very disappointing, with dirty looking grey sand and crowds of people, I couldn't get away quickly enough. From Venice I went to Trieste, and then down the Dalmatian coast. Split was an interesting old town, people still dressed in their traditional costumes, men in baggy trousers and white silk shirts with coloured embroidery, riding on tiny donkeys so small the riders' feet were practically on the ground. I loved Korcula, the only island that still had forest on it. All the others had been denuded of trees for building ships for Venice, and then introduced goats kept down any regrowth, so in my time they had bushes of thyme, rosemary, and other wild herbs only about three feet high. I watched the ship building in Korcula; the wood was not bent, but cut along its natural curves and the boats fitted together without nails.

Dbrovnik [*Dubrovnik*] was the highlight of this trip. Not yet discovered as a tourist resort, it was a walled medieval town full of interest. The whole coast was subject to violent storms, and as the market square in Dbrovnik had buildings around three sides and was open to the sea on the fourth; there were strong iron rings set into the walls of the buildings with ropes strung through them. If there was a strong wind one had to cross this square hanging on to the rope and go around the three sides, otherwise one could have been blown into the sea by the wind.

I would have liked to go on to Tirana in Albania, but was told so many horror stories about bandits that I gave it a miss. This was another area that I would have loved to see again, now gone, of course.

After this long detour I am now back in Freiburg. We had a rather nice system in Germany where there were only very few compulsory lectures in each course and for the rest one could pick one's own preferred lecturers. These got a percentage of the money students paid to attend their lecture, so it paid them to be interesting and popular. As I have always been able to learn better by eye (reading) than by ear, I only attended lectures that I enjoyed, including some that had nothing at all to do with my courses, such as psychology. I also went with friends who did medicine to their lectures, and later, back in Berlin, watched some of the world's great surgeons at work. I remember one Professor Sauerbruch, who told us about a girl born without a vagina, whom he operated on because she wanted to get married. He used part of the colon to put in the place of the missing vagina, pulling down and reconnecting the bowels. If he had used a piece of bowel from further up, it would have produced gastric juices whenever the rest of the bowels did. He told the girl to come in if she became pregnant, as she would need a caesarean, and heard no more for years. Then he met her one day in the street with four small children, who she told him had been born perfectly normally. Much to his surprise the piece of bowel had expanded just as a true vagina would. Another time he had a very pretty little girl aged about two was wheeled into the lecture room in her cot, and he got one of the students to feel in her mouth. She had a lump on the roof of her mouth, which he said was an incurable cancer and would kill her painfully in a few more months. He said that this was one of those cases when a doctor might wish for the right to practice euthanasia, but warned of the dangers of this. He said he once sent home a man whom he had diagnosed as dying of an incurable cancer, to die as he thought, only to meet him some years later fully recovered from what turned out to be a form of tuberculosis of the bones. At that time many lecturers still hadn't quite accepted woman students. One such called up a girl student and asked her what was the part of the human body that could expand most. She got embarrassed and started to stutter and blush, and he said: "I am sorry to disappoint you, but it is the vagina."

I enjoyed chemical practicals, which consisted mainly of analyzing substances and giving the elements in it and quantities of each, as well as such things as making soap from lye and fat. I had trouble with this, as one of the by-products is glycerine, and I could never find it in my product. I ended up cheating and buying the required amount of glycerine at a chemist. Unfortunately at that time, about 1931, there was already a rise of anti-Semitism. It didn't affect me all that much personally, though on one occasion I came in to discover that all the chemicals in my jars and bottles had been changed around, but there was one very Jewish looking student who was really persecuted and though I never had the courage actually to interfere I hated to see it.

In Freiburg I also did another experiment, which was to get drunk. This was actually the second time in my life, as when I was just three I once went into our dining room after my parents had given a dinner party, emptied all the dregs of glasses into one glass and drank them. I then went into the hallway, collected all the cushions and pillows I could find which to my then size seemed to make a heap about six foot high, climbed on top of it and went to sleep. During my childhood I was never given alcohol and not even tea or coffee until I was about fourteen, when my father gave me the occasional taste of wine at meals so I would know how to deal with alcohol when meeting it outside the home. However, I never took to either the taste or the effect of either wine or beer. In Freiburg my landlady and some friends took me up to an inn on the top of a hill, reached by going up zigzag roads through lawns and flowerbeds, and I quite deliberately drank enough to get really drunk, just so I could see what it felt like. Strangely enough it did not affect my memory, though one always reads that drunks do things they do not remember the next day. However, it did do away with my normal inhibitions. I remember clearly looking down the hill and thinking what a waste it was to walk around all those paths, so I lay on the ground and rolled down the hill, where eventually my party picked me up when they got down by a more conventional route. I then started singing loudly in the streets on the way home, despite my companions' attempt to keep me quiet. I can't remember having a hangover the next day either. However, this was certainly the last time in my life I ever drank to any extent, and I still don't like either the taste of alcoholic drinks or the effect they have on me.

After three years in Freiburg I returned to Berlin. My father by then was living in two rooms in an old hotel near the business, so again I found students digs, this time with a shoemaker and his wife. My father used to invite me to dinner every now and again, but I didn't see all that much of him.

The shoemaker was a great believer in horse betting and kept giving me tips. Not being a gambler I never followed his advice, but just for the fun of it wrote down his tips and how much I would have won or lost if I had bet, and as I expected, found that at the end of term I would have been quite a bit out of pocket. My dislike of gambling went right back to my early high school days, when we went on one of our monthly excursions. In fine weather we took a train to some place like the Havel lakes and hiked, then caught a train back home, or in bad weather we went to some museum or the zoo. On this occasion it was a hot day, and we all had money for lunch. At lunchtime we called in at an inn to eat our sandwiches and drink lemonade. However, I saw one of those one-armed bandit machines, and spent all my money at it. Though I was extremely thirsty I had to do without a drink as all my schoolmates said they would have happily shared their drinks if I had forgotten or lost my money, but seeing I was stupid enough to gamble it away it served me right, and I jolly well could do without. I hated gambling ever after.

Professor Hermann Pohle, Curator of Mammals

As I had always wanted to go on expeditions I wanted to do some kind of doctoral thesis which entailed collecting my own material. I had decided my main love was mammals, with birds a close second, so I went to the Curator of Mammals [*Professor Pohle*] at the Museum of Natural History and asked if he would accept me as a pupil. I told him about my wish to go collecting but that my father could not afford to finance any proper expedition to places like Africa or South America. He said that he had just had a Palestinian (Israeli) girl called Aharoni who had done her thesis on the Muridae of Syria and Palestine, and he also had recently had a visit from some people from the Turkish Ministry of Agriculture asking for advice and help with plagues of rodents, so that if I did my thesis on the Muridae of Asia Minor it would link up with Miss Aharoni's work, and I would get permits and assistance from the Turkish Government. This is what I eventually did, though like all his students I had to undergo a trial period spent in skinning and stuffing a variety of old specimens that had been preserved in either alcohol, or worse still, in formalin. During this time I read what little was available on Asia Minor, and also paid a Turkish student to teach me some of his language, orally only, as I didn't want to bother learning the Arabic alphabet which was still used for writing. Actually Turkish is a very easy language in some ways, as the grammar has no exceptions at all; if one knows the way one plural is formed, that is the way all plurals are formed, and the same with conjugation of verbs. All one really has to do is learn vocabulary, and a few conventions, for instance the Turks shake their heads for yes, and put their head back and click their tongue for no. The Turkish language has nothing in common with Arabic, but is more related to Hungarian and Finnish, but in writing, as in newspapers, nearly all the words used are from Arabic.

I also took some riding and shooting lessons, and never got terribly good at riding, but then, one just walked the horses. I remember the first time I went to the rifle club and asked to be taught. Again women were not commonly known to do such things then, and the young man who was supposed to test me out gave me an old muzzle loader elephant gun and told me to shoot at a target. Fortunately my father had warned me to hold the gun tightly against my shoulder, as the gun had a terrific kick. Some older man came along when he heard the terrific bang and told off the young fellow, saying I could have broken my shoulder. However, I had managed to hit the edge of the target and though bruised was not seriously damaged, so I was accepted. I got pretty good at target shooting, but never really mastered clay pigeon shooting. I hated seeing groups of young Brown and Blackshirts practicing pistol shooting with human shaped targets.

Finally, as I had never actually done any collecting, I went to a little place in Bavaria and did some collecting, bringing back a collection of small rodents, shrews, and so on. Though my father paid for my trip, an old (Jewish) man [*Oscar Neumann, a well known ornithologist who ended up in Chicago*] who had once been rich but was now quite poor and who used to amble about the museum where he knew everybody, got me orders from the Field Museum in Chicago for birds, and from the Rothschild museum at Tring for fleas and certain butterflies.

Dr. Oscar Neumann

So one day in early spring 1933, I set off for Turkey in the famous Orient Express (third class, of course). Trains then had four classes, the first was heavily upholstered; second class rather like our one class trains nowadays with some leather upholstery; third class with wooden seats; and fourth class was just empty trucks without any seats, and one sat on one's luggage or the floor. First class had two beds in sleepers, with bedclothes and morning tea provided, second class had three beds in each tier and only a blanket provided, and there were no sleepers at all in third or fourth class. I was interested in seeing the different looking types in the various countries we passed through, and was impressed with the Bulgarians, who often had clear grey eyes with long black lashes. I remember a young Rumanian telling me all Rumanians were liars and never to believe anything they said.

Fortunately I had always had good health, though at one time I had been allergic to lots of things. I would get hives and my blood was full of eosinophil cells, and medical students used to ask me for specimens for their slide collection. Anti-histamines were a new thing then, and my doctor gave me a series of three anti-histamine injections, each of which raised an enormous hive on my buttock, but after that I had no more allergic reactions, and the extra eosinophils disappeared from my blood samples. I also had arthritis more or less all my life. I had no more tonsillitis after having my tonsils partially removed at the age of eight, but of course my tonsils grew again. When I was about nineteen I was quite badly crippled with arthritis, and spent a whole winter not being able to straighten my back. The doctor thought it was the infected tonsils that caused the trouble and sent me to a woman surgeon who this time took out the tonsils properly, again with local anesthetic because they were so enlarged that she might have cut into some vein and caused a hemorrhage. I asked her to let me see the tonsils and she did so, showing me the pockets of pus and explaining everything. I had to stay in hospital for a week, and I was told not to drink alcohol, as some other girl was given wine by her family to celebrate her homecoming and had hemorrhaged to death. After the operation my arthritis improved a lot, and I could sleep quite comfortably on a wooden seat wrapped in a blanket, or on the floor.

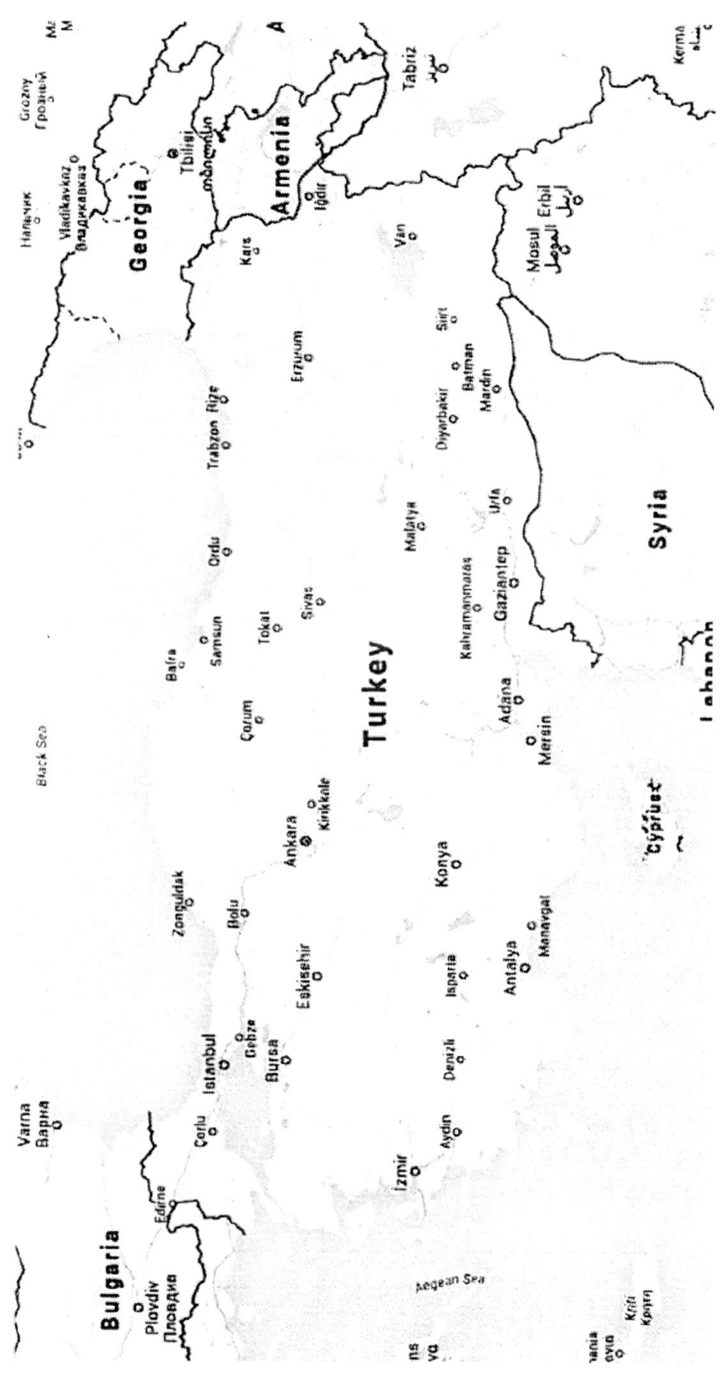
Turkey
Syria
Georgia
Armenia
Bulgaria
Black Sea
Aegean Sea
Tbilisi
Vladikavkaz
Grozny
Kars
Iğdir
Van
Tabriz
Erbil
Mosul
Siirt
Batman
Mardin
Diyarbakir
Erzurum
Trabzon
Rize
Urfa
Malatya
Ordu
Gaziantep
Kahramanmaras
Sivas
Tokat
Samsun
Bafra
Adana
Mersin
Çorum
Kirikkale
Ankara
Konya
Zonguldak
Bolu
Manavgat
Antalya
Isparta
Eskisehir
Gebze
Bursa
Istanbul
Denizli
Varna
Çorlu
Aydin
Izmir
Edirne
Plovdiv
Kriti

ASIA MINOR

I arrived in Istanbul in spring 1933, and stayed there for a few weeks, finding my feet so as to speak. Turkey was then a very interesting country, having been for the previous ten years or so under the dictatorship of Mustapha Kemal, later known as Ataturk. He had been an army officer under the Sultan, and after the war, when the British had occupied Constantinople, he was sent to Asia Minor to demobilize Turkish troops. Instead he set up an opposition government with a new capital at Ankara, made war on and drove out the Greeks, which included massacring about 200,000 of them in Smyrna, and set about westernizing the country. Though on the whole a benevolent dictator to his own people, he enforced his wishes pretty ruthlessly, making an example of people who continued wearing the fez for instance, by hanging some of them in public places. By the time I arrived his government was well established, and favoured by most people.

I forget how I got to know a group of Germans and Austrians, possibly through the German consulate in Istanbul. The name was changed from Konstantinople since this was Greek, but a scholar told me that actually Istanbul was equally Greek, being the local dialect version of "en ten poleyn", or "into town". The town was divided into three main parts, Stamboul being on the European side of the Bosporus, and Galata and Pera over the bridge on the Asiatic side. Stamboul was the old part of the city, with its mosques and palaces and the famous bazaar; Pera was where most foreigners lived.

I stayed at a hotel in Pera, and one of the first things I learnt was that Turkey was a veritable heaven for bedbugs. They were everywhere, and as Moslem religion does not permit killing of animals other than for food, they were quite unmolested. The first night I spent in this fairly good hotel I counted thirty-eight bug bites on my lower arm from wrist to elbow. I eventually solved this problem by making a sleeping bag out of a mattress cover with a drawstring I could tie round the neck. Over my head I had a piece of muslin, which was tucked into the bag so that only my face was exposed. For some reason bedbugs don't bite people on the face, or not me anyhow. Fleas also abounded as did lice, and the Turks would gently remove them and throw them out of a window on some passerby. Before I came to Turkey there had been also hordes of feral dogs all over Istanbul, which was rather dangerous as rabies was endemic. Again the Turks could not actually kill them because of their religion. They solved the problem by catching all the dogs and taking them by boat to a barren rocky island where they gradually starved to death, the stronger eating the weaker ones. It didn't matter to the Turks how cruel they were to animals as long as they didn't actually kill them. In this case a French glove manufacturer had offered to pay a small sum for each dog, kill it humanely, and use the skin for glove leather, but this offer was refused.

The Germans I got to know in Istanbul were mainly young girls about my own age, some working as governesses or office workers, others waiting to be repatriated after a failed marriage to a Turk. It happened frequently that a German girl married a Turkish student, who while he was in Germany behaved like everybody else. However, on going back to Turkey with him the girl would find that she was expected to conform to rules applying to Turkish women, including quite often accepting another wife or two, and many couldn't take it. I did some sightseeing in the old city, and was very interested in the Bazaar, which was enormous, with streets of brass workers, carpet sellers, goldsmiths, etc. I learnt to look out for traps, such as an apparently old brass table having a design of a railway train on it, and to tell whether a carpet was really old by testing the colours. The best old vegetable dyes were colourfast, whereas the modern product of the time used aniline dyes which ran when wet.

I began to realize that it would be impossible for a lone woman to travel in Asia Minor. Fortunately I got to know a minor official from the Austrian embassy called Sepp Finger, who was due for quite a lot of long service leave. Finger spoke not only Turkish, but also Persian and Arabic perfectly, and had the kind of pleasant easygoing personality very useful in Turkey. His hobby was collecting folklore, and he offered to come with me as interpreter and male protector, pretending for the purpose to be my maternal uncle, which in the Turks' eyes made him like my father. It was he who told me the story that exemplifies the difference between Prussians and Austrians. During the war, when of course the Turks were on Germany's side, a German officer came to a Turkish supply post, wanting some things.

"Come in," said the Turk, "Fine morning isn't it? Sit down and have a cup of coffee."

"I don't have time for that," said the German, "I just came to ask you if you can let me have ...?"

"Sorry, I don't have that," said the Turk.

A while later an Austrian officer came in. He accepted the invitation, exchanged small talk with the Turk and drank coffee for a while, then said,

"Look, could you possibly let me have ...?"

"Of course, dear fellow," said the Turk.

I was lucky when visiting the Hagia Sophia, which was originally a Byzantine church and is now a mosque, to see wall paintings that had been hidden under whitewash for centuries and had just been exposed again on command from Kemal Pasha. The Moslems take their religion very seriously of course, though the Turks on the whole not as much as the Arabs or the Persians. They interpret the commandment about not making images to mean that one must not draw, paint or sculpt human figures or even animals and their designs are almost always geometrical. It was good to see those perfectly preserved biblical wall paintings and mosaic floors that had been hidden from sight possibly for five hundred years. It was also interesting to go to the bazaar with Finger, who was on friendly terms with many of the stallholders. Generally the Turks don't like any foreigners, and Persians, Armenians, and Levantines, among others were only allowed in Istanbul, and not anywhere else in Turkey. Tourists, who were few and far between in those days, were suspected of being spies, or else would-be exporters of antiquities. Asia Minor is of course full of the latter (just think of Troy, with its thirty-six layers of towns) and Kemal had brought in a very useful law that made excavation an offense, unless done with permission from the government. In all too many cases local peasants would find an old town or burial site, dig down looking for coins or jewellery and destroy everything else in the process.

After my stay in Istanbul I went on to Ankara, where I had to see the Minister of Agriculture who would give me the necessary official permits and support to do my collecting. I had been warned not to travel first class in the train, as the bugs and other vermin were much worse in the upholstered seats than in the wooden ones of the cheap class. Ankara was almost completely a very modern city, having only a small section that still showed some of the original little town. Like Canberra it was built entirely as a capital and seat of government. There was a national university, and at that time many of the professors were Germans, who lectured in German with a Turkish student translating. They had been told that eventually when sufficient Turkish students had graduated, they would be replaced by Turks unless they could lecture in fluent Turkish by then, but most didn't bother learning the language. For transport Ankara had what they called captie-catchtee, minibuses holding seven or eight people. The principle was that the first passenger would say where he wanted to go, the owner/driver then stood outside shouting his destination, and anyone going in a similar direction would also get in. The buses had no timetable, but left whenever they had a full complement of passengers.

At this point I better give some idea of the geographical features of Asia Minor. It is really a peninsula, roughly like a long rectangle with Black Sea on the north, Mediterranean on west and South Russia and Persia in the east. There are mountains right along the Black Sea line, the Pontic Mountains, and again along the southern line up from the Mediterranean, the Taurus Mountains. A dry high plateau is in the central part.

In Ankara I was told that foreigners were not allowed to go anywhere east of the Euphrates River, nor into the western area within a couple of hundred miles from the Mediterranean. This was because of the fear of spies, fear of Russians in the east, and fear of the Italians, who were then fortifying the island of Rhodes within sight of the west coast. I was allowed to go anywhere else, but had to report to the local police station immediately on arrival, tell them how long I expected to stay and where I was going next, and then report again before leaving. My passport had a long piece of paper glued into it on which my comings and goings were registered.

The Turkish police were actually a part of the army, and were always sent to a part distant from the one they came from in case they were not impartial. All male Turks had to do military service. Those who could read and write served two years, and those who couldn't three years, with the first year being used for education. I only ever met one able bodied young man who escaped military service. He happened to be from a very high mountain area which was too cold for fleas, bugs, and so on to survive, and had developed no immunity to them, so he got violent allergic reactions and nearly died, and eventually was sent back home. The Minister of Agriculture gave me a letter to all the officers of his department, asking them to assist me whenever they could, which proved very helpful.

One afternoon during my stay in Ankara a German entomologist asked me whether I would like to accompany him on a walk in the countryside to observe and catch some of the local insects, such as scorpions, tarantulas and centipedes. We were turning over stones in a small gully when suddenly about a dozen men surrounded us and started to fight my companion. I was ignored, except for one boy about 15 or so who tried to stop me from getting back up to the level of the plain. However, I got back up and luckily saw a troop of soldiers marching along not too far away. I called out this news to the German, who repeated it in Turkish, whereupon all the men ran away and we got home without further incident. I wondered what those people had been after, as we didn't look terribly prosperous, but I had been told that some Turks would murder you for a pair of boots. On returning to Ankara and talking about the incident I was told that a few weeks earlier an Austrian lecturer and his wife had gone for a walk in that area, and that the man had been badly beaten up and his wife raped.

Before leaving for Turkey I had of course studied what information was available about my field. It is really surprising, considering how close Asia Minor is to Europe and how easy to get to, how little it had been explored. My plan was of course to obtain specimens from areas that had been missed by previous travellers. Zoologically Asia Minor is very interesting, being on the crossroads of different fauna areas both from east to west and from north to south. For instance in the north there were ermine, martens, stags and pheasants, in the south hyenas, leopards, mongoose, and near the Syrian border, gazelles. I had no definite itinerary, but wanted to go to places that had not been visited by collectors before and in as many different fauna regions as possible.

After obtaining the necessary permits I returned to Istanbul to pick up my camping and collecting gear and Sepp Finger. One of the most valuable pieces of advice I had been given in Germany was that only badly planned and executed collecting trips led to "adventures", and never to take silly risks. So for the first place to collect in I picked Bolu in the Pontic mountains to which there was a bus service. This is about a hundred kilometres as the crow flies from Istanbul, but at least twice as far as the road wends. The bus, like all Turkish buses, was completely overloaded, luggage was piled high on the roof, and passengers who couldn't fit in the bus sat on top of this. The roads were absolutely shocking. Between Istanbul and Bolu we passed over 36 bridges, and at each someone had to get out and walk across, testing every board in case it had rotted through. The Turks had odd ideas of westernization. We passed many villages which had built concrete pools holding about two feet of water and shaped like the Sea of Marmara, located about a kilometre outside the village, when the money and effort would have been much better spent repairing some of the dangerous bridges. Also schools were invariably built well outside the villages, entailing long walks for the pupils. Turkey had been largely an illiterate country before Kemal Pasha, who brought in universal education to age ten at least.

The Pontus area is very beautiful. The whole area is so thickly wooded that in those days timber could only be cut in the areas nearest coastal towns, which had been cleared and the forest replaced by scrubby regrowth. All the rest was covered by magnificent pine forests with huge trees, lichens hanging from branches rather like Spanish moss because of the high rainfall, and masses of rhododendrons everywhere. Oleanders were also very common and occurred on the edge of the forest, in clearings and near the coast. It is interesting that the ancient Greek writer Herodotus told of a poison honey in that area, which made soldiers who ate it go mad. This was long regarded as one of the author's tall stories, but we now know that the honey from nectar gathered by the bees from oleander is really poisonous, with symptoms as Herodotus described them.

After a short stay in Bolu we hired packhorses and went east to another mountain town called Tosya. The Turkish packhorse is an unfortunate creature. It is used from the time it is a yearling, and is always completely overloaded. A normal load consists of two saddlebags holding about a hundred kilos each, with a large Turk riding on top. Feeding is rare and the animal normally depends on what it can graze during the night and rest stops. As a result horses are skinny, undersized, and nearly all have knock-knees on the back legs. Geldings were the most desirable mounts, as with stallions and mares one ran the risk of unwanted excitement should two caravans meet and a mare be in season.

In Tosya we met the local officer of the Department of Agriculture. I chiefly remember him because he had a large hole in his nose, the result of an untreated boil that broke through to the inside of his nose. This man had a really beautiful horse, and when we asked him how he managed to get it he said that it was just one of the local kind, but as a foal had been so weak that the owner didn't expect it to live and so sold it to this man very cheaply. Just by proper feeding, and not riding it until it was old enough, it grew into a magnificent specimen by local standards. He said he was due to go on an inspection trip for the Department and suggested we travel with him. This took us into the higher mountains. It was quite an experience. The lower reaches of the Pontus have extreme humidity, about 2000mm a year, but the humidity decreases quite suddenly at a higher level and just above the limit of forest growth one stands in clear blue sky looking down on an endless sea of clouds, which covers the entire lower land right up to the sea. It is too wet for wheat; the peasants grow maize and rice, and also a lot of fruit trees and very good tobacco.

While the larger towns in Anatolia have hotels, or rather caravanserais, usually built round a central yard in which the animals are kept, the smaller villages had the tradition of making guests welcome. Some villages had a special guesthouse that was only used by travellers, in others the peasants took turns in providing accommodation and in either case the villagers provided the food, always the best they could afford. In the richer villages they might kill a fowl, but generally the food was pillav, a kind of fried rice, maybe with some eggs fried in lots of fat. The bread was the unleavened kind, like flat plates, and was used instead of cutlery to mop up fat. Everybody ate lots of garlic, and in sheer self-defense I too started to eat this so I couldn't smell it on them. There were times in Turkey when we lived for weeks on unleavened bread just rubbed over with a bit of garlic. In the fruit growing areas there generally was also a "traveller's tree," the fruit being reserved for travellers only, and even the smallest children knew not to touch it. To offer payment for the hospitality would have been a deadly insult, so having been warned in advance I carried things like Woolworth costume jewellery, to give as presents to wives or children of the host.

There were no chairs and tables; one half lay on the floor round a low platform to eat. Only the oldest men sat with us, while the young men and women served the food and did not eat till we were finished. Also, it was the old men who knew and told all the folklore, unlike Germany where the Brothers Grimm had got most of their material from the old village women. I soon understood Turkish sufficiently to understand and enjoy the conversation. I was interested to find that many of our German fairytale motives also occurred in Turkey, for example Big Claus and Little Claus and many others. There was one character rather like our Till Eulenspiegel called Hodja Nasreddin, of whom lots of funny stories were told. He was supposed to be a real person, and later in Konya I saw his grave, which typically had a large and heavy stone door with an enormous stone padlock situated in an otherwise open space. One story I remember was this: Hodja was sitting on a tree, sawing off the branch on which he was sitting. A passing traveller said, "Look out, you'll fall." "Nonsense," thought Hodja, who went on sawing, and in due course he fell with the branch. He ran after the traveller and said, "You must be a great fortune teller, tell me when I am going to die." No denials helped; he insisted, and to get rid of him the man finally said, "You will die after you have sneezed three times." Hodja tried hard not to sneeze, but in spite of his efforts he eventually sneezed once, then again, and finally a third time. He immediately said, "Now I am dead," and he lay down not moving with his eyes closed. In due course the family came, thought he was dead, and put him on a bier to take to the cemetery. (Turks don't get buried in coffins.) When they came to a fork in the road they stopped and started arguing about which way was the shorter road. Hodja eventually got tired of this, sat up and said, "When I was still alive, I always used to take the left fork."

Another folk tale was about a peasant who had a very clever daughter. He went to the Sultan and boasted how he could solve any problems. The Sultan said, "I shall give you a problem, if you solve it you shall become one of my advisers, if not you will be beheaded." The man came home and lamented about his lot, the problem seemed insoluble: "I give you a ram, you make me a rug from his skin, a meal from his flesh, and give me back the ram unharmed." The daughter said: "That's easy. You shear the ram and I will spin the wool and make a rug from it, then you castrate it and make a meal from the testicles, and then return the animal." The man became an adviser to the Sultan, and the daughter one of the Sultan's wives.

The average Turkish peasant was very poor. Everybody had to pay a tax on every head of stock he owned, and also a general tax of about six dollars a year. If they could not pay they could work off the debt by doing roadwork. One constantly saw gangs of people on the side of the road, breaking stones into gravel. At first I thought they were convicts, but they were just people working off their taxes. In the rice growing areas malaria was rife and one saw many nearly naked children with hugely swollen stomachs because the spleen was enlarged by repeated attacks of malaria. Better off were the peasants who grew opium poppies. This was a strictly controlled crop, that had to be licensed by the government, and all the opium was sold to it.

The coastal area of the Black Sea has very many remains of ancient Greek settlements. The Greeks called the Black Sea the Pontus Euxinus, which means the hospitable sea, and we were told at school that this was one of those cases where they tried to pacify the gods by calling them something pleasant, as they called the Furies the "gracious ones," as in fact the Black Sea is much given to sudden severe storms. However, scholars I spoke to in Turkey thought that it was really a hospitable sea for them, as everywhere they came they found Greek settlements already in existence. Here also are many remains of the Crusader times, ruins of castles, and so on.

From Bolu we went on to Tosya, which lies further east, in a high plateau that shows some resemblance to the inland plateaus. The inhabitants there grow mainly rice in small irrigated paddy fields, each surrounded by a low dam. When I was there they had a plague of the little rice hamster, and this was my first experience of such a plague. As is generally the case, in the early days of the plague most of the specimens caught were pregnant females, whereas towards the end, when food supplies ran low and the plague animals resorted to cannibalism, it was the adult males that survived, which is the reason that it always takes such a long time for a species to build up again after a plague.

From Tosya we caught a bus back to Ankara, and from there went to Inevi, right in the middle of the central plateau, and close to the Tusshollu, one of the saltiest of the saltwater lakes in the world. Interestingly not far from this there was a freshwater spring and a small swamp area containing such things as the Northern water rat, though it must have been cut off from the northern river system for several thousand years. Here again we found an example of the misapplication of westernization. People here used to build their houses from mud bricks, which were very effective in keeping the place cool in the daytime and warm at night. However, now they were building with concrete, which in contrast was hot by day and cold at night.

The inland of Anatolia is full of archaeological remains. One can tell tombs from old settlements, as the tombs have a kind of pyramid shape whereas the towns usually leave hills wider and higher at one end with a kind of narrower tail. In places where there had been digs as many as thirty-six layers of settlements were found, one on top of the other, starting right back in the Neolithic and progressing through Hittite, Byzantine, and right up to the fairly recent past. Some of the old settlements may have been destroyed by fire or war, but generally it was a matter of the water supply drying up, the place being abandoned and covered over by sandstorms, and later resettled if a new spring developed. Sandstorms were frequent in the area and the fine dusty sand penetrated everything. It even got into the works of a watch packed in a suitcase right among clothes and I was glad that I had mainly metal boxes.

The peasants in the central parts of Turkey grow a short hardy kind of wheat and keep herds of goats, including Angora goats, and fat-tail sheep. I went on further east to Konya, a very old town with some very beautiful old mosques and other old buildings with magnificent stonework carved and decorated, and beautiful mosaic floors. Then we went down nearer the Taurus Mountains to Eregli and to Karaman, which is halfway up the Taurus Mountains. I realised the necessity of the government ban on unauthorized digging up of antiquities when we were told in one village that a grave had been dug up; in it was a very well-preserved body of a young woman, still fully dressed. The villagers promptly divided up the clothing among themselves, only to see it fall into dust in a few days after exposure to the air. All that was left were a few blue glass beads, the remains of an armband, and these were not of any value being widely found everywhere. The grave by the description was from the Byzantine times. At another place I was offered a Hittite seal to buy. However, I was a bit worried about breaking the law when I had had so much assistance from the Turkish government and I refused to buy, after taking a rubbing of the seal. Later at the Berlin Museum I was told that this seal was a tremendous specimen, so I hope it got somewhere safe eventually. I was also told of two brothers who found a whole library of stones with cuneiform inscriptions somewhere east of Kayseri. They removed them to a cave which they thought would be safer, just keeping a few to show foreigners who might be profitable customers. This was during the Kurdish wars, the two were killed, and no one knew where they had buried the plates.

From Karaman I went up into the high mountain area of the Taurus to Ermenek. The Taurus Mountains are of course very different from the Pontic region. There are far fewer rivers and the climate is Mediterranean. Instead of apples, pears, peaches and oranges the people grow edible chestnuts and other southern things, and the forests consist of leafy trees such as walnut, chestnut, olive, and of course the cedar of Lebanon. This is so common that whole villages are built from it. There was a house being built just when we came to Ermenek and it smelled just like a freshly sharpened pencil magnified a million fold. All these wooden houses were magnificently carved and decorated, the carving being of course geometrical and then painted mainly blue and green. As always people looked down on the traditional, and a few ugly concrete buildings were very much admired.

On the way we passed the river in which Barbarossa (Redbeard) had been drowned when going on a crusade. I was not at all surprised; I tried to have a bath in the icy cold water and was nearly torn away from the branch I held onto because the river was running so fast. Keeping clean was always a problem in Turkey. Mostly one had to be satisfied with washing face and hands. The Turks only eat with the right hand, using the left for cleaning themselves after using a toilet, which is just a hole in the ground with two marks where one puts one's feet. No toilet paper, just a jug of water and, as I said, one uses the left hand for cleaning, so it is never used for eating. There are of course steam baths in the larger towns, but it takes nearly a whole day to visit one and go through all the different stages of first getting used to the heat, then the actual steam, then spending so much time in each of progressively cooler rooms. Women have their separate days, of course. Once when I got desperate I asked for water in my room, then covered up the window and cracks, got undressed, and had an all over wash. On emerging I found a crowd of women, all very concerned that I might got pneumonia from such imprudence.

We also passed a now well-known place that has so much lime in the water that each little runnel has built itself a bed several feet high out of the lime that deposited out of the water. The man who charged a small fee for showing this would throw a rose in at the top of the little canal, and it would emerge completely coated with lime further down and could be kept indefinitely.

I had a few bad moments during these travels. In one village the headman put an edible toadstool on my plate, which was riddled with cooked maggots. I said to Fingers, "I can't eat that," and he told me I must, it would be a terrible insult not to. I still said I couldn't and he eventually saved me by waiting till we were unobserved and then taking the morsel and eating it himself. Another time we had been travelling on packhorses for three days, much of it along the side of a mountain completely consisting of black obsidian. The path was about two feet wide and wound round the mountain, so one could see about 1000 feet above, and there was a 2000-foot drop to the right. This was bad enough, but eventually we came near the village of our destination and found it was on the other side of a wild mountain river, flowing over rocks way below. A tree trunk was the only way to cross to the other side. I said I just couldn't cross this. Finger said, "You must, you can't go back alone the three days we have come, and there just across is our village." Eventually he got a ball of string out of our gear, gave me one end to hold and said, "Follow me across, holding on to this and not looking down." I knew as well as he that had I fallen the string was no help at all, but somehow holding it enabled me to cross the river. This was one of the worst times of my life, just the same.

The last spot on this trip was Tarsus (of St. Paul fame), quite a large town not too far from the Syrian border. From there we returned by train to Ankara and Istanbul, and I returned to Germany to spend the winter doing some more work in the museum.

The following spring I returned to Istanbul. Fortunately Finger was prepared to go with me once more, as though by now I could speak Turkish quite well, it still would have been impossible for a woman alone to travel in Turkey at that time.

We first went to Brussa, which is on the southern shore of the Sea of Marmara and on the foot of Mount Olympus. This is not the one in Greece where the gods are supposed to live, though presumably the ancient Greeks living in that area named it Olympus because they thought that gods lived there also. Brussa was the nearest I could get to the western area of Asia Minor, which was out of bounds for foreigners. I collected from sea level to high up Mount Olympus. In one village people showed us a very beautifully embroidered wedding outfit that had been in the family for generations. I wanted one of the girls to put it on so I could take her photo, but she refused, being frightened of the savage punishments for wearing non-western clothes, so eventually I put on the outfit and Finger took my photo in it. It is interesting that when I left Turkey, of all the things the Customs officer looked at, the only thing they confiscated was this photo, which they thought would give Westerners a terrible impression of the new Turkey. Fortunately I had the negative. I then went to Antalya, which is on the south coast, but much further west than Tarsus, in fact due south from Istanbul. This is off the main range of the Taurus at the foot of a very high mountain, and I was particularly keen on collecting on this mountain, which had not previously been visited by any zoologists. Unfortunately I picked that particular moment to get malaria, and by the time I had recovered sufficiently the police had caught up with my plans and told me I was not allowed to go. I am sure I would have found many interesting things, including quite possibly a new Apollo butterfly for Rothschild at Tring.

My last visit that summer was to Rize, which is right at the Eastern coast of the Black Sea, not too far from the Russian border. This is the part of the Pontic region with the highest humidity and the highest mountains; in fact the mountain range behind Rize is a continuation of the Caucasus. Its height is 3700 metres, or over ten thousand feet. Whereas in the lowlands the peasants grow the usual crops of maize, rice, fruit, tobacco and even tea, the parts above the tree line are used for pasture for the cattle in summer. I had been collecting on the coast and up some distance into the mountains when we found some villagers who were about to go up to just below the perpetual snowline, and were willing to let us come along. The country there is so rough that packhorses cannot be used, and the women carried all burdens. As a result many women died in childbirth, and in my time the government had established a clinic to help and advise these women. It was found however, that the men would not let their wives attend the clinic; they said it was cheaper and easier just to get another wife.

People in Turkey generally thought foreigners were either spies or collecting antiquities for illegal export. They could not understand why I was collecting rats and mice, and it would have been useless to tell them about science or museums, so Finger made up a story that mice had long tails and many children, and my specimens were going to be used to make a fertility drug for women who couldn't have children.

We spent about three days walking up the mountain and there was no well-defined road, only cattle tracks going up and down into and out of creeks. Eventually we came to the summer grazing area. This would have been early in July, as the winter doesn't end until June, and the first snow falls again in September. The Turks had a shed in which they kept the milk, which did not go sour in the high mountains, in wide flat wooden pans until the cream set on top. They then made the cream into cheese. I had previously tried camel milk, which I didn't like, and which often had urine splashed into it during milking, but I had loved the rich milk of buffalos, which was yellow and tasted like cream. In any case, the villagers gave us cream and cheese as part of the deal, but otherwise we had brought our own food.

This was a very beautiful area and full of interesting wildlife, including snow fowl, chamois, and so on. Unfortunately I had not been allowed to take a rifle, and these animals were so shy one could never get within shotgun range of them, but could see them way up on a high mountain on the other side of the valley. I had brought my tent from Germany; it had a waterproof floor and was small and just for sleeping. One morning I woke up to find that it had snowed during the night and the tent was covered with several inches of snow. That day the peasants got ready to return to their village. Unfortunately Finger's boots had worn out and so he had to do the entire return journey with native type footwear. To make this you stand on a piece of fresh green hide, which is then cut around and pierced with a knife round the edges, another strap of green hide is threaded through this and tied round your ankles. The trouble is of course that one can feel every stone through them.

On returning to Rize we found that we had caused quite a panic. There had been rumours that we had been kidnapped by bandits or even killed and the police were both relieved when we returned and annoyed with us. Furthermore my father in Germany had trouble getting money out to me, the Germans having just brought in laws restricting the taking of money out of the country. So I thought it best to return to Germany, even though it was not very late in the season.

In Turkey I gave away my cheap Woolworth watch, which had served me well through both trips. Ironically I bought an identical one on returning to Germany and this stopped after three days. I was told that these cheap watches were welded into the case and could not be repaired. I took one live specimen with me, a large horned owl that I acquired just before going home. I thought to give this to the Berlin Zoo, but found that it was not wanted. Luckily, as I lived in digs, I was able to pass it on to a fellow zoology student. I also brought back a Saluki or Persian greyhound. A pair of these had been presented to us as a special mark of esteem and Finger kept the male, while I took the female. The salukis of this area are smaller than those of Persia, where they hunt gazelles, and are used to hunt hares. Unlike greyhounds which have the intelligence bred out of them, they are highly intelligent as well as very beautiful, and mine proved to be an ideal city dweller, being content to spend days lying quietly with elegantly crossed forelegs as long as I took her for a good run at least once a week. I tried to give her exercise by letting her join a practice run with greyhounds, but found that once she discovered the hare to be artificial she lost interest and refused to run after it. I used to take her to the Grunewald and let her run madly round and round a large clearing. Another woman with a saluki, a breed then very rare in Europe, told me a story that proves these dogs' intelligence. During one of the rabies scares when all dogs had to be muzzled out of doors, her saluki used to run off behind bushes and return without the muzzle. Eventually she got a heavy metal muzzle, which he could not dislodge. He came to her and indicated that he wanted her to follow him and led her to the place where he had discarded all the other muzzles, as if to say, "Well, if I have to wear the thing I would prefer the light leather one."

I would have loved to make a collection of Turkish rugs. These are very distinctive, each village having its own traditional designs and colours, some being famous for their product. Carpet and rug making was still done as cottage industry, though unfortunately often modern aniline dyes were used, but one could have bought very good rugs quite cheaply, only I never had enough money to spare. In one town in Eastern Anatolia I was shown through a government carpet factory. The workers were all children, girls between eight and 13 years old, the idea being that their smaller hands were able to make smaller knots and a finer end product. I was told that no cruelty was involved in this child labour, the girls spent several hours per day at school, were well fed and treated, with the money they earned being a considerable help to their impoverished families. In addition each girl when leaving the factory was given a bonus, which amounted to quite a good dowry. Apart from these woollen rugs there are also felt mats made, chiefly in the cotton growing areas. Felt making is an interesting process to watch. On a large level floor with a frame around it about thirty centimetres or so of either finely teased short bits of wool or cotton are strewn, the whole well shaken in all directions so as to mat the fibres, then wet and pressed with very heavy weights. Other layers may be added to give the required thickness. On the last layer a pattern is created by cutting strips of felt of a contrasting colour and arranging them on the surface before pressing.

I did make a collection of guest towels. These too were different in almost each village and seemed to show the origin of the population. They were made from a kind of huckaback cotton, and used after meals, with a dish of water, to clean hands, as of course there were no knives and forks. Each towel had a border, about three or four inches wide on either end. Some had coloured floral designs, others geometrical designs, and in one place at the Black Sea the embroidery was drawn thread work done with silver and gold threads.

On returning to Germany I spent the next fifteen months or so completing my thesis, which entailed a couple of visits to London to study types in the Museum for Natural History, and obtaining on loan some further types from a Russian scientist, pieces from the far east where I had not been allowed to go. As my father was dead by then, I was determined to leave Germany as soon as I had obtained my Ph.D. and again through the good offices of my Professor at the Natural History Museum was asked by some American Museums whether I would like to collect for them in Northern Australia.

NAZI GERMANY

There was always a certain amount of anti-Semitism in Germany and much more in the East, where there was a constant trickle of Russian and Polish Jews coming to escape from pogroms in those countries. There was less in places like the Rhineland, where the Jews had been living for centuries with a lifestyle much like that of everybody else. Politically I grew up in a Social Democrat democracy, but there were many people who still hankered after the "good old days", including the aristocracy and old army people. The old German flag had been red, white and black, the new one was red, gold and black, and on public holidays one could see peoples' political opinions by the colours of the flags they hung out. Also, on the seaside, the "castles" surrounding the beach chairs would often be decorated with red, white and black flags, and later, during the early days of the growth of Nazism, also with swastika flags. However, on the whole there was not a great deal of discrimination. After the 1918-19 revolution a law had been brought in that all children had to spend at least the first four years of their schooling at state schools, so that there was none of the enmity between Catholics and Lutherans, the only non-Catholic group in Germany, and I was quite surprised to find in Australia all those different brands,

Methodists, Anglicans high and low, Presbyterians, Baptists and many more. My high school had Catholic, Lutheran and Jewish girls and no troubles between them. My cousin, who went to a conventional German school, said that apart from having Jewish religious instruction he did not feel any different and was not persecuted. One generation earlier there still has been some discrimination, for instance to advance in the army and the public service it was an advantage for a Jew to become a Christian. There was a joke about the man who went to the Catholic priest and asked to become a Catholic. "My son," said the father, "I see you first became a Lutheran before coming to me. Why was that?" The man replied, "Well, when people asked me my religion and I said Lutheran they would say: and what were you before? And I had to say Jewish. If I join you and they ask that question, I can say Lutheran."

Certain areas of Berlin, like Lichterfelde and Potsdam, were noted for anti-Semitism, also certain places on the seaside. I remember once being taken to the island of Helgoland (which was fortified and used as a base by the Nazis and blown up after the war), and seeing not one republic flag on the sandcastles.

My mother, who did not like many of her relatives, often called the Jews "a small but nasty race" and many people, including my parents, expected that in another two or three generations the Jews would have become so assimilated as just to be Germans. Most German Jews considered themselves Germans of the Jewish religion, except recent Eastern immigrants who still stuck to the old ways. For this reason I did not believe in Zionism, the movement for a Jewish state (Israel) in

Palestine. I felt the trouble with the Jews was that they kept themselves apart and Zionism was doing just that. After all, with all the migrations that had gone on in the world in the past two thousand years, if everybody wanted to go back to where his ancestors had lived two thousand years ago few people would stay where they now lived.

At that time there were published magazines called *True Stories, True Confessions* and *True Romances*, which I read whenever I could borrow them. I remember reading a story about a Jewish girl, not looking it, who went to an American university, was asked to join a sorority, got engaged to a fine upstanding wasp boy and then the horrible truth came out and of course everybody dropped her. This was the main reason I refused when my father offered to send me to Stanford University.

The Nazis were just a joke at first, and probably would have stayed a minor splinter party except for the Depression, which hit Germany worse than any other country. We had a system of voting still used in most European countries, proportional voting. This on the face of it is the fairest way. If a party gets ten percent of the votes it gets ten percent of the members of Parliament and so on. Any party that doesn't get a minimum of votes loses its deposit. One voted for the party and not for individual candidates. In practice it leads to unstable government. Rarely has one party been an absolute majority. There may be up to forty parties, some large, and some just splinter groups like the landlord's party that wanted to increase rents, and the tenants' party that wanted to decrease them. In Germany for ages we had the Social Democrats, just left of centre, as the largest party that governed with help of a few similar ones. When their government failed during the Depression, Brüning, who came from a good old family and had been an Army officer, was the leader of the next largest party, the Catholic Centre Party, and Hindenburg appointed him Chancellor. Hindenburg had been one of the chief generals in the First World War and had been pulled out of retirement in his eighties and elected President. Brüning thought he could improve conditions in Germany if the treaty of Versailles was revoked, because it still required huge payments of reparations. Unfortunately the French and others would not agree at all, so he too failed. Then Hindenburg's son, who like so many staunch nationalists rather favoured Hitler, persuaded his senile father to call on Hitler to form a government. Actually the Nazi Party had only got 19% of the votes at the previous election and Hindenburg didn't really like Hitler, who was lower class and had only been a corporal in the war. However, the deed was done and one of the first things the Nazis did was to burn down the Reichstag and blame it on the Communists, outlawing that party. The first concentration camps were built not for Jews but for political opponents.

A few months later Hitler held another election, and this time it was announced that the Nazis had got 98.9% of the votes. This of course was quite ridiculous, as we all knew. On the other hand voting tickets were numbered, and the numbers written on the roll beside the voter's name, so that theoretically it was possible to find out how someone voted, particularly in small rural areas where the odd brave dissident would promptly be sacked by the Lord of the Manor.

During the early time of Nazi rule nothing really terrible happened to the Jews, and many kidded themselves that persecution of the Jews was going to be dropped from the programme, or at least that people who had served in the war would not be affected. Shortly after that I went to Asia Minor. When I returned things had changed considerably. Hitler had certainly created a lot of employment, simply by making large-scale war preparations. The famous Autobahnen (ancestors of freeways) were one of those war preparations. There were mass meetings in halls and on streets. I remember once Hitler was supposed to speak somewhere and our housemaid went to hear him. She came back full of excitement about how wonderful he had been. When I asked; "What did he actually say"? she replied, "Well, I couldn't really say, but he was wonderful."

No doubt Hitler was a great orator who had the secret of getting people enthralled. Also the Germans had been starved for pomp and circumstance during the rather drab times of the Republic. I remember some years earlier we had a visit from king Ammanullah of Afghanistan, quite an unimportant figure on the world stage, and the Berliners went absolutely mad with excitement. So the Nazi rallies were popular for that reason too.

During my first sojourn in Asia Minor came the first real official persecution of the Berlin Jews. Houses where Jews lived and businesses owned by Jews had windows smashed and JEW written across the doors and windows. That is when my grandfather died, in September 1933. He was in his late eighties, and went out and tried to tell the storm troopers how honest he had always been, (I remember he objected strongly to silk stockings because he didn't think they lasted long enough), and what a good German he was. I don't think he was actually injured, but died of the shock and upset of the thing.

By the time I returned from Asia Minor for the second time, things had taken a decided turn for the worse. The racial laws had been introduced, making sexual relations between Jews and Germans a crime and letting Jews only stay in Jewish owned places. So I had to find a new landlady, a middle aged Jewish woman who lived somewhere in Charlottenburg. She had one son in his early twenties who escaped to Holland just a step ahead of being arrested by the Gestapo. Apparently he came home one night from a lecture sopping wet and told her he had been thrown into the Spree by a group of Brownshirts. He saved himself by hiding behind a bridge column with only his nose out of water till they had gone. As soon as he got home he packed a few things and took the next train to Holland. In the morning an official party of Gestapo men came to arrest him. At that time it was mainly people who had at one time been members of some left-wing group that got into trouble. Another time my landlady stood in a butter queue. This was during the time when Göring announced "Guns before Butter" and everyone had to queue. A policeman stood by to watch the people, and when a woman started to grumble he said, "What are you complaining about, you voted for this." Shortly afterwards some Gestapo came and took him away and we heard later that he had shot himself at the police station. Whether he did, or they killed him, I do not know. "Aryan" shops had to put signs in their windows saying, "Jews not wanted here". One day I went to my hairdresser to find one of those stickers on his window and of course went to find a Jewish hairdresser. A few months later I met the hairdresser in the street and he asked why I had stopped coming. I said, how could I come when you have this sign in the window and he told me that he had to put it in, or he would have ended in a concentration camp as he was already in trouble with the Nazis, having been at a compulsory Nazi meeting and raised his hand with a cigarette in it for the Hitler salute.

There was a tabloid paper called '"Der Stürmer" published by one of the head Nazis, and this was displayed on stands on nearly every street corner. The stands were wooden and the frame was painted red with swastikas all over, all pages of the Stürmer were nailed on to the blackboard in the middle. They contained such items as stories about a nasty Jew who seduced a nice Aryan girl, giving street names and house numbers, also stories of how girls having affairs with Jews had been shaved, stripped and flogged through the streets. I was told that the addresses given in the articles were completely fictitious, some of the streets existed, but not the numbers given.

It was during this time that my father killed himself. He had for years lived with a very nice young woman who became a good friend of mine, and he was blackmailed at work by the head accountant, who later became managing director when the firm was given to Aryans. My father discussed this with me for quite a while, and I tried to tell him that a man of his ability should have no trouble making a new start in another country, and he actually said he would do so, even had his teeth attended and bought a lot of new shirts, but then he killed himself instead of going to South Africa as he was supposed to do. My friend never married anyone else and I corresponded with her till she died of diabetes about 1960.

[*Richard told everyone that he didn't like goodbyes at trains. Then he went to his office building and turned on the gas in the company kitchen, after taking sleeping tablets. When he was found he was not dead but in a coma. He lingered for several days while Gabriele sat by his bed hoping he would die, as if he had lived he would havè suffered terrible brain damage. Oral account.*]

It was after this that I decided I would leave Germany, and indeed Europe, as soon as I had got my doctorate. Matters improved in 1936, as the Germans wanted to make a good impression on foreigners who came to the Berlin Olympic Games. (Following completion of her thesis, Gabriele was required to take an oral defense examination. She had three examiners, each of whom independently gave her a grade, with the lowest grade normally being the one awarded for the whole exam. Two of the examiners gave Gabriele the highest possible grade. The third examiner asked her only one question: "What scientific evidence proves that the Jews are an inferior race?" She replied, "There is none," and he promptly failed her. To fail this exam meant she could not be awarded a PhD. However, the normal procedure was waived, and she was given her degree with the lowest passing grade. Oral account.)

Before leaving Germany I decided to go on one more trip. My friend, whose Aryan appearance was a good protection, and I went to North

Germany for a change, visiting Bremen and Lübeck and then the Lüneberger Heide, moorland with heather and gorse and blueberries growing.

At that time it was getting difficult for Jewish people to go to the more desirable places in the world. There were just too many refugees looking for somewhere to go. My younger cousins, Hilde and the Colman boys, had been sent to French secondary schools in 1933. Hilde went on to University, where she met and married a young Frenchman. The marriage didn't last long, but gave her French citizenship. The Kochmanns (Colman is how they anglicized it), also matriculated, then the elder started work, while the younger one did a course of textile designing. They went on to the Argentine, but were advised that their chances would be better in Australia, and with sponsorship by the Jewish community in Australia came to this country, first Ulli, then Gerald, and they managed to get their parents out too, just before the war. The U.S. was getting very hard to get into; they had a quota for different nationalities and that for Germany had been overfilled. My aunt Mummi Danziger and her family went there. They had quite a lot of money of course, but even so had a lot of trouble. In those days immigrants still had to stay in Ellis Island to be vetted, and they had a handicapped child. They employed a very good lawyer who gave a heart-rending description of the terrible fate that awaited them if they were turned back, and got them permission to immigrate. They bought what sounded to me like a hobby farm in Connecticut.

Australia was even more difficult, and by 1937 about the only way you get permanent residency was to be sponsored by Australian relatives.

I had other problems too. When I was quite young, my parents, who could see that I wasn't going to be very good with money, (I could never manage my pocket money very well), and also were afraid of fortune hunters, had made a joint will saying that I was not to come into the complete control of the estate till I was twenty five, and in the meantime my financial affairs were to be managed by a solicitor appointed by the Government. Then, when my father tried to alter this after the Nazi take-over he couldn't, because my mother was dead and the will had been a joint one. The best he could manage was to be permitted to appoint an Aryan lawyer of his choice, which of course was much better than having the Government appointing a good Nazi. However, this man, though well-meaning, shared with many of my relatives and friends the attitude that anti-Jewish ideas were not really serious, and he was not at all in favour of my giving up nearly all I owned and leaving the country. Also my grandmother then suffered from senile dementia and had reached the stage of having to go into a nursing home. Though my aunt had looked after her, my father had been financially responsible and I was told I would have to deposit a sum sufficient to secure my grandmother on the income thereof. This was only a problem because by then the Nazis had brought in a law making all Jews deposit in cash or negotiable shares a sum equal to one quarter of their total estate, as valued by the Nazis. My Grumach shares were valued at three times their face value, so I had to deposit all I had for this purpose alone, leaving nothing for a fund for my grandmother. As it happens she died just then after a fall, which was the best thing for her and certainly made things easier for me.

My father had had a fully paid life insurance in a Swiss Bank and the Nazi authorities told me I could keep half this (M1500) if I brought the other half back into Germany. The Germans then were very short of foreign currency to buy essential war materials. Not long before the Germans had built an airship called *Hindenburg* and had to fill it with hydrogen, because they could not buy helium, and it promptly exploded on its maiden flight.

I could, of course, have gone to Switzerland pretending I was just going on holidays, identified myself, and got the whole amount, but I was both too cowardly and too law-abiding to do this. Also it meant I could buy all my clothing and equipment in Germany. I was a bit sorry when I found that my normal German passport, still valid for five years or so, was taken off me and replaced with one stamped "Non-Aryan" and valid only for two years. This meant that at the end of two years I would have become what was then called Stateless, which made it much more difficult to get into any country. Also, as I only went to Australia with a permit to stay two years (to collect) I could not possibly bring out my furniture and other household goods, which I had to leave in storage and eventually lost for good. However, I did get out before the worst happened.

Gabriele Neuhäuser. 1937

AUSTRALIA

As I was only able to take a small amount of money out of Germany but had quite a lot in that country, I spent what I could before leaving, buying as much as possible of my camping and collecting equipment and clothing. I also decided to go to Australia first class. This entailed getting several evening dresses, for which I never had any use after the voyage, and it was in fact a mistake. I left Germany on the *Narkunda*, an elderly boat of the P. & O. line, in June 1937. I found the approximately six weeks trip dull, never having been enamoured of the sea. I knew English reasonably well, but had nothing in common with the other passengers, many of whom were former Anglo-Indian types. The boat's library was pitiful and rarely unlocked, and I had absolutely no interest in the activities provided, for example playing deck quoits, walking several miles round and round the deck, or dancing. I spent much of my time doing the petit point work on the evening bag now belonging to Rayna, and one of the few occasions when another passenger talked to me was when the wife of General Birdwood, the only "important" passenger, told me that Queen Mary did that kind of work. The sea was calm and boring, the greatest excitement being the sightings of a few dolphins and flying fish.

There was a swimming pool on deck, which the tourist class passengers were allowed to use once or twice a week. I never did; I had no togs with me, and in any case couldn't swim very well. I had learnt as a child just the old-fashioned breaststroke, and I could float indefinitely on my back, but that was all. I had been taught by a queer method, a harness round my waist was hooked into something like a huge fishing line and this held me up while I practiced the strokes. When he thought I was ready, the instructor released the catch, and I swam on my own without even knowing it.

The food on board was quite good. One had to wear evening dress for dinner, and the important passengers sat at the Captain's Table. I had been told about the funny rites of baptism performed on those crossing the equator for the first time, and made sure to stay in my room on that night. On the night of the fancy dress ball some people had brought costumes, others were good at improvising, but I just didn't attend. As we got nearer to Australia there was supposed to be a big party. I did go to this and even tried to join in, when suddenly everybody was told to be quiet as the New Zealand Government was sending a radio message to General Birdwood, who had been head of the Anzacs and was going to visit New Zealand. Next day I heard one of the Anglo-English men say what a pity it was that this message had come at this particular night, as it had completely destroyed the party atmosphere. He then glanced in my direction and said: "Even she was doing her poor best."

We stopped at Aden (uninteresting), at Bombay, where I had a look around and saw the public wash ground where hundreds of Indians washed the city's clothes, the Street of Jewellers and the Street of Barbers with many tiny stalls as shops, of which I still have photos, also I saw even then the extreme crowds and huge masses of children.

The next stop was Colombo, from where I joined a bus-trip to Kandy. I saw the temple of the Holy Tooth, which is supposedly a tooth of Buddha but is really some fossilised large animal tooth, and very much enjoyed the beautiful Botanic Garden.

Bombay. Street of Jewellers - 1937

In Colombo the boat replenished its supplies of fresh fruit and vegetables. From then on everybody called mandarins by this name, previously they had been called tangerines. I got my first taste of some tropical fruits. I didn't like pawpaws at all; they tasted all right but had a horrible smell. However I loved Mangosteen, a small green fruit with a flesh rather like a custard apple, not sickly sweet but with a most beautiful taste. I later read Wallace's book *The Malay Archipelago* (he was the man who deduced evolution before Darwin), and he called the mango the king of fruits, and the Mangosteen the queen of fruits. I was disappointed to find they were not grown in Australia and interested when I saw just a few days ago that there is now a yellow fleshed

Mangosteen which can grow in less tropical climates and will shortly be available in Queensland.

Towards the end of the voyage I got to know a girl about my own age, also Jewish, who had been sponsored by a family in Perth and was of course travelling tourist class. Her sponsor met this girl in Fremantle and invited me to go for a sightseeing trip with them. I enjoyed this and was particularly impressed with the Swan River, which was the deepest blue I had ever seen, much brighter than the Mediterranean at its best. Even though it was middle of winter the weather was fine and many wildflowers were already out.

After this welcome break I rejoined the *Narkunda* and went on to Sydney. My first visit was to Mr. Troughton of the Australian Museum, to whom I had a letter. Mr. Troughton was charming to me, and I did not discover till many years later, when I read the History of the Queensland Museum, that in fact he was very much opposed to my plans, seeing that most of my specimens would go to America, and he had tried all he could to stop me getting the necessary permits. I had no intention of collecting in the mostly well-known southern parts of Australia, but hoped to do my travelling in North Queensland, the Northern Territory, and eventually the Kimberleys. I spent about a week in Sydney, and having got to know a middle-aged woman who ran a very small tourist business, went on several trips with her. She didn't run buses but took small parties of up to five or six people in her large car. This way I saw French's Forest, where we met an eccentric old lady who lived in an old tram, and had a day trip to the Blue Mountains.

Since permits to collect in the Northern Territory had to be obtained in Canberra, I went there next. Seeing Canberra now, it is hard to believe what it was like a mere fifty-five years ago. Back then there was one small area containing all the living quarters and the only shopping centre, and a few dozen large public buildings scattered about the bush and connected by dirt roads lined with little trees, only one to three feet high. There was no public transport so one had to walk for miles to get from one ministry to the next.

The one thing that really impressed me in Canberra was the extreme snobbishness and class-consciousness of the inhabitants. A young typist had offered to take me to the Minister I had to see. Later another woman also offered, and when I told her that Miss X had already said she would take me, she replied: "Don't you think it would be better if you were introduced by a secretary rather than a typist?" This was quite typical. I didn't do much good obtaining permission to collect in the Northern Territory; in fact I was told that it might be better if I started off in a more civilized part of the country, for example Queensland. On I went to Brisbane, where very fortunately for me Mr. Longman, the Director of the Queensland Museum, was much more helpful. He not only helped me to obtain permits to collect protected fauna, but also offered, in return for obtaining some of my specimens for his museum, to attend to sending my collections overseas.

The Queensland Museum in those days had just a skeleton staff. Mr. Longman had a secretary, Miss Murphy, and there was a librarian, Miss Watson, who was a staunch communist and who later married Pete

Thomas of the Trades and Labour Council; he subsequently wrote a booklet on the Mount Isa strike. Apart from a few attendants or guards in the public part of the museum that was about all, apart from a few field naturalists who pursued their own interests. One of these was an old man called Mr. Young, whose interest was fossils. Both he and Mr. Longman invited me to their homes. Mr. Longman lived in Chelmer in an old-style timber house, on a site sloping right down to the river, with its own little jetty. I have heard that this has been bought and restored by an architect and is still much as it was in my time. Mr. Young lived in Graceville and all I really remember was a large English oak tree in the middle of his backyard, a most unusual sight for Brisbane.

I had bought a Chevrolet utility truck for £326, and Mr. Longman suggested that as I was quite unfamiliar with Australian roads and conditions, Mr. Young should accompany me on my first trip.

Queensland at that time had one of its usual droughts, and much of the west was as bare and level as a billiard board, so one could drive all over the place. If there was no road, one just followed other tire tracks. We went inland to Hughenden; a couple of things I remember are the Cactoblastus Memorial Hall erected in honor of the beetle which exterminated the Prickly Pear pest, and the mud baths in Muckadilla, which were supposed to do wonders for arthritis. After seeing many of the well-known spas in Europe, with their luxury hotels, casinos, and so on, I was amused to find a tiny township with perhaps twenty inhabitants, a wooden shed erected over a small pool of black hot mud, and four people sitting in this and playing Five Hundred on a board laid on top of the mud between them. Our final destination was the Atherton Tableland, so on reaching Hughenden we went northeast straight along the newly constructed road to Mt. Garnet. Apart from an official party, we were the first people to travel over this road, which went more or less straight along the top of the Great Dividing Range. Since it was recently graded it was very much better as well as shorter than the old road, though possibly not as interesting. The road was such a novelty to the previously very isolated station people along it that everybody wanted us to call in and stay with them. We spent one night at Oak Park with the Nimmo family, and were shown over the station, including the children's swimming hole, which they shared peacefully with some freshwater crocodiles. I was told about the Oak Park Races, an annual event that brought many hundreds of visitors from all over Queensland and beyond.

Another call was at the Wilson's place. They had not been there very long and seemed very poor, living in a shack with lots of children. One girl had been bitten on the neck by a redback spider and had almost died; she was still pretty sick when we were there months later. Mt. Garnet is on the western dry part of the Tableland and is not very attractive, so we went straight on to a place called Evelyn Scrub, where we stayed the night with a fat red-faced old lady, another acquaintance of Mr. Young. I got into trouble there, through my less than perfect knowledge of the English language. The lady mentioned she was a very sick woman, and I said, "I don't believe it," and was told off severely for calling her a liar. What I meant of course was that it was hard to believe as she looked so healthy, but it turned out she had very high blood pressure.

We then went on to Cairns, where Mr. Young left me and returned home by train with my thanks, having first introduced me to Mr. Flecker and Mr. McDonald at Kuranda.

Alone again, I returned to the Tableland via Yungaburra. The road then was one-way, being so narrow and winding that two cars, or more likely trucks, just couldn't pass, so there were set times for going up or down and a manned booth at either end where one had to report, to avoid having someone still on the road when it opened for traffic the other way. I stayed first at Lake Barrine, which is a very pretty lake right in the middle of the rainforest, with quite a good hotel. I hadn't picked a very good time, as the cast of the Australian film, *Tall Timber*, which was shot on the Tableland, was staying there and the owner was all excited and preoccupied with them. Also I found that this was not really a good place for collecting. Possibly because of the presence of feral cats, there were few small ground animals and the area even then being a National Park, I could not collect protected fauna. Also, as I soon discovered, wildlife is not really all that abundant in the depth of a rainforest, concentrating mainly on the edges of big shrub and open forest. I spent a few days setting traps and looking around, going some distance by car. This is where I had one of my narrow escapes from a potentially serious car accident. I had seen a small creek at the bottom of a steep incline on the side of the road, pulled the car off the road and climbed down to set traps and inspect the area generally. Getting back into the car I turned the steering wheel the wrong way while trying to back out, and found myself half way over the drop. I had to sit perfectly still for the next half hour or so as any move might have sent the car right over, and it also needed my weight in the driving seat. Eventually a utility truck full of strong young men came by, and three of them got onto the running board, their weight steadying the car enough for me to get out, after which one of them backed the car back on the road again. (I wasn't ever much good at backing, and haven't improved with the years.)

Next I went to Yungaburra, a cheaper and much better place for collecting. There was open forest, and much of the original scrub had been cleared for farming, but there was one isolated large patch of rainforest still standing, though this too was scheduled for clearing. This meant that there was a considerable concentration of fauna in the remaining rainforest, where in fact I collected all seven possums native to the region, with such things as tree kangaroos also being very plentiful.

In spite of all my previous experience, I always felt somewhat guilty about killing animals, rationalizing that as so many of them were going to become extinct anyhow with the destruction of their environment, it was important to get at least some specimens preserved in museums. In this case I felt better about my collecting, as the animals in this particular patch were in any case doomed.

I generally tried to get to know the local people who might know something about the whereabouts of rare species, and in some cases offered to pay for specimens in good condition. One man whom I got to know in this way was a timber-worker called Sid Liptrott, whose face and head were strangely disfigured. I found later that he had been raised in an orphanage, and his looks were due to his being kicked in the head repeatedly. Unlike many of the locals who looked at my specimens in surprise and said that in all their lives in the area they had never known them to exist, Sid was interested in nature and very knowledgeable, as well as being a good shot. He asked if he could go on with me as my assistant, and when I told him that I couldn't afford to pay him, he offered to come just for his keep. As I intended to go to Cape York next, I accepted this offer. Returning to Cairns I sent off the boxes of specimens I had so far collected to Mr. Longman, and while making enquiries about the Peninsula did a bit of quick sightseeing in and around Cairns. I got to know Mr. Flecker, a local dentist who was the founder of the Field Naturalist Association and was particularly interested in the poisonous box jellyfish, then unnamed, which eventually got named fleckeri after him. I went to Green Island which then was quite undeveloped, with only a few people in tents camped among the bushes. A great difference from the same Island twenty years later, when it had a hotel, lots of tourist shops, and masses of people. I also saw the Barron Falls when I was going in the train up to Kuranda. This was before the hydroelectric scheme, and the falls then were a really majestic sight. On each journey the train stopped on the railway bridge right in front of the falls, so one got a very good look at it.

Kuranda even then was a nice little town, and famous for its railway station, which had won the prize for the best in the state so many times that it was no longer allowed to enter. The whole station was a mass of flowers, tree ferns and other ferns, and interesting plants. I found that the normal way to get to Coen was rather tedious and took up to three weeks. It entailed taking the *Wandana*, a small coastal steamer that went from Cairns via Thursday Island to the Gulf country and back, as far as Port Stewart. As the river mouth was too shallow for the *Wandana*, passengers were deposited on a bare rocky island in the Bay, and sometimes had to wait there several days till the tide was right for a smaller boat to take them to Port Stewart. Nothing was provided for the wait, one had to take one's own food and water. From Port Stewart a truck driven by Mr. Shepherd from Coen in the Cape York Peninsula brought goods and passengers to Coen. Not liking the idea of all this I looked for alternatives, and found that a Cairns jeweller, Tommy Macdonald, who had been a fighter pilot during the first world war, owned a two-seater Piper and accepted charters. So I squibbed the *Wandana*, sending Sid Liptrott off on it with all the gear, and did the trip in the plane. Macdonald was a most reckless pilot and several times I expected to run straight into the side of a mountain. However, all went well. I inquired at the jewellery store about Tommy many years later, when he was in his eighties and retired but still came into the shop and told everybody how much better it had been run in his day, so apparently he survived his hair-raising flights and died peacefully in his bed.

Coen in 1937 was an unusual place. The entire white population of the Peninsula was then about fifty people. In Coen there were three local families, the Armbrusts, who owned the store, the Thompsons, who ran the hotel, and the Shepherds, with Mr. Shepherd having the contract run to and from Port Stewart. Each also had a cattle station. I heard a story that Mr. Shepherd once arrived at Armbrust's station just on lunchtime and was invited to dinner - roast beef, of course. "That isn't bad beef I grow," he said. "You must come and have a meal at my place some time to see what yours is like."

Apart from these locals (Mr. Armbrust's Christian name was Coen, because he was the first white baby born in the town), there were also a married postmaster with an eight-year-old daughter, a schoolteacher, and three policemen who serviced the entire peninsula. There was also an old somewhat eccentric chap called Forsythe, who lived just out of town beside an old gold mine and made his living putting the old mullock heaps through a cyanide process. I chiefly remember him for wearing pajama tops as shirts.

Some miles north of Coen was Batavia, being run as a tin-mine by the Fisher brothers, who employed quite a number of people. Many years later one of them recognized me at an Orchid Society meeting in Cairns, where he was then living and driving heavy equipment he owned for the City Council, leaving his wife to look after his thousands of orchids.

All these people, while they were in Coen, ate at the Thompson's hotel, as did I. The dining room had a very long wooden table with benches either side, and the top ten feet or so of the room was protected by wire netting and contained Mrs. Thompson's large collection of native orchids, with Cooktown orchids from pure white through to deep purple. Mrs. Thompson's daughter, Eileen, was then at home having her fiancé inspected by her mother (Mr. T. died before my time). Eileen was a nurse, and her intended a pharmacy assistant, but he was most interested in natural history and kept asking me to tell him about my collecting. I met Eileen again about twenty years later at the CWA Club in Brisbane. Once again she recognized me - I must look odd - and she told me that her husband, Lea Wassell, had in fact become a very well known naturalist who many times took interstate and overseas scientists around and had quite a few things named after him. He had died young, but lived the life he loved.

I did not of course have my car with me, so depended on local transport. I would have liked to go to Ebagoola, where the ant-bed parrot had its home, but it was just too far and hard to get at. I did some collecting round the open country near Coen, but then wanted to go near rainforest again. As I depended on packhorses I employed a young Aborigine and his wife, and that is how I got to know [*my future husband*] John, who warned me that, being from a mission, the young man was not reliable. He said that the tribal aborigines were very good, but the missions wrecked their way of life and they could not be trusted.

These were still the "bad old days" in some respects, though no longer quite as bad as when Coen Armbrust was a boy; he told me that back then the whites went for a weekend black shooting, as in later times they went pig shooting. However even when I was there, the police rounded up tribal blacks unless they were working on some station, marched them in chain gangs to a mission, and told to stay there or they would be sent to Palm Island. I have no doubt that actually they would have been better off there, but they couldn't bear the thought of being away from their family and tribe, so that this was a very effective threat. Mrs. Shepherd told me that particularly Lockhardt Mission had a very bad reputation. The missionary provided them with a basic ration of tea, sugar, flour and tobacco and then told them to live off the country, hundreds being cooped up in an area that would normally have provided for one or two families. He also made them wear clothes, and they didn't know to take them off and dry them after swimming or otherwise getting wet. As a result of this and malnutrition most died within nine months or so after arriving at the mission, but the missionary kept them on his books and was sent support from the south for the supposed numbers he told them he had.

Anyhow, seeing I was determined to get to the rainforest, John took pity on me and offered to go along. He owned three very good packhorses and one smallish riding horse, supposedly half brumby, called Ned Kelly after the famous Australian outlaw because it was very hard to catch. Once caught and saddled it would give an experienced rider no further trouble.

John had been on the Peninsula about ten years. When he first came to North Queensland he got a job as stockman, and later head stockman on a cattle station, until his horse fell on him and he broke his hip and it was five hours before he was found. After several months in hospital he was told to avoid rough riding in future so then he took a job helping an old chap with his dairy farm outside Cooktown. The man told him if he stayed with him he would leave him the farm, but John said he didn't want to be slave to a bunch of cows for the rest of his life. That is when he got himself a Miners' Right, allowing him to prospect for gold, and came to Coen, where he got friendly with the much older Stanley Boyd, and worked mates with him for years. Boyd was an interesting character. After his father had left her he was raised by his mother, and she, being a bigoted Catholic, brought up the boy with the idea of making a priest out of him, as she said, to atone for the wrongdoings of his father. He was sent to Nudgee College, but turned violently against Catholicism. After leaving Coen, Stanley Boyd eventually lived in Cooktown, where he started the local museum and was a very well known identity.

Since this was during the Depression, prospecting was one way of keeping off the unemployment rolls, and while John and Stanley Boyd never struck it rich, they always managed to find enough to live. They got on well with the Aborigines and learnt a lot about living off the country from them. Just a little before my time two southern ladies drove a baby Austin up the Peninsula, and then wrote a book about their adventures. John was rather amused to find them saying that once, camped near a waterhole, they narrowly escaped being massacred by blacks, since they found bare footprints all around their tent in the morning. Actually what they saw was the footprints of John and Stan Boyd, who were camped nearby and early in the morning went to the hole to get water.

We eventually left Coen, and after two and a half days of riding came to the edge of Rocky Scrub, the rainforest round the Rocky River. At this camp we killed fourteen deathadders before setting up our tents. It was a ,marvellous place for collecting, with the typical Cape York fauna, related to that of New Guinea; Cuscus, Palm Cockatoo, Eclectus Parrot, many fruit pigeons, etc. It was also the home of the Taipan, which had not then been officially named but was locally known as MacLennan's brown snake, after the collector who first described it.

This is also the only time I came across the telepathic powers of the Aborigines. I had heard a lot about this, how a whole family started wailing and mourning at the exact time when a relative who had been sent to Palm Island had died, but always doubted these second- and third-hand reports. In this case the black "boy" came to John one morning and told him that one of the policemen in Coen was leaving to come up with such and such horses and would be with us in a couple of days. Sure enough the man came, and when told about the message he said that we were told just when he had heard he had to go and decided what horses to take. This being hilly and heavily timbered country, there were no smoke signals used.

After about a fortnight we were running short of flour and certain other foods, so sent off the black couple to get us more supplies. Days passed and it became clear that they would not return. We were eking out our supplies with local food. Once half a dozen scrub turkeys flew up on a tree, and John asked me to sit there while he went back to the camp for a gun, another time he pulled a half-grown wild pig, squealing madly, into the camp by the tail, and held it while Sid got the gun and shot it. I must say that it wasn't much to eat. The Cape York wild pigs are the descendants of the original pigs released by Captain Cook, and when caught very young and fed proper pig food taste exactly like tame pigs, but when living on bush tucker they are very rank. Scrub turkeys taste very nice, but scrub hens, which live largely on insects while the scrub turkey lives on berries, don't taste very nice at all. In the end we had to return to Coen because of diminishing supplies. Once again Sid and the heavy gear went on the *Wandana* and I chartered Tommy Macdonald's plane. Sid left me in Cairns and returned home. Before leaving the North I had another go at going to the Bloomfield River where the Bennett's Tree kangaroo lives in the upper reaches, but only got as far as Daintree and realized that I would not have the money or facilities to make this spot work out. Instead I decided to go to Mount Molloy, west of Mossman and in the upland forest country. I squibbed the "jump-up" from Mossman, which is only six miles, but three of them practically straight up without any stopping places. I was told that two or three cars usually travel in convoy, one going a certain distance and then stopping with a member of the previous car standing by to put rocks under the front wheels. Then this second car would go up first and the procedure would be reversed. Anyhow, I decided to do things the easy way, going right back through Cairns and the Tableland, about 150 miles all told. Mount Spurgeon is near Mount Molloy. Mount Spurgeon wasn't a bad place for collecting, having several flying gliders and other fauna I hadn't come across elsewhere. What made it better is that a local man turned out to be very knowledgeable and obtained many specimens for me I might not have found on my own, including the two kinds of native cat. Unfortunately this man had been shot in the head during the First World

War and was left with some after effects that made him very difficult to get on with. He took offense at nothing at all, and one could never know how he would react. If I thanked him when he brought an extra good specimen he would say "Don't thank me, you're paying me", next time, if I didn't, he would say, "You might at least say thank you". I managed to avoid really bad upsets but was quite taken aback when he offered to come further with me. Somehow I managed to dissuade him without upsetting him too much. From Mt. Molloy I went on a bit further to Mount Carbine, which then had flourishing wolfram mines. These were small one-man operations, each man digging out the very rich ore and bagging it. There was one woman running a place. Her husband had blown himself up with gelignite, and other men used to do the geligniting for her, but otherwise she did all the work herself. Just before I came a man had been told to leave the town after unacceptable behaviour, and he revenged himself by cutting the telephone wire. The wire was strung up along trees, and he cut it at one tree, bent over the two ends and nailed them back just an inch or so apart. It took the locals about six weeks to find where the break was. I was also told about an eccentric old man who lived a hermit's life out of town, and who used to kill a beast any time he came to town. He just cut out the bits he wanted and left the rest to rot. So, any time he was seen approaching, all the locals went out bearing gifts of fillet steaks, liver, and so on, to stop him before the act.

I felt I wanted to give the islands another chance. Having found the fauna of the smaller ones very restricted, I decided on Hinchinbrook, which is much larger and covered with hills and big scrub. The starting point is Cardwell, with a rather atypical population nearly all of Scottish descent and fairly inbred. At the time an eccentric Englishman was living in Hinchinbrook. He would take visitors if he liked them, and had built a few cottages to accommodate them. He provided in addition citrus fruit from his trees, and fish from his fish traps, but all other food had to be brought in by the visitor. I found once again the fauna of mammals very restricted, but the birdlife was more interesting. The worst part of this stay was a pet bull, nearly full grown, which wanted to play with me. It was the only survivor of an earlier attempt to bring cows to Hinchinbrook. All died through a mishap in landing, except this then very young bull calf, which the owner hand reared and still played with, mock wrestling with it. I, not being all that strong, was rather intimidated by the beast. The owner tried to fence it off, but it would just walk around the sea end of the fence at low tide. I enjoyed watching the fish in the trap, and had my first taste of such things as turtle meat and eggs (these weren't very nice, tasting rather sandy), and stingray, which is good eating when young.

On the other side of the island lived the only other inhabitants, an illiterate and probably slightly retarded man and his wife. I was told the story of his wife reading to him a bundle of old newspapers someone had given them, and when he heard that England had gone off the gold standard, he promptly dug up a small hoard of gold sovereigns, took them to Cardwell and offered them to a local for sale at a pound each, thinking he was cheating the buyer when at that time a sovereign was already worth a lot more.

It was high time I had a look at the west, so I went south to Townsville and straight west to Cloncurry. The drought was in its third year and as before, the western plains were as flat as a tabletop, with no marked roads at all and car tracks going all over the place. Not a sign of any plant life, apart from a few trees near dry creek beds. I spent a few days in the Post Office Hotel in Cloncurry, then the best hotel, and once again run by an eccentric, a very fat old lady who only took guests she liked and approved of.

I soon found that Cloncurry was a hopeless place for collecting, being by western standards a large town of about 2500 people and having been much larger in the past. Half wild goats were roaming everywhere, and apart from kangaroos there was little native wildlife. Trying for a smaller place I first went to Quamby, a few miles north, but found this not much of an improvement. Finally I went to Malbon, a small railway township on the Mount Isa Line, right at a railway bridge over the Cloncurry River. This turned out to be a much better place with vegetation and a few waterholes in the river, and hilly country with rock wallabies and some quite interesting birds, including a spinifex wren, which had previously been known only from Western Australia. I also found a young lad who used to earn pocket money getting young Cloncurry Ringneck parrots out of their nests and selling them to dealers. He knew hollow trees where bats spent the day, so I made quite a good collection of tree dwelling bats which previously I had found hard to get hold of, unlike those bats that live in caves. I was at that time not terribly affected by the heat, though one day the thermometer on the pub verandah showed 113° Fahrenheit in the shade.

I was just about ready to leave Malbon when the drought finally broke. I was down in the dry riverbed one morning collecting my traps, when I heard a roar and saw a huge wall of water approaching. We had actually had no rain in Malbon at the time, but apparently there had been heavy rain further up the river. I just had time to get back up to the top, before the wall raced down, and the Cloncurry River, dry for several years, ran a banker. Then it started raining in Malbon and didn't stop for three weeks. Much of the country was flooded, and the railway bridge over the river was under water. We saw a whole mob of kangaroos starving to death on a high bit of ground because they could not get through the surrounding floods. The refrigerated train that took fruit and vegetables to Mount Isa once a week was stranded in Malbon, and as the town ran out of food we used to say that at least we wouldn't starve, if the worst came to the worst we could break into the train and get food.

Eventually the rain stopped, but it was another three weeks before the water had receded enough to clear the railway bridge. I was anxious to leave, as I had already spent nearly three months in Malbon, far more than I had intended, but wasn't game to drive the car over the sleepers of the bridge. However, one of the locals finally did this for me, and I got back to Cloncurry. There was a terrific difference in the look of the country, what had been bare flat plain before was now covered with grass and herbage, and wildflowers about four feet deep, and one had to keep well on the roads that had had the grader over them.

The next place I stopped at was Pentland, which was out of the black-soil plains and in low open forest country, with patches of brigalow *[Acacia harpophylla]* here and there. This again turned out to be a good place for collecting, the fauna being quite different from either that of the far west or of the coast. The brigalow had some very interesting birds I had seen nowhere else, and other wildlife was also plentiful. While I was in Pentland there was one of those occasional epidemics among the koalas, and one could see dead ones lying under trees every morning. The koalas had been totally protected by Act of Parliament many years earlier, and were expressly excluded from the fauna I was allowed to collect. I wrote to Mr. Longman and asked him whether it would not be permissible to take animals that were already dead, but was told that under no circumstances was I to touch any of them, which at the time seemed an awful waste.

Still going south I stopped at Rockhampton, the main interest being the railway which went right through the main street of the town, like a tram, and the Botanic Gardens which were old and very beautiful. Once again looking for a small place to go collecting, I picked on Byfield, which was small enough not to have a hotel, so that I had to find board and lodging with a local farming family. The local crop was mainly bananas, and I was interested to see them ripened artificially. A hand of grass green bananas was put in a large earthenware pot with a small piece of carbide (as used in the lamps, there not being electricity in the place) and next morning the bananas would be fully ripe. Byfield then still had a lot of the original countryside, and was the world supplier of the so-called Byfield Fern, which is actually a cycad widely used by florists, and which I was did not grow anywhere else, nor had any method been found to grow it from seed or otherwise propagate or even transport it. I did not find anything very exciting in Byfield, so did not stop there too long.

John and I got married at the Registry Office in Cairns, with two people from the next room acting as witnesses. I used to stay at Hotel Pacific whenever I was in Cairns, but we decided to stay at Hyde's Hotel, which was then supposed to be the best in Cairns. Actually I didn't like it as much as the Pacific, as it was right in town instead of on the waterfront overlooking the sea, and was also much older, with decor being rather Edwardian. This is where I made another bad mistake. I had already lost my mother's emerald ring coming to Australia, stolen from my cabin, no doubt by the stewardess. However, as there were notices up about leaving valuables with the purser, I never dared report the loss. The rest of my family jewellery was packed in two large trunks, which during my travels were stored at a firm specializing in storing and sending goods. I took John to this place, opened up the trunks and showed him the jewellery, giving him my father's watch but putting everything else back. I should of course have taken the things back to the hotel and opened them in the privacy of our room. As it is, a number of people were working on repairs to the roof of the next-door building and could have easily overlooked us. In any case next morning we had a call from the police, saying that during the night Bryce's storage rooms had been burgled. Nothing was touched except my trunks, and nothing was taken from them except the jewellery and an old box camera, which was found in a Cairns park a few days later. However no trace of the jewellery was ever found.

BRISBANE 1938-1945

John decided that in order to provide for any future family and me he had to return to the building trade. The question was where were we going to settle. I had liked Perth on my short stay there when I first arrived in Australia, and suggested that we have a look at this. We exchanged the Chevy Ute for a sedan (another mistake, as John would have found a utility much more useful later on) and drove down, in easy stages, chiefly along the coast, via Brisbane, Sydney, Melbourne to Adelaide. There we were advised not to try to drive to Perth, as the road was terrible and there was no water available for most of it. So we left the car in Adelaide, which we both liked very much, and took the train to Perth. We both liked the town, and I sent a parcel of dried wildflowers to my friend in Germany [*Margaretha Hornauer*] but John decided after some enquiries that he would prefer to go back to Brisbane as a place of permanent residence. So back we went, this time taking alternative roads and seeing places like Mount Gambier, which we had missed on the way down. In Brisbane we stayed at first in Oxford House just near the Methodist Church in Ann Street, which was the kind of place that country families stayed at and it was pleasant and quiet. During my first stay I had stayed at the Canberra, also in Ann Street but on the corner of

Edward Street. This I found terribly noisy, the front rooms facing Ann Street got hymn singing half the night from the *[Salvation Army]* Peoples' Palace just across the road, as well as traffic noise. The back of the Canberra was right over a railway tunnel, with the steam trains blowing their whistle every few minutes, and also my room, though several stories up, was right over the kitchens and I got a lot of food smell. Anyway, John went around making enquiries about the chances of setting up as a builder in a small way and got quite a bit of encouragement. The first thing we had to do was to find a place to live, so an estate agent, with whom John got friendly, R. S. (Bob) Malloy, took us about and we saw lots of Brisbane which I haven't ever seen since.

("There was a safety deposit box in Amsterdam which contained some diamonds my father had bought. I wrote to an acquaintance and asked him to take these out and send them to me. He asked me if I wanted someone to accompany him, and I said no, but I am sure he did not send the largest stones to me. However, I took the stones he did send to Hardy Bros. and got £500 for them, which paid for the first house we bought in Brisbane." Oral account.)

We ended up buying a block of land in which is now Hawkins Drive in St. Lucia, and was then called Coronation Drive, just about five minutes walk from Ironsides School which was then new. This block was level about 40 feet back and then sloped down very steeply. When cleared of the scrubby second growth, it had a magnificent view over the river and the Indooroopilly golf links. We built quite a nice brick house, with a red tiled roof and a living-dining room making the most of the view, and then John started on his building career. However, he was just too honest to make much of a financial success of it; other builders used to employ tradesmen and make them sign for the correct wages but actually pay them laborers' rates, also John refused to accept slightly damaged parts, such as baths or sinks with a tiny chip where it didn't show selling at much reduced prices, when the specifications said that only first class stuff had to be used. Accordingly the other builders got rich whereas John barely made an adequate living. Our house was nice but rather isolated. It was the first house in the street, beyond the Ironsides State School, which was then quite new and about five minutes walk from us, and at the end of the bus line. All my life I had been a frustrated gardener, and in fact during our trip to Perth had bought Brunnings' *Complete Gardener*, and read every bit of it during the train trip to and from Perth. Unfortunately this was written for Southern conditions and rather led me astray. I marked lots of plants I wanted to grow, only to find later that these would not do well in Brisbane. While our house was being built we stayed at a flat in New Farm, quite a nice one with the then very popular Rosenstengel furniture (now highly collectible), which was very well built from good timber, but which I, unlike John, didn't care for, as it was done in an imitation Tudor style which was pretty uncomfortable, particularly the dining room furniture. My own tastes ran to the Swedish style modern, then still unknown in Australia, except that I didn't like the knock-kneed looking legs. Also this flat had, as most places in the days before DDT, lots of cockroaches. Not far from this flat was a small nursery, run by the daughter of the man who started it, Mr. Matthew, after whom a very deep mauve

Lagerstroemia was called. She told me quite a lot about gardening in the Brisbane area and gave me one bit of very good advice. "Grow what you see doing well in other gardens and if you must try things you aren't sure about, don't put them in prominent positions." I later met her again when she ran a small florist business in one of the Brisbane Arcades.

My garden in St. Lucia was fairly conventional in the flat part in the front lawn, two rose beds and a hedge of a large single rose with wavy petals called "Mefrouv de Ness." At the back we had lawn and clothesline on the small flat section, then two flights of curved stone steps round a rockery lead to the steep bit at the back, in which I planted mainly shrubs and not too many trees as I did not want to cut off the magnificent view. At that time a Mr. S. B. Watkins, who was the Government Analyst, used to write the gardening column for the Courier Mail, and I once wrote to him for advice. He wrote back offering to visit me on his pushbike as he lived not too far away in Toowong, halfway up Mount Cootha. I gave him a bougainvillea of a then new colour, which wasn't doing well for me, and many years later wrote to him again from Mount Isa, when I got a letter back saying he remembered me well, and thought of me often when admiring the magnificent bougainvillea he had from me. He asked me to visit him when I was in Brisbane, which I did and I enjoyed the day very much. He had several large blocks of land, much of it still bush, and a wonderful garden; he specialized in camellias but had all kinds of other things. My bougainvillea had grown into a giant specimen that went right over a huge pergola in his backyard. I kept spasmodically corresponding with him and once sent him a carton of grapefruit from my tree in Mount Isa. He wrote back saying that if it grew so well there it was a wonder no one was going in for commercial citrus growing. Mr. Watkins kept writing his column almost until he died in his eighties.

I got rather worried when I didn't get pregnant straight after marriage, and after about three months went to a very good German refugee doctor, who had got a medical degree from Edinburgh University. He gave me some simple advice that worked, so Rayna was born thirteen months after we got married. I had no trouble during pregnancy, no sign of morning sickness or anything like that (nor with later pregnancies either) but certainly made up for this at the actual birth. I was in labour for four days, the last of them almost continually, and by that time, having had no sleep or food, "dropped my bundle" as the doctor put it, and just screamed. The doctor did not believe in giving painkillers as they might affect the baby. I remember the ward sister coming in and telling me to stop, saying nobody could get any sleep, and my replying: "Why should anybody sleep when I feel like this?" Eventually she came back and said she had phoned the doctor and he had allowed her to give me a needle. She said, "I won't give it to you till you stop that screaming," and I replied: "I am not going to stop till you give it to me," after which I must have gone to sleep. Eventually the doctor decided to use instruments, and Rayna was born at 11 a.m. the following day. When I woke up from the anesthetic there was the doctor saying: "You have a lovely daughter." "Never mind that," said I, "Has the war started yet?" "Forget about the war, you have a lovely daughter."

I was of course concerned because of our attempt to get my young cousin Inge, Lilli and Fred's sister, to Australia. Anyhow the war broke out a day later. (September 1st, 1939).

I kept hemorrhaging for about a week, then my temperature shot up, no doubt with what used to be called puerperal fever that killed lots of women, however by that time the first sulfa drugs had come on the market and I recovered quite quickly. However I was not allowed even to sit up in bed for twelve days. Rayna was quite badly marked by the instruments and half her face appeared to be almost paralyzed. *[A forceps scar has lasted a lifetime.]* Also her liver didn't start working for a few days. In fact I had to stay in hospital for a full month just because she was not well enough to leave and go home. I was in a single room and got very bored. I was told it was absolutely essential that Rayna be breast-fed, so persisted in spite of getting repeated abscesses. This was a nuisance, as I had to take her off the affected side, breastfeed on the other side, then weigh her and make up a bottle for the missing amount. No sooner was one side healed (with help of sulfa drugs) than an abscess started on the other side. However I kept breastfeeding her till she was eight months old. When I first came home I had a girl from the Mothercraft Association staying to help for the first few weeks. Being a summer baby Rayna lived mainly in singlets and nappies, and for going out in a couple of rather nice playsuits I bought in a Chinese handcraft shop in the Brisbane Arcade, blue like her eyes with nice embroidery. She was almost bald when she was born, and then very fair, long and fairly thin. She was always a fussy eater, and as there were at that time no readymade baby foods apart from a terribly insipid cereal called

Farex, when she got onto a mixed diet I spent quite a while preparing vegetables, rubbing them through a sieve, only to have her spit out the first mouthful and refuse any more. I got very frustrated about this. She strongly objected to eggs and turned pale at the sight or smell of liver. We had an old-fashioned electric stove which took about ten minutes to heat a hotplate and then had enough stored heat to go on cooking for another hour, so a lot of electricity was wasted.

John would have loved to enlist as soon as war broke out, but I begged him to wait, as apart from having such a young and delicate baby I was wondering about discrimination, having heard stories about this from the First World War. So John postponed ideas of war service for the time being. He had of course to give up being a speck builder, and in any case with diminished bus services the St. Lucia place was both too expensive and isolated for us, so we sold this house and bought a second-hand war-service home on Waverley Road in Taringa. John bought a bike and worked building war-related buildings in Rocklea, a long way from us, so he had to leave about 5 a.m.

The former owner of our house had been a rather eccentric Christian Scientist woman with two children. I never met her but was told that she used to do naked sunbathing in her yard, that she nearly let her daughter die from diphtheria, not believing in doctors and depending on prayer, and that once, while her daughter came to her crying that a bee had stung her she said: "You shouldn't say that, dear, you should say, 'a little insect kissed me.'"

The front of our house faced a paddock where we could often pick mushrooms, with a small store at the bottom end facing the street. A private bus-line ran to and from Brisbane through Taringa and Toowong, and the bus driver was very nice. He knew all his passengers and would stop at their houses and not just at regular bus stops. My neighbours were on one side a Mrs. Bock, who had one boy then about six or seven, on the other side a Catholic family called Walsh. Mrs. Walsh had a sister who kept a cow and during the war made her own butter and sometimes sold me some. She also gave milk to a poor woman with a large family, but was stopped by the health department and told she had to throw away what she could not use. This seemed terrible to us at the time, but cows in those days quite often had tuberculosis, and I later saw two children with bone tuberculosis in Townsville Hospital, after which I could appreciate this law.

At the back in Payne Street Indooroopilly lived Mrs. Kerr, who became and still is a very good friend. [*Mrs. Kerr remembered that Gabriele stuck her face through the hedge in the back and said, "Will you be my friend?" Lesley's account.*] Her neighbors on one side were the Herrons, a cranky old couple with a middle-aged daughter who had been engaged for nearly twenty years and when she eventually married had her husband collapse and die during the wedding night. These people never talked to anyone unless it was to abuse them. On the other side of Kerrs were the Mahers. Mrs. Maher had four children, and all but the elder boy gave her a lot of worry. One boy seemed at one stage set to become a juvenile delinquent, the elder girl was very plain and either very neurotic or even psychotic, and the younger, a very nice looking girl, married a man who physically abused her and she died very young of kidney trouble. In spite of this Mrs. Maher always seemed bright and cheerful, as did Mrs. Kerr, who also had had a far from easy life.

Mrs. Kerr's father had been a heavy drinker and this alone made her childhood difficult. Then came the Depression. Her father and brothers were unemployed, her elder sister had a good job in a dress factory, and her mother used to go out doing cleaning for people. Laurel left school as soon as she had passed the state Scholarship exam at just thirteen, and spent the next six months walking all about the Valley and into the city asking everywhere if there was a vacancy. After six months she was actually offered two jobs at the same day, and took the one at T. C. Beirnes, then one of three big Valley stores. She got three shillings per week, which she handed to her mother, who gave her back threepence. She could never afford to buy lunch as she was expected to wear gloves and a hat and also to use make-up at work to make her look older, so she needed to save her money for these things. She blamed her bad skin on the cheap powder she used on her face during that time. She got married at eighteen to a young man who worked at a tinning plant working over vats of acid, which might account for his getting emphysema later in life, though he was also a smoker. When she was fifteen her father once took her into the Valley at night to see some fete, and promptly went into a pub and forgot about her. A strange man asked her what she was doing alone and she said that she had come with her father and where he was. The man took her to the hotel, got the father called out, and told him off about the danger he had left his young daughter in, giving a vivid description of what could have happened to her. This gave her father such a shock that he actually stopped drinking and didn't start again for many years.

When I first met Mrs. Kerr she had three boys all round Rayna's age. Mrs. Kerr was a very intelligent woman with a great sense of humor. Drew, the eldest boy, was good at English in school, but bad at math. Unfortunately he had a teacher who used to hit him on the head and had him in such a state of fear that he couldn't do well at anything, so he left school at fourteen and became apprenticed to a painter. He later married a girl he had been going with since they were both at school and had three very good-looking children, but the marriage didn't work out. He started drinking and she divorced him. He looked like going the same way as his uncle, who after being a brilliant young man and co-founder of Premier Blinds, became a derelict on skid row. Fortunately Drew met a woman a little older than he, who was an abandoned wife and thought he was just wonderful. This was apparently just what he needed; he stopped drinking, pulled himself together, and is now a high executive in Bergers' paints with a beautiful house on the Gold Coast.

Donald, a year older than Rayna, was always my favourite, a very bright boy. He did much better than Rayna in the Scholarship exam and started high school but left after one term, I think because his father made him feel he ought to be earning and not be a burden on his family. He became apprenticed to a baker, passed with highest marks for his year, but then decided not to go on, as by then bread had started to be produced in factories, for example Tip Top. So he joined his brother in painting jobs, then got a job in Premier Blinds, and was sent as manager to the Cairns branch. After a while he and a workmate set up their own business, Northern Blinds, and he made so much money that he could afford to retire at forty or so. He got very interested in orchids, having married a girl from Babinda whose father was an orchid grower, and later helped me quite a bit when I got interested in orchids. He bought a beautiful place in Kuranda and made a very nice house and garden, but eventually returned to Cairns because his wife, who was a keen golfer, wanted to be there. Fairly recently he sold the old house in Cairns and bought a new place on a hillside with wonderful views.

Mrs. Kerr's mother, who had both diabetes and pernicious anaemia, was very sick, blind and dying for years, and Mrs. Kerr nursed her through it all. Then her father, whom she had never really liked, became senile though physically all right, and every time a home was mentioned pretended to have a heart attack, so Mrs. Kerr, taking shares with her sister, had to nurse him. Eventually the old man had to go into a home, and funnily enough, once there he liked it very much, and even refused to visit them because he didn't want to leave the place. Later still Mr. Kerr spent several years in very bad health, at least four of them bed-ridden with emphysema and progressive heart failure, and once again she spent all her time nursing.

By then they were living with their daughter Sharon and her husband in a granny flat their son-in-law had built, in the next street from where we lived in Clontarf (on the Redcliffe Peninsula).

When we moved to Taringa, our new house was on the typical Queenslander high posts with a long flight of stairs front and back, and the garden had the usual little house [*outhouse*] in the back corner. There were two large mango trees near the back fence which produced good crops every year. I set out to plant a lot of shrubs along the paling fences and also a largish rose-bed in front of the mango trees. The first year while the roses were still small I planted eleven tomato plants between them, with a six-foot stake beside each; I trained each plant up the stake, taking off all side shoots. This was one of those English type tomatoes with very large clusters of medium size fruit of very nice flavour, and I got enough from those eleven plants to give away to all the people in the area.

When we first moved I had a fright, as we had left all the garden stuff on a bench under a house, and there I found Rayna, then only maybe 15 months old, all covered with a white powder, which turned out to be arsenate of lead. I put her in the bath and made sure every bit was washed off, and fortunately she had not eaten any, as a test at the hospital showed. After this, one of John's first jobs was to build a childproof cupboard for garden poisons. Rayna had a playing pen and also a high chair that would convert into a low-chair, all turned wood, and no doubt a collectible nowadays. I got quite good at looking for redback spiders which used to like dark corners and lived in the lavatory and under the house, and once I even found one under the seat of the high-chair. Rayna was a pretty child with large blue eyes, a rather olive complexion and by then a deep gold hair, perfectly straight. She was very late learning to walk. She actually was sixteen months old before she walked. Then I began to notice that she had become very knock-kneed, so I took her to the hospital. At the children's hospital at that time they had a Dr. Crawford who told me that unlike bandy legs, knock knees never straightened without treatment. He said the two things that could be done were either to break and reset the leg-bones, or to put the child into splints for about six months. I squibbed the operation and opted for the splints. (I later felt I may have done the wrong thing, as a little boy in her kindergarten had the operation and was back, cured, only a few weeks later.) A special orthopedic shoemaker attached to the hospital made the splints. They consisted of high boots with metal bars right up to the waist, where they ended in a waistband of leather. At knee-height there was a pad on the inside with straps that buckled on the outside of the knees. The things had to be left on all the time, day and night, only being taken off once a day for bathing. The idea was that the constant gentle pressure on the knees would eventually straighten the legs, and that was actually the case. I had to take her back every month, but even in between had to put the straps into the next hole, as they became loose. I remember once we were going home to the tram-stop and the conductor looked at us coming, holding the bell-pull. I thought he was waiting for us, started picking Rayna up and running, only to see him pull the bell, and the tram went off when we came close. I thought it was a very poor joke at the time. When the splints were on people used to talk about the poor little crippled girl, and I got to noticing just how many children and adults were knock-kneed without apparently worrying about it. Rayna didn't seem to mind the splints, in fact when we handed them back after she was finished with them she was quite upset and said: "Where is the man taking my big boots? I want my big boots."

When Rayna was about two, I became pregnant again, but unfortunately got dengue fever, of which there was an epidemic just then, and after running a very high temperature for several days eventually ended up in hospital (public ward) with a miscarriage. I was very upset, though the doctor told me that it was probably the best thing, as the fever would have badly damaged the fetus. I remember we were told not to ring the bell during visitors' hours, which is when the actual miscarriage happened, so I just got out my washbasin and put it under me. Later when the nurse discovered the contents she told me I should have rung the bell, so what was one to do?

Mrs. Kerr had looked after Rayna; in any case her children and Rayna were constantly playing together, either in her yard or mine, with a convenient hole in the fence. Graham Bock, who was a bit older, also came to my place a lot, but I eventually had to ask his mother to keep him away, as he became very insolent, refused to go home when I told him, and lay on the floor saying "make me". Mrs. Bock was quite offended, but got over it eventually.

John by that time was working for a firm called Chesterfield and Jenkins, and doing war jobs on the Downs and in places like Toorbul Point (near Bribie). He was a foreman by then and put in charge of quite large jobs, and they didn't want to lose him. This was of course a reserved occupation, and every time he tried to enlist they got him pulled out again. Eventually he said, "If I can get into the Air Force, will you let me go?" They agreed, not thinking that he had a chance as he was thirty-six by that time. However, he was accepted (in ground staff) and even took the command course, from which he could been exempted because of his age. He then was sent to New Guinea where he spent the remainder of the war, writing such uninformative letters as: "We have now left where we were and have got to where we are now"; all letters of course were censored. During his final leave I got become pregnant again, and Lesley was born in 1944, while her father was in New Guinea. I used to send him madeira cakes, as he did not like the fruit cakes which were the normal thing in parcels to servicemen, and he wrote once that these were so popular that he was lucky to get more than a slice or two, while the tins of fruitcake were just lying about. While in New Guinea he spent some of his spare time making "foreigners"; he made a small ashtray out of a back of a shell, with threepences and an ornament out of three rifle shells fastened to a board, the centre one having a plane in flight made from silver coins. I still have these, but unfortunately one of my children took the plane to school one day and lost it. He also made me a lovely box in shape of a book where the back pulled out as drawer, all made from different woods beautifully inlaid. This too is now lost.

Mrs. Kerr, who already had three boys each two years apart, had her fourth son about a month after Lesley was born. Actually we had expected to be in hospital at the same time, but I was early and she late. We both went to the Woman's Hospital, I in Intermediate and she in the Public Ward, but she said this was a mistake because with the Depression over the only women in the public ward were prostitutes and the like. Even the Intermediate wasn't up to pre-war standards of course; they used pillowcases for nappies and were too short staffed to change them frequently, with the result that Lesley was raw with nappy rash when I got her home. Fortunately an ointment called Ungvita, which strongly smelt of cod-liver oil, fixed matters in a day or two. I had made arrangements for Rayna to go into a Red Cross children's minding place while I was in hospital, as of course Mrs. Kerr might have been away too. She visited Rayna there after a couple of days and was so upset over the conditions she found that she took Rayna home immediately and looked after her.

I was only in labor for three days with Lesley, and had far less trouble with abscesses while feeding her. I did get one and was put on sulpha drugs to which Lesley turned out to be allergic, her face swelling up to about twice its natural size. She was of course born in April, and I had been warned not to wean her during the really hot weather because of a chance of gastroenteritis, then a killer of artificially fed babies, so tried to feed Lesley till she was eleven months old. However, she started to lose weight, and on testing it was found that actually my milk had by then lost its nourishment.

As I did with Rayna, I used to leave Lesley in the City Hall nursery when I had to go to Brisbane, and she would go peacefully to sleep. On just one occasion I persuaded Mrs. Kerr, who had to go into town herself, to leave John there too. He screamed when she left him, and she worried about him and phoned the place after about twenty minutes, when she was told, "For goodness sake come and get him, he hasn't stopped screaming since you left." By that time Rayna was three and in a kindergarten [*nursery school*] on Stanley Terrace. She really enjoyed the kindergarten, except for the mixture of pumpkin and mashed potatoes they got for lunch. After lunch they had a nap, then were taken to the bus stop and put on their respective buses. Rayna used to nurse a cheek full of those vegetables right through her nap, and spit it out from the bus window. Occasionally I took the children to Sandgate on the train (steam), taking a washer and towel to clean them up, as they always emerged covered in soot. I remember one time when Rayna did not wait for her bath till we got to Sandgate, but went, fully clothed, into one of the goldfish ponds in Anzac Square. Once I rented a flat in Sutton Beach in Redcliffe to give the children a proper seaside holiday. However, they didn't seem at all excited about it, and I found the place overrun by cockroaches, which were even in the ice-chest, so cut my losses and returned home the next day.

I used to go to Brisbane fairly often, as I used the then School of Arts Library in Ann Street, which was handy both to the bus stop and the City Hall. When the children were old enough to walk I used to take them in occasionally, and give them cheap treats. We went up the City Hall Tower lift, and halfway the lift stopped so we could look at the works of the clock, and then went right to the top. The City Hall was at that time the tallest building in Brisbane and from the viewing area gave panoramic views. Then we went by tram to the Botanic Gardens, back by another tram up Edward Street, with sometimes a ferryboat ride across the River and back, and all this was free or nearly so.

When Rayna was a baby we took her to Ann Street Presbyterian Church to be christened. This was the first time I had seen a church service in Australia. I got embarrassed when we had to come to the font with Rayna and the Minister talked about how beautiful it was to see young parents bringing their babies to be made Christians. When John went to pay him, he was talked into becoming a member of the Church Committee, but it didn't last long - he got disillusioned when he found that all everyone was interested in was the amount of money in the 'Collect'.

John was away when Lesley was a baby and Mrs. Kerr said she was having the Methodist Minister christen her son John at the house and invited me to have Lesley "done" at the same time, which I did. It was quite a party, though as John was already about six months old the long heirloom christening gown really didn't fit him. Anyhow, this is how Lesley came to be baptised Methodist, and Rayna Presbyterian.

Both my children cried a lot during their first few months. With Rayna I hadn't done much knitting as she was a summer baby, however, for Lesley I knitted at least five dresses as well as a large shawl, and of course booties and gloves. Much of this effort was wasted, as at home she lived in flannelette nightgowns and she didn't go out all that much. I gave away most of the knitting practically unused, but seem to remember I sold the shawl. I then learnt to smock, and smocked baby dresses for Lesley and also a few things for Rayna. The worst part was to pull the material together, the actual smocking I enjoyed. Lesley was quite different from Rayna, she weighed about the same but was shorter and fatter with a round head and a mass of dark hair, which everybody said would fall out. However it never did, and she kept on having brown hair and grey eyes and her father's very fair skin. In spite of their physical differences lots of people claimed that they could see a resemblance between the two. Lesley was also very different in character. Rayna had never sucked her thumb; Lesley started to suck hers when only tiny and didn't stop for many years. During her first cold winter I made her flannelette mittens to keep her hands warm at night, but she kept screaming till I finally cut a hole into the left one and pulled her thumb through so she could go on sucking it. She had a pink and blue bunny, made from some velvety material, stuffed with cottonwool, which she loved and used like a security blanket. She used to hold bunny's ear in her hand and tickle her nose with it while sucking her thumb. She called it "Nunny" and after she was walking it got very dirty and had to be emptied of stuffing and washed. She would stand under the clothesline with her arms up crying, "Nunny, nunny, nunny," till I could finally give it back to her. Later it was kept in her cot, and as with a security blanket, when she hurt herself she would rush to it, grab the ear, and stand there sucking her thumb.

Following John's wishes both children were sent to Sunday school at an early age. Lesley loved this and was particularly impressed with a trick that converted pink water into white to illustrate how Jesus washes white your sins. Rayna, when asked how she liked Sunday School said, "All we do is colouring in and read stories that are supposed to be true, even the teacher pretends they are true." However, she attended Sunday school so regularly that she often won the attendance prize, and in her first year at boarding school came second in the State in Bible knowledge. The prize was a complete Shakespeare and she said she was glad she hadn't won first prize, as that was a Bible.

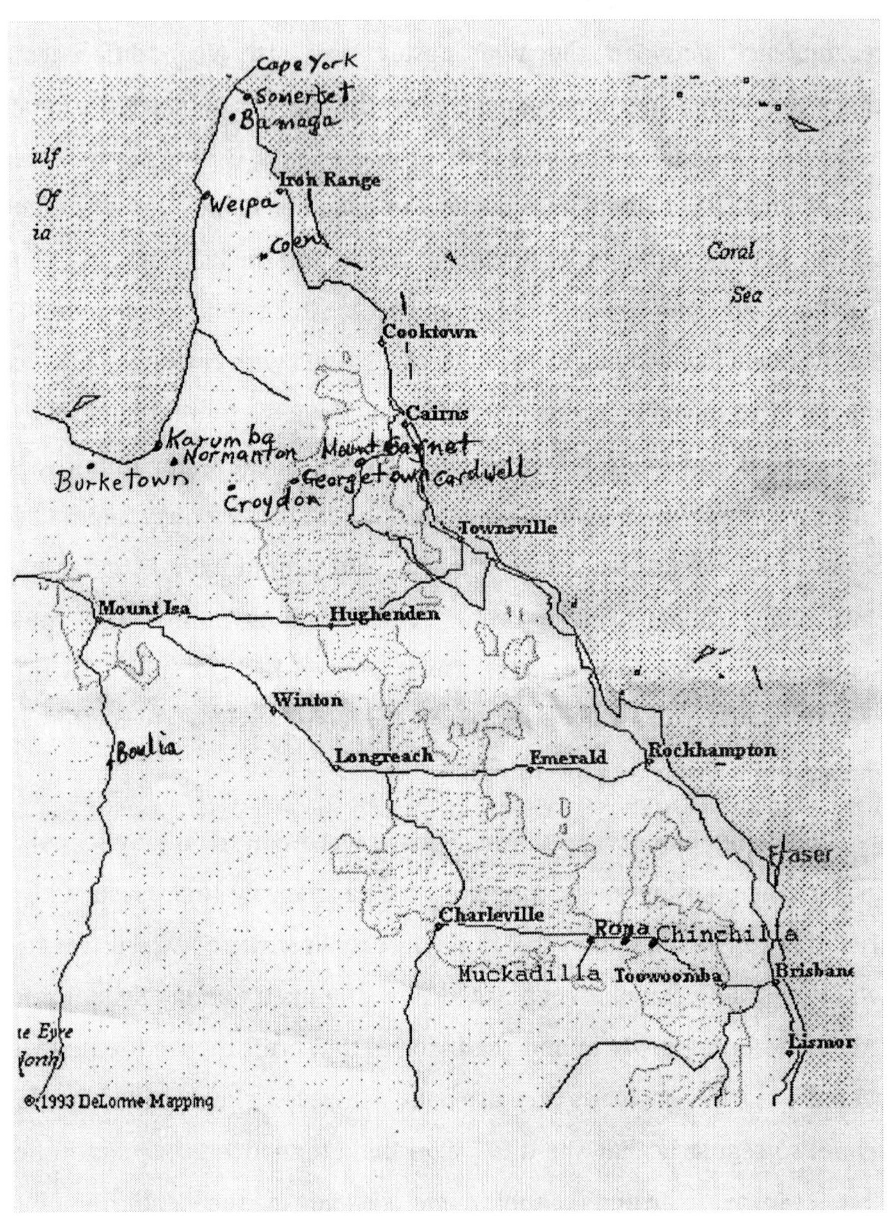

Queensland map, hand lettered by G. Scott.

NORTHERN QUEENSLAND, 1946-1949

Just after the war ended I had a letter from Mr. Tate asking me if I felt like collecting for the American Museum of Natural History again. I regarded this as a joke, as I had two children aged six and two. When John got de-mobbed a few weeks later and came home I showed him the letter, just for fun. Much to my surprise he said: "Well, I feel I'm not ready to settle down to a humdrum life yet, so how about we sell this house and I buy a surplus army four wheel drive truck, build a caravan onto the back of it, and we can go? I could help with the collecting, and do some prospecting and a bit of contracting work on stations."

Well, that is what we ended up doing. I enrolled Rayna, who had had nearly a year in Taringa School, in the state Correspondence school, making arrangements to be sent several weeks' supply of lessons at a time, as we would not always be within reach of post offices.

We had of course to go to places where I hadn't already collected. We started off once again at the Atherton Tableland, but this time just outside Ravenshoe, in an area with somewhat less rainfall, though still enough for thick rainforest. We camped in a clearing at the edge of the scrub, near a dairy farm belonging to people called Turner. There I once again marvelled at the Australian habit of segregating the sexes. The man was rather stupid, the wife quite intelligent. Even so it was taken for granted that John and Mr. T. would go into one corner to talk while the wife and I were left together. The main excitement during this stay was the time when I nearly started a major bushfire. I tried to light a cooking fire and it got away from me at a great rate. Fortunately the men were close by and managed to beat it out just in time.

We tried to get to Chillagoe, which sounded like an interesting place, but could not reach it even with the four-wheel drive, as there were numerous creek crossings with very steep banks, so we had to turn back when we got about half way.

We then went back to Hughenden on the Mount Garnet Road, and I found it quite interesting to see the change the war years had wrought. All the local station owners had made a lot of money selling beef to the army and built magnificent houses. We called in on the Wilsons, whom I had visited with Mr. Young, and once they recognized me they were very friendly, but warned us that the station owners near the road had become tired of travellers expecting free hospitality and were no longer thrilled to see them. We had no intention of stopping at any of them, but ended up having to ask help from the people at The Lynd as we had trouble with the truck. In Hughenden John got to know the local shoemaker, a man called Mottershead, who was badly crippled because when he was young and silly he insisted on getting up and going to a dance just after an appendix operation, with the result that he got peritonitis and was left with a permanently crippled hip. He knew the district very well, and told John about all kinds of places where gold had been found in the past, and in fact offered to go with us and show him the places. We first went to a place called Diggers Springs, back up the Mount Garnet Road for a little way then left, which is to the west. I asked about a beautiful permanent small rock pool that I had admired on my first trip, and was told that some idiot had broken down one side of it so his horses could get to the water, whereupon the water all ran out and that was the end of that.

We camped at Digger's Springs for a while and I did some collecting while John did prospecting. Mottershead took a great fancy to Lesley, then about 2 years old. He used to recite "The Drover's Dream" to her. Diggers Springs was a nice camping place with clear permanent water. There was a little swampy spot where sun-dew, the insect eating plant grew, and I often wonder whether this would have been something new if I had collected some. I had acquired a yeast-bottle and started making bread, as I never cared for damper. Like most beginners I did the usual thing, burying some dough that had not risen, only to find that the sun's heat fermented the dough and it came up like a giant mushroom. Rayna was doing her correspondence lessons at a great rate, usually finishing a week's work in about two days. I had been told that mental arithmetic was usually a problem, so to make sure of this I improved the shining hour by making the problems harder, for example, instead of asking how much do a dozen bread rolls cost if one is two pence [*pennies*], I would say, "How much do a dozen and a half cost if one is two and a half pence?" I also got books for her to read from the correspondence school, but never enough, so I wrote to the country extension service about borrowing them. I told them, to their delight, that she wasn't keen on

Enid Blyton books, which along with the "*Biggles*" books were then the main reading for many children.

John and Mr. M. used to go to Chudleigh Park Station occasionally and be given some meat; eventually the manager gave them a rifle and said to shoot a barren cow when they needed meat, in return for culling out some longhorn bulls. We built a trough of canvas and made our own salt meat.

Somewhere along the way we had acquired a very nice cat, which travelled with us and who was Lesley's special pet. After some time at Diggers Springs we moved to a place called Boyd's Springs. This was a place with a large hill on which in the early days some Afghans had found gold. They had taken out the rich pockets, but when John took samples at random the whole went to about a half an ounce per ton, not enough he said to bother about at a time when gold was £2 per ounce, though perhaps viable for a company with machinery. When we left Diggers Springs we could not find the cat anywhere, and after spending about two hours looking and calling eventually reluctantly decided to leave it behind. When arriving at the next camp Lesley got out of the truck, and said, "*There* he is." The cat had been sitting on an axle of the truck and obviously had not moved all the time until we stopped again. On one of my walks looking for wildlife I came across a waterhole about a mile from our camp, where in the late afternoon a large mob of black cockatoos used to come to drink. One day I took Rayna along to see this, and as we went down to the hole a bunch of cows with a bull came along the track, also to get a drink. We scrambled to the side away from the track and the cattle of course took no notice of us. Another time John came home with a sugarbag full of black bream, which he had caught with a bent pin and bits of salt beef from a small but deep rock pool in the otherwise dry river. It was a welcome change from a rather monotonous diet. He went back a few days later, taking Rayna, but though the waterhole and fish were still there, not one of the fish would bite. I was pleased that John took Rayna, as he nearly always refused to take us anywhere, for instance to the stations. He kept on saying we might hear swear words, and he would have taken the children had they been boys.

I had found by that time that collecting was no longer even marginally viable. The Museum still paid us the same as they had before the war, while all expenses had gone up a lot. I also forget our exact itinerary. I know we spent some time in Blackwater, a few miles north of Rockhampton, and not far from Olsen's Caves. Sometime also we went to Mount Spec, northwest of Townsville, which was one of the nicest camping places I remember. This was in the days before the reservoir was built. The road up to Mt. Spec was very steep and narrow with lots of hairpin bends and I was always glad when we didn't meet any timber trucks. The summit was covered in dense rainforest, but once again we picked a site on the edge of the scrub but in the forest country. An old army camp had been here during the war and we stayed in one of the surviving huts. Wildlife was abundant, and I particularly enjoyed the yellow robins, which were so tame one could practically touch them. There were also many bowerbirds and the two Australian birds of paradise, here called riflebirds, and many possums and gliders as well as other small mammals. Many years later when we lived in Mount Isa, John and I went back to Mount Spec during a holiday. By that time there was no trace left of the old camp, and most of the country had been fenced. This was after the lake had been completed, and we went right round it on the scenic road all the way through rainforest. We stopped as near as we could to our old camp (on the old Charters Towers road) and I was thrilled actually to see a yellow robin once again.

Before we returned for our second stay in Hughenden, John got a job building some new shearers' sheds in a station near Richmond. We went with him and stayed at an old shearers' shed. It was drought time once again, and I found some interesting small flat-headed marsupial mice that lived in the cracks in the black soil. One night we had a very heavy storm and I believe my children still remember being told by their father to sit under the big table, in case the roof collapsed. John decided he better find some carpentry work to help our shaky finances, which is why we went back to Hughenden. We camped at the Hughenden showground, which had showers and lavatories. About twenty feet away a shearer and his wife were also camped. One day, while Rayna was doing her schoolwork I saw the man standing at the door of his van exposing himself. I did not want to tell John, who no doubt would have picked a fight with the man. He was obviously sick, and had rather a nice wife. So when the children and I went into town for some shopping I told a woman I had got to know about it, and she suggested we should move into the empty allotment next to her house, put a box on either side of the fence and use her facilities. I told John about this offer, saying it was much handier and less lonely for us, and we moved. He was working by that time, and I took Rayna along to the local school and asked about enrolling her. Doing the correspondence lessons so much more quickly, she was actually within three months of the grade three, and after a short test the headmaster said he would try her in this and if necessary put her back later. However she had no problems, and within a short time was about halfway in her class. She had been five and a half when she started school, so she was not really too young for this class.

John had taken another contract and was going to be away two or three weeks. He took one of the boxes at the fence for his food and substituted another, which unbeknownst to us had a broken board spliced together with a piece of wavy metal. When I stepped on this to get over the fence, it broke with me and took a long slice out of my leg. Looking down and seeing the blood running out of my shoe, I called to my friend, who gave one look and called the ambulance. Two men arrived and were going to carry me to the ambulance. "Nonsense, I can walk", said I, stood up, and promptly fainted, the first time in my life. I was taken to the hospital and stitched up and bandaged, and told to take it easy for the next ten days or so. John was told about my accident at work and broke all speed limits to get to the hospital. However, finding me quite all right apart from a bandaged leg, he soon got over his fright and soon forgot I was supposed to be an invalid. A few years later we spent a seaside holiday in Townsville and I scratched my leg on an oyster rock. This scratch got infected, and oddly enough the infection spread to the old scar. Fortunately by that time penicillin had become generally available and it soon cleared up the infection.

At one stage, possibly after our first stay in Hughenden, or more likely after another stay at the Atherton Tableland, where John was very proud to shoot several specimens of Hypsoprymnodoa, the day-feeding marsupial that is a sort of living link between bandicoots, possums and wallabies, we intended to go from there through to the Gulf country and then back to Cloncurry. I got pleurisy and a friend took me to the hospital where I was told I should postpone the trip for a few days at least. We weren't pleased about this, as it was getting late in the season and we could expect storms at any time which might make the Gulf rivers impassable, but it couldn't be helped. We went right through Einasleigh, Georgetown, and Croydon, as far as Normanton. Early on this trip our cat died of feline enteritis and I am still convinced that Lesley caught it, as she vomited yellow foam exactly as the cat had done. Fortunately she was only sick a few days and recovered without treatment. When we got to Normanton we found that the trucks with the wet-season supplies had already come, and no further supplies were expected till after the wet. There was no petrol for sale in Normanton, and it looked as if we might be stuck there for the next four months or so. Actually we were lucky even to get to Normanton as one evening we got bogged crossing the Gilbert River, and if there had been a storm that night, we could have easily lost the caravan and all our belongings. However we were lucky as it didn't rain, and John managed to extricate us the next morning.

In Normanton we were camped once again on the town common, near the public baths, which consisted of a small wooden building through which practically boiling water ran from a bore. I found the place very uninteresting and didn't look forward to spending months there, though John was assured that there would be plenty of work for him. After a couple of days a man told John he had bought an army surplus building and was in difficulties about putting the roof on. He told him that if he put the roof on for him he would give him enough petrol to get us to Cloncurry. This John did, while I kept hoping all the time that the rain would hold off just a bit longer. Camped near us was a family of Indians, who had a sideshow snake-charming act, and who also wanted to go to Cloncurry. They suggested that we should travel together, so we could help if either got into difficulties. So eventually we got to Cloncurry, and once again camped at the show ground. This is where I saw the Indian Rope trick. Not the one from the story books with the boy climbing up and the man climbing after him and throwing him down in pieces, but just the rope rising unsupported several feet in the air. I still don't know how this was done. There was nothing but bare ground, the rope was examined by several people and had no gimmicks in it. Neither did the Indian have anything like a magnet on him, and as we were standing all around him, some behind him, it couldn't have been mass hypnosis.

From Cloncurry we returned to Richmond. It was November when we were in Normanton, and we spent Christmas in Richmond, or at least near it on the sheep station. I remember this, because we ordered a case of mixed fruit from the Brisbane Markets as a special Christmas treat for the children and the railway sent it to Winton by mistake, so that when we eventually got it the contents were a mildewed mess and I was only able to save a few oranges.

By this time I started to worry about Rayna who was tall but extremely thin and on our return to Hughenden I took her to a doctor who said all she needed was a diet with plenty fresh fruit and vegetables, and to take her to the coast. John had another contract to do, so we went off by train by ourselves. I had booked sleepers from Townsville, but by this time the wet season had well and truly started and the train the previous week had been unable to run, so the people who had sleepers on this got preference, and we had to accept sitters. I paid for three seats, but our companions turned out to be a young coloured woman and her three children, and shortly after departure her husband, who had a seat in some other carriage also came along, so we ended up with about two seats. I got no sleep at all and decided to interrupt the journey in Rockhampton and stay there till I could get sleepers for the second night. After all that time in the bush, I was down to my last dress, and shortly before getting to Rockhampton this split right along the back, so the first thing I had to do was to go into Woolworth and buy another dress to wear, not one I would have chosen under different circumstances. We managed to get sleepers for the following night, and went to stay at a place in Sandgate, another holiday hostel of the Country Women's Association. I hated this place; the manageress was one of the few people I ever really disliked, which was no doubt because she disliked me. The only other people there were a mother and thirteen-year old son from Thursday Island. The boy was due to be interviewed for entry into the naval college. I still remember this boy was given a table napkin, and when I said why he, and not my children, this woman said, "Your children aren't used to them, " which was quite true, but I still didn't like it.

Rayna and Lesley, Brighton. c. 1949

There was a great housing shortage still, but I managed to find a place in Brighton, outside Brisbane, a large old house belonging to an old lady called Mrs. Warren. She had already rented half her house to a young couple, Mr. and Mrs. Blake. He, later Dr. Blake, became Government Botanist, and they built a very nice house at the Gap in Ashgrove, where I visited them. They were bush lovers and spent much time at Binna Burra, going for long treks with their little girl, Betty, who kept up well though she was only two at the time. Anyhow, Mrs. Warren rented me a large bedroom with a kind of built-in balcony upstairs, and a portion under the house made into a living room/kitchen. Mrs. Warren and Lesley took a great liking to each other. Rayna started school at Sandgate and made friends with a girl called Pat, who was an adopted child. Unfortunately her adopting mother died when she was about twelve, and the father didn't care about her and wanted her to earn as soon as possible. So though she was very bright and did her Scholarship at eleven (the normal age was thirteen or fourteen) she left school and got a shop assistant's job. Actually she was not much good at math, and unfortunately their teacher had a habit of making any pupil who got less than eight out of ten sums right stand on his seat, and then caning them on the back of the legs. I remember how shocked I was when I saw the welts on Pat's legs. Eventually he hit her on the chest and her mother went to the school to complain. About the same time the old headmaster, who was an alcoholic, finally retired and the new man started off by confiscating all the teachers' canes and saying if anyone was really so bad he had to be caned it should be reported to him and he would do the necessary. I thought of this when later I read the autobiography of a teacher in which he said, "Anyone who hits a naughty child ought to get a job looking after pigs, and anyone hitting a child for being stupid ought to be in the pigsty."

Our neighbors on one side of Mrs. Warren's house were an old couple; he was a retired railway worker. They told us how they lived and saved on wages starting at ten shillings per week and rising to thirty shillings, from which they bought their own house and a couple of others to rent. On the other side lived yet another schoolteacher. This man was apparently very popular with his colleagues and pupils but let his frustrations out on his wife, whom he regularly beat up. He loved his two children and never touched them. His wife died not much later of a brain tumor, and the son committed suicide in his first year at university in spite of doing well in his course, possibly the effect of his traumatic childhood. All this reinforced my dislike of physical violence, but I must admit did not stop me from spanking my children, generally when I lost my temper, though I always felt ashamed afterwards.

After John finished his contract he came down to Brighton, and I tried to persuade him to stay in the area, as there was plenty of work and a great shortage of tradesmen. However, he decided he didn't like the coast and returned to the west. He phoned Mount Isa and asked if any jobs were available for carpenters, and on receiving an affirmative reply went there. He stayed at the barracks for a little while and then took advantage of the scheme by which the Mount Isa Mines Company gave materials to any tradesman wanting to build a house, with an option of renting it on completion. The rent was nominal and included free electricity; five shillings per week for a two-bedroom house, seven and six for a three bedroom one, and ten shillings for a very large family home. As soon as the house was finished John sent for us to come up, and so began the twenty years that we spent in Mount Isa.

MOUNT ISA

The children and I arrived in Mount Isa early in 1950, after John had built the Mines house we were to live in. The Mount Isa Mines Company (M.I.M.) at that time would let tradesmen build houses, providing materials and other tradesmen as necessary (for example, electricians) and then giving the builder the first option of renting the place. When John first came to Mount Isa he had lived at the Company barracks with the other single men. At that time there were about 7000 people in the town, and nearly 3000 of them lived at the barracks. The turnover for these was very high, about 300% a year, but M.I.M. would give preference to people returning for the second time, probably thinking that if they came back after knowing what the place was like, they would be more likely to stay.

Our house, the medium size three-bedroom kind that rented for seven shillings and sixpence per week with electricity free, was in rather a nice part of the town. Actually the Leichhardt River [*which was a dry sandy river bed for most of the year]* divided Mount Isa into two parts, the Mine Side and the Town Side. We lived of course on the Mine Side, in South End, quite close to the end of the lease, which was surrounded by a fence, and just one street in front of "Nobs' Row" where all the high executives lived. I was amused recently to see that the National Trust has now listed the house occupied by the then Managing Director, Mr. Kruttschnitt. It was called Casa Grande and was only built in 1949.

Our street, Devoncourt Street, was quite short and only had a few houses in it. On our side there were the Goodwins right at the end, a family with ten children, rather a nice woman, but the husband and the older boys were rather rough diamonds. On the other side there lived the Stewarts -- he was another carpenter, and also a member of the Pipe Band. At that time M.I.M. was very proud of its local bands and would go out of its way to employ people who were good band musicians. Mr. Stewart used to march up and down his verandah playing the bagpipes for hours. Beyond the Stewarts, on the next corner lived the Dents, with six children aged from seventeen to three.

To get back to Mount Isa in general, the town side was not terribly well developed. Unlike our area which had red soil, though rather stony, the town side had horrible soil, and the only people who lived there were those not employed by M.I.M., railway workers, local shopkeepers, and so on. M.I.M. used to let school teachers and people like that stay at their barracks, which were somewhat divided on class lines, depending on Company employment.

There was a bridge across the Leichhardt River and a street with one row of shops on the other side. There was a chemist, a Greek cafe, a jeweller/watchmaker, a paper shop, as well as three hotels, the post office, a baker, and a few others I now forget.

The Company ran a community store on the Mine Side, a large dark wooden building where one could buy anything from furniture to food.

The customers did not pay in cash but gave their (or their husbands') pay number, and the cost of the purchases was deducted from the next pay. If one had spent too much one got what was called a three star pay; for the pay amount there were three asterisks. Once a week the train came in with a refrigerated carriage with fresh fruit and vegetables, and on that day one got up early and stood in a long long queue for many hours to buy the weekly requirements. If one was late one might miss out altogether, and whenever the trains were held up by wet weather or strikes one just did without. Generally people used powdered milk, though while we were in South End there was a man who for a while came around with a cart selling fresh milk from a few cows he kept on a small property outside the lease. This milk, however, had rather a funny flavour from some weeds the cows used to eat.

People called Brazil had befriended John before we came up. The man was an electrician and a Catholic, his wife never changed her religion but the two daughters were brought up as Catholics. I remember her telling me that her young daughter came home from convent school very upset one day because one of the nuns had told her that her mother would not be able to go to heaven. After that, I think, she sent her to the state school. I saw the eldest girl just once in Brisbane, when the Mount Isa Silverband, the other M.I.M. sponsored band, was giving a free concert in King George Square, and Shirley Brazil was the only girl in the band. I can't remember whether we had a utility truck [*pickup truck*] or what kind it was, but I think we must have had, as we visited the Brazils who lived quite a distance from us. Later Mr. Brazil set up first as representative of General Electric and then in an independent business, and we actually bought our first refrigerator from him. John had always been totally opposed to buying things on time payment, but I pointed out to him that we would spend as much on ice each week as the repayments and still have to save the money for the frig, doing without in the meantime, so eventually he agreed to this purchase. During our first Christmas the weather was exceedingly hot and our fridge started to defrost. Mr. Brazil arranged for us to have a new 'tropical' engine put in it, after which it performed perfectly for the rest of its life. It had no freezer apart from two small compartments holding aluminum trays, to be used for ice blocks or homemade ice cream.

When we first arrived the inside of the house wasn't quite finished, particularly the partition between the kitchen and living room, which only had two uprights for the future doorframe. I promptly ran into one of these and got a black eye and John was quite worried because he said people who did not know us would think that he had beaten me up. *[Wife beating was not uncommon in this alcoholic town.]*

John had suggested that we get a dog, and I bought a very nice Border collie pup, which was only eight weeks old, too young, as they thought in those days, to be immunized against distemper. However John said not to worry, as there had never been any distemper in Mount Isa. The inevitable happened, the first and worst distemper epidemic happened just after we arrived, and our pup got the disease. At that time we had the annual wet season and the river came over the bridge. I waded through ankle-deep water to get to the chemist on the town side to get some medicine for the pup, and by the time I got back the water was knee deep and people formed a human chain to cross. A few hours later the bridge was four feet under water and impassable for over a week. This happened quite often and meant that people who got caught on the wrong side couldn't get home, or to work. Unfortunately the medicine did not save the pup, which started having convulsions and had to be shot to end his suffering.

Rayna was eleven and Lesley nearly seven when we came to Mount Isa, and both were enrolled into the Mine School, which of course was much smaller than the school in Sandgate they had been going to. Sometime during their time there the headmaster had all the children do an I.Q. test, and told me that my children were among the top in those tests. However I later found that quite a few of the boys in particular considered the matter a huge joke and deliberately gave silly answers, which might have accounted for the generally very low results.

Before coming to Mount Isa I had made arrangements with the then School of Arts Library in Ann Street in Brisbane to have books sent up for the children and me. This library was later taken over by the Brisbane City Council, and its head librarian, Mr. Muir, became City Librarian. I had also acquired a radiogram and began collecting 78-rpm records mainly of lighter classics. Radio was a problem for quite a while; we could only get Radio Australia during the night and nothing at all in the daytime. This was a disappointment for Rayna who had been in the ABC Argonaut Club and actually managed to become a "Dragonstooth", her name in the club was Pentiselea 49. The children got marks or blue certificates for letters, stories, paintings, music, etc. They sent in and got,

I think, a book prize for six blue certificates and became Dragonsteeth when they had fifty points. Of course not being able to hear the program she had to drop out of this.

My children soon got to know the Stewart and Dent children, though they never had much to do with the Goodwins, probably because they went to the convent school. When her children told Mrs. Dent that I was keen on reading she sent a message to say that she had quite a number of books that I was welcome to borrow. I went over, was asked in for a cup of coffee, and this became the beginning of a long-lasting friendship. Mrs. Dent, like Mrs. Kerr, did not like going out much, and had the reputation of being a snob. The social life in town at that time was restricted to drinking at the pubs in town, the Country Women's Association, various church groups, and the Mary Kruttschnitt Club on the Mine Side. This last was definitely somewhat snobby, the standing of a woman depending on how high up her husband was in the Mine's hierarchy. My husband at the time being just a carpenter, I couldn't have joined if I had wanted to, and Mrs. Dent told me that by the time they had made up their minds that she was good enough to join, she decided that they were not good enough for her. She was an interesting character, and certainly dwelled a lot on her family background. Her mother had been a Spode, the last surviving descendant of the famous English china manufacturer, and she was very proud of this. Mrs. Dent's father had a small cattle station in the Mount Isa area, and I think eventually worked for M.I.M. Mrs. Dent was sent to Blackheath, the Presbyterian girls' school in Charters Towers, where she was quite unhappy, and at eighteen she married. Mr. Dent was about twelve years her senior and a diploma engineer. During the war he could not enlist, as he had damaged both kneecaps in a Mine accident earlier on, so decided to do his bit by working as maintenance engineer for the Red Cross. Women and children were either not allowed to stay or were discouraged from staying in Mount Isa during the war, so he took his family to the Blue Mountains where he bought a derelict apple orchard. Mrs. Dent told me that she could never later bring herself to pay high prices for inferior apples after seeing thousands rot on the ground there. In the Blue Mountains she made friends with Dymphna Cusack and Florence James, the authors of such books as *Come in Spinner* and *Caddie*. Dymphna Cusack was very left wing; Florence James after getting a divorce from an unsatisfactory husband went to England with her two children, became a reader for the publisher Constable, and still occasionally visited Mrs. Dent in Nambour after she moved there years later.

In spite of a rather restricted education Mrs. Dent was very intelligent, had a great sense of humor, and was a voluble talker who never seemed other than full of fun and games. She had seven children then, the eldest was then at Thornborough, the boy's school corresponding to Blackheath, and later at Queensland University. There he became editor of *Semper Floreat*, the student paper, and leading light of the theatrical society. I remember he once played Hilary in a performance of "A Fruity Melodrama". He always wanted to be a teacher in a private school and never deviated from this, becoming eventually Queensland's youngest headmaster at Toowoomba Grammar School. He died rather young of cancer. Carol, the next child, was not academically interested and was so unhappy at boarding school that her mother finally agreed to let her come home and leave at fourteen. She then worked as shop assistant and married a young Czech called George Feurich, who started a photographer's business in Mount Isa, where she still lives.

By going interstate Mrs. Dent's children, the younger ones at least, lost a year's school; they were put back a grade on returning to Queensland. This meant that the next three children were all in Rayna's class at school, though a year or two older. Mina and Marian became Rayna's friends. Marian had a twin brother, Peter. Unlike the other children in the family, both had very red hair, but otherwise they weren't at all alike. Marian was a fat baby and Peter small and skinny. Mrs. Dent said it was quite comical to watch them as babies, when Marian sat and Peter, who walked very early, ran all around and over her. Peter, by the way, was one of the boys who deliberately gave silly answers to that I.Q. test. He was seventeen when he passed Junior and insisted on leaving school, though his parents encouraged him to go on. All he wanted to be at that age was a ringer on a station. His parents said if he left school he would have to do an apprenticeship, so he did Fitting and Turning. His best friend, a very bright boy, was doing a diploma course and talked Peter into doing this as well. Peter did all right, except failing math every year. Their mother had told all the Dent children that nobody in the family could do math. After finishing his apprenticeship Peter decided he had been silly not to go on to university, and took adult matriculation. He again failed in math, but was granted the certificate and began an engineering course. He apparently worked like mad and did not take part in any activities at the university, scraping through the first year getting a post in Math, doing better in the second, and then suddenly doing really well and graduating with nearly all distinctions and high distinctions. He became one of M.I.M.'s bright young men and eventually worked up to just one step below the top. However, after being given the job of hatchet man during one of M.I.M.'s purges, he left them and got a job with another company.

All this of course is going many years into the future. As I said before, after Mrs. Dent sent a message saying she could lend me books, I got into the habit of dropping over frequently. In turn I lent Mrs. Dent books I thought might interest her from the Brisbane Library, also 78 records I kept buying as I could afford them.

I had been making my children's clothes since they were babies, and Mrs. Dent asked me if I would make some for Marian and Mina, which I did with the proviso that they would do the hand finishing themselves. I had always let Rayna have what she wanted, at one time a very bright red dress and lots of Woolworth special jewellery. I felt that it was better for her to get these things out of her system; otherwise she might want to wear a bright red dress at sixty. I had acquired an electric sewing machine, the first model with a knee control and I still have this, as I never in later life did enough sewing to feel the need of something better. Actually when Rayna was twelve she bailed up and asked me to buy her dresses, as mine always had a home-made look. She also decided that my ironing wasn't good enough and started doing her own, much to my delight. I must say I never had any real aptitude for dressmaking. I had tried to do courses a couple of times, but each time was put off by having to learn drafting patterns and things like that when all I wanted was hints on the practical side of sewing. I tended to take shortcuts that turned out to be long-cuts, never tacking anything, but just pinned it at most, and generally spent more time unpicking where I had gone wrong, than actually doing the work. Also I hated the hand finishing and never basted any seams.

Mina Dent showed an early aptitude for dressmaking and quite often when she and Marian were going to the pictures that evening, would run up dresses for both of them in one afternoon, which always looked very nice, though not properly finished inside.

Lesley was nearly three years younger than Noela, Mrs. Dent's next child, and two years older than Julie, but used to play with both of them. Noela tended to make a convenience of Lesley, encouraging her if she had nobody better on hand, and telling her to get out when she had another friend her own age about. If that kind of thing happened to Rayna she would just go home and read a book, but Lesley would be quite heart-broken. Julie was a sweet little girl. She was named Julie Ann Frances after Florence Hastings (James') children, Julie and Frances, and if asked her name would rattle off Julie Ann Frances Hating Spode Dent, rather like Rayna at an earlier age, who when asked her name would say "Rayna Scott Waverly Road Taringa."

Shortly after we came to Devoncourt Street a bricklayer called King built a house across the road from us, and his wife gave piano lessons. Rayna said she wanted to learn, and had lessons for some time, having to practice on Mrs. King's piano, but eventually gave up and decided she would rather listen to records of great pianists. Mrs. King had a daughter, Deanna, about Lesley's age, who went to the convent school and played sporadically with Lesley. She told Lesley about the beauties of being in the Brownies and actually got her to join, but as their group consisted all of Catholic girls they weren't very nice to Lesley and she refused to carry on.

Though my memory on the whole had always been excellent and I used to be able to memorize a long poem just by reading it through once or twice, I had a rotten memory for numbers or unconnected words. I had a lot of trouble remembering John's pay-number, 1721, until he gave me a "donkey-bridge" by saying: "Just remember, when Lesley is seventeen Rayna will be twenty-one." I still remember this number after more than forty years. Also sometime later a woman gave me her phone number, 693, when I had no pen to write it down. She said: "Just remember it is seven away from seven hundred." This too I never forgot. I remember the other tenant in Mrs. Warren's house in Brighton, Mrs. Blake, told me that she used to be a very dreamy kind of person and in her job as receptionist had trouble remembering phone numbers. She found that in the long run it saved her time to memorize them in the first place rather than keeping on to have to look them up. Even now I sometimes forget the rest of a phone number I looked up during dialing and have to look it up again and start over. I made a mistake too with Lesley's birth year, when I enrolled her in school in Mount Isa, saying she was born in 1943 instead of 1944. As a result she had to run with children a year older at the school sports and was most annoyed when the teachers told her she was eight, when really she was only seven.

At the first Church of England Flower Show and Fete we went to, a puppy was raffled as the prize to whoever guessed its name correctly. I allowed Lesley to enter (the ticket cost sixpence) and she picked Dusty for a name, and won the pup. I was never sure whether she really picked the correct name, or whether they just gave the pup to her because she seemed so very much in love with him. Dusty was a bitser, coloured like an Alsatian and undoubtedly with some dingo thrown in, and we had him for years.

Apart from the picture show on the Townside we had very occasional live performances by companies coming up from Brisbane. I remember two I went to with Mrs. Dent. One was a concert by the Queensland Symphony Orchestra (I think it had a different name then, and I remember being rather annoyed because the conductor told us before starting that people weren't supposed to clap between movements of a symphony or concerto). I knew this of course, but realise that probably many in the audience didn't.

Another time the Lyric Opera came up and performed *Rigoletto*. This was in the middle of a very hot spell and I felt sorry for the actors. Not only did they have no proper scenery, as the one they had brought up in their mobile carriage didn't fit into the low hall, but also they must have been extremely uncomfortable in those heavy and hot fur-trimmed velvet gowns. I remember when Rigoletto bent over the dying Gilda to sing his last aria, seeing the sweat from his face dripping onto the poor girl's face, I thought she must have been very tempted to move.

Another time we had a ballet coming up and the performance was held in the old Methodist Church hall on the town side. The stage was rough and not built for such doings, so it was quite funny to see the dancer looking so light and graceful, while their footsteps on the wooden stage sounded like a herd of elephants.

When Rayna was about fourteen, and Mina and Marian a bit older, they all went to the Fellowship of the Presbyterian Church. The minister was friendly with one of M.I.M. Department heads and they started a light opera company. The three girls were asked to join and sang in the chorus of two Gilbert and Sullivan operettas, first *Trial by Jury*, and then *Pirates of Penzance*. This was the first time I had heard much Gilbert and Sullivan and I really liked both the music and Gilbert's clever words. After the Pirates Mr. Walker got transferred and the company folded, but it was fun while it lasted.

I was a member of the Country Women's Association (C.W.A.) but didn't attend to their meetings, just paid my dues because this enabled me to go to the association's holiday places. There were huts in Kissing Point, a suburb of Townsville, and we went there a couple of times. They were in a nice cool area of Townsville right near the beach, but very primitive, just a bare hut with one large table and a couple of benches and a part up each side, one step higher, with beds and cots. There was a stove and an ice chest and electric light, but one had to bring one's own bedclothes. There was a shark-proof enclosure in the water but this hadn't been maintained and one could see large holes in the wire netting at low tide, when the structure was exposed. I had been told only to go swimming when the tide was going out, as the sharks then didn't come close in, and we had no trouble. Two days after returning home, I read that a man had been bitten by a shark in that enclosure, and another at Arcadia on Magnetic Island. I scratched my leg on a post with oysters growing on it and this became infected and also spread the infection to the old scar I had on my leg from falling through a box in Hughenden. Fortunately by this time penicillin was available and I got an injection, which cured me quickly. A woman from a sheep station stayed with her children in one of the other huts. She saw me do knitted lace work (a housemaid had taught me to do this when I was quite young) and asked if I would do her a set of tablemats for pay, which I did, but of course got very little for. She was another snob, who told me she had booked her daughter into a New South Wales boarding school, as she didn't think the Queensland ones were good enough.

We took a boat to Magnetic Island once, and went up Castle Hill, the hill which keeps Townsville so hot in summer, and which the Yanks had offered to demolish when they were there during the war. (The offer was indignantly refused.) We also used to go along the beach towards Cape Pelerandra round some rocks, under which on low tide we found some very nice cone and cowrie shells.

The second time we went to Kissing Point I offered to take Noela Dent. As it turned out this was unfortunate. First the trip itself was uncomfortable. We had had a rat plague in Mount Isa, a native rat which was so numerous that if one looked out of the window at night one could see the whole ground moving. They came into the houses too, and I once put a loaf of bread on the table, turned to get the knife and turned back to see two rats eating the bread in broad daylight. Towards the end of this plague the feral cats, owls and kites had also bred up considerably and eventually no doubt many of these also starved. Our train was held up for nearly a week in Richmond after wet weather. Fortunately we had a sleeper, but the rat plague was also in Richmond, and as many people ate in the train and spread crumbs and things around the rats came right into the train. The Railway Department reduced the prices in the dining room, but I used to take the children for at least one meal a day to the town's best hotel. Some of the travellers who were returning from holidays were quite broke, others, who could afford it, took a plane home. Eventually we arrived in Townsville, and then both my children, one after the other, got some kind of gastric trouble, which fortunately didn't last long. Then Noela got sick and I first thought that she had the same thing my children had had, but she didn't improve and started complaining of pains in her legs and having trouble walking. As there had been an epidemic of polio I got very worried and took her to the hospital, where they diagnosed rheumatic fever. I visited her every day and stayed an extra week, but eventually had to go home leaving her still in hospital. I felt terrible about this, though of course she may have got the sickness even if she had stayed home.

I had taught Rayna to knit at an early age, and when she was about eleven she won a first prize at the Church of England Show for a dressed doll, having knitted not only dress, bonnet and booties, but also singlet and panties for a small baby doll (gloves too). The Stewarts had moved to another street and our new neighbors were the Moys. He was a butcher, and got us a proper butcher knife only normally available to the trade, which I still own and use.

I had also started teaching Rayna and Mina German at their request. This was all right when we started on a book called *I Can Read German* (*Ich Kann Deutsch Lesen*), all about a family of humanized water rats and the doings of their three children, but when it came to having to learn grammar and vocabulary they both lost interest. Mina had asked me to tell her bad words, and once when the three girls went to the town picture show she for some reason called the man in front of her "ein alter Esel – an old donkey." He turned out to be a German, turned round and said to her in German, "you are a silly little ass too," to the girls' embarrassment.

I used to do a lot of baking in those days, and for birthdays went to quite a bit of trouble, making "frogs", "niggerheads" (I am sorry but that is what they were called) and Berlin Buns, a kind of doughnut without the hole, but with a jam filling, which was made from a yeast dough. It was quite a lot of work, and I only did it occasionally during the cool weather. The buns were cooked in hot fat and rolled in caster sugar when cooked, and a crowd of children used to stand around ready to eat each batch as it came out of the pot.

John had made friends with Mr. Dent, who loved the bush and often took his family on trips, sometimes including us. This is how I saw Riflecreek Dam, then the only dam for Mount Isa with lovely clear water. The caretaker being someone the Dents knew well, we got permission to walk around the dam, and the children could swim below the dam in the overflow. John and Mr. Dent also used to go to Karumba on the Gulf for fishing trips, and sometimes on longer trips along the Birdsville Track or something similar. The Birdsville track was little travelled in those days and one had to report at the police station on both ends so search parties could be sent if anybody didn't arrive at the other end. About this time some friends of the Dents from their days in the Blue Mountains arrived in Mount Isa, Mr. U. and his wife and two children. Mr. U. started a steam laundry on the Townside, having been promised the Mine's business. M.I.M. at that time was trying to help the town to develop, and eventually closed down the community store to encourage business development on the Townside. I didn't like Mr. U., who seemed very opinionated. His wife and children all worked full time at the laundry and he spent quite a lot of time at the Dents. I remember having a great argument with him once when he said dry sand was heavier than wet sand. I proved that he was wrong by putting equal amounts of wet and dry sand on opposite sides of a balance scale and he still said he was right and if I used a cubic yard of sand I would see he was. So I ended up not going to Mrs. Dent's place as much. About this time too, M.I.M. brought out a new set of rules for occupants of Mines houses, giving M.I.M. the right of inspection anytime and of taking houses off people at a week's notice. This didn't appeal to John at all, and he decided to build us a house on the Townside.

Actually things had been changing since we came to Mount Isa. At first we had Mr. Kruttschnitt as Managing Director and Mr. Hilton, another American, as General Manager. Charlie Hilton was extremely popular. He used to drive around the lease in his black Pontiac car and stop and talk to people who were working in their gardens, asking if they had any problems. People could always come to him for help and advice. When he and Kruttschnitt retired he was a hard act to follow and the next man, a Mr. Gross, was very unpopular, perhaps because nobody really could live up to Hilton.

Next came Mr. Fischer, who had been at Broken Hill. He had a very nice wife, plain and without any snobbishness; in fact she discouraged this activity among the wives of executives. There was a story about her being at a party where the talk got onto washing machines. "I don't need one," said Mr. Fischer, "I've got one," pointing to her. The next morning she went out and bought the most expensive washing machine she could find. Unfortunately later on she and her two small grandsons were killed in a plane accident when returning from a holiday.

Mr. Foote, the next Managing Director, had a wife who originally disliked being the big shot in the town and would have preferred a more private life just for herself and her family. However, she adjusted admirably and became quite good at being hostess at big functions.

To return to our doings, John talked to Mr. King, the bricklayer, and they looked over the Townside and took up perpetual miners' leases on two adjoining blocks, the idea being that they would build houses from the usual hollow concrete bricks, helping each other with their respective trades. John took me over and I was shocked to find the "soil" to be a mixture of schist rock and white bull dust and the two blocks themselves about ten minutes walk from town with just bush all round. Mr. King drank a fair bit and John used to get annoyed when he didn't turn up on the building site. Eventually however the brickwork was finished. Then Mr. King became ill, and was first diagnosed as having hookworm, a disease one gets on the North Coast by walking bare-footed on contaminated soil, but whatever it was killed him. The M.I.M. tradesmen held a working bee and finished his house, but I don't remember Mrs. King ever living in it. I think she sold it and left Mount Isa.

After our house was finished we moved of course. We had electricity and town water, but the flow of this was very poor; it used to run from the taps only between about midnight and five a.m. and one had to fill baths and containers during that time. We had a septic system with a trench along the western side of the house and we built a tall trellis along this and planted a couple of grapevines, which grew like mad and gave us shade from the westerly sun, and also grapes. We could not water them at all, but the grapes had their roots in the septic trench, which both watered and fertilized them. We planted some Athol Pines along the border between our and King's house; these aren't beautiful trees but with oleanders some of the few that don't require watering. We also had a fairly large fowl house in the back corner (we had a corner allotment) and I planted a mulberry just outside this. It was a seedling and turned out to be a male, so after a couple of years we pulled it out and started again with a cutting from a female tree, which flourished and provided us and the fowls with masses of fruit in season, and the fowls with shade from the western sun. We had a concrete brick garage in the backyard, which however John used as workroom and kept his vehicle under a carport built onto the side of it. I planted a fig tree there and for some years got very good crops of figs (a fruit I don't really care for).

Later a tiny beetle, which rather like a fruit fly filled the fruit with maggots, infected it and I eventually pulled it out. When we first came to Joan Street there was still quite a large heap of sand at the back of the house, and a pair of spotted pardalotes built their tunnel next in it. I tried to keep the local cats away from it by barricading the surrounds with spinifex and had a rather silly feeling that if they reared their young successfully it would be a sign that I would get away from Mount Isa some day, otherwise I would be stuck there forever. Fortunately for the birds and my peace of mind they did rear their young all right. Though from a landscape point of view I preferred the Mount Isa region with some hills and mainly red soil to the deadly black-soil plains. However, I disliked Mount Isa, mainly the very hot summers, which were worse on the Townside; the hollow bricks kept the hot air in them all night, and in the morning, even though it may be quite pleasant outside, the walls would still feel hot and the temperature in the house over ninety. I used to spend much of my time at night lying in a shallow bath of, by then, cool water, reading and rarely got more than four hours sleep in summer, which lasted at least five months.

By the way, in view of the recent referendum on daylight saving which was overwhelmingly disliked in the north and west of the State, it is interesting that the schools in Mount Isa used to start in summer at 8 a.m. and let the children out early, reverting to the normal times during the cooler months.

After moving I didn't see much of Mrs. Dent. After the first two or three years the town got sewerage and I was able to have a proper garden. John got a friend to dump about ten inches of topsoil from a new open cut onto our allotment, which helped a lot. We pulled out the Athol Pines and discovered that they had already put thick roots under the foundations of the house, even though they were about thirty feet away from it. I planted some more fruit trees, a grapefruit, a mandarin orange, and a Meyer lemon, all grafted trees bought from a nursery M.I.M. maintained, and they quickly produced increasingly large crops as at that time we had no fruit fly in Mount Isa. One year we had about three thousand grapefruit from our tree most of which I gave away, as John was the only one in our family who liked them.

All this gardening and the sewerage system was made possible by M.I.M. building a new and much larger dam at a place called not very imaginatively the Thirteen mile, where eventually quite a large lake formed with facilities for boating, fishing and swimming, all well away from the part the water supply was taken from. This lake, Lake Mundarra, became a popular picnic spot. It was stocked with fish and people used to get quite good catches of fish. John however would never do any fishing there (there were too many people) and his fishing was restricted to his trips with Mr. Dent to Karumba on the Gulf.

We often saw the proverbial blue moon because of the dust haze; in colour it was a definite light blue; this happened several times every year. One trouble with the water from Lake Mundarra was that on occasion, usually after rain, the water became very brown, full of mud. I had for years been making my own ginger beer with a "ginger beer-starter", but had to stop, as the dirty water killed the yeast. We had an infrequent phenomenon of a sudden mass of little things like small horseshoe crabs in puddles on the side of the road after rain, also occasionally small fish and lots of tadpoles. People used to say it rained these, but it was more likely that they bred from eggs surviving in the ground from previous rains. There would also be masses of frogs, both tree frogs and the large green kind, which also aestivates. After we got the water and soil I built a fairly large rose-bed, ordering my roses from a Southern firm, and they did quite well, though in summer the flowers would open and die in half a day, but during the colder months I had some good roses. I also grew some carnations, which were John's favourite flowers. Between the rose bed and the house John built me a large aviary, which we later divided into two, one for native finches and one for budgerigars, chiefly, though I also had a couple of African lovebirds and Quarrians. The finch aviary had shrubs planted in it, but nothing could grow in the other, as the parrots killed all the plants. I finally had success at breeding, which had always frustrated me when I had kept birds in cages. I also got a pair of canaries, but these apparently breed better in cages, mine used to lay eggs and hatch young all right, but somehow the first female I had kept begging the male for food, and then eating it herself, instead of feeding her young. When I replaced her with another female, the young got fed all right, but somehow the food would stay stuffed in their crops and not be passed on to the stomach, so they too died. I also introduced a pair of European goldfinches, and found one of them cross-breeding with a canary. These young were reared successfully, but didn't look as nice as either of the parents. The lovebirds used to lay infertile eggs, so no luck there either. However, some of the finches bred regularly, and so did a pair of king quails which ran about on the floor of this aviary. It was very nice to see first the parents sitting on the speckled eggs, then the whole family walking about, mum first, then the tiny striped babies, a little over an inch long, then dad. One trouble was that these quail are highly territorial, so as soon as the young males got their adult plumage the father would peck them to death unless I removed them first.

I used to go in and inspect the budgerigars' nests every day, and handle the young trying to keep them tame. Some refused my attentions from an early age, but others remained very tame and would come and sit on my hands or shoulders when I entered the cage. It was such birds that I gave to any dear old ladies who wanted a pet. I once gave one to a girl who used to let it fly in her garden, where it would sit high up in a large gum tree and still come to her when she called it. I later generally charged a small sum for the birds, not because I wanted the money but because people tend to value things more when they have paid for them. I remember one woman coming to me for a bird as pet for her children. Two days later she came back and said the children had knocked the cage off the table, could I give her another bird. I refused. Once I came home from shopping to find the budgerigar aviary wide open and two very small girls playing with the water dish, making mud pies. Many of the birds had got out, which worried me as they had babies in the nests, but fortunately they all hung about and we eventually got them all back with a kind of butterfly net. After that I put padlocks on the gates.

After John built me a bush-house, I started a cactus collection, and intended also to grow foliage plants. I had no intention of growing orchids, but I found that foliage plants were difficult because of the dry climate, and got talked into trying a few orchids. At that time an orchid society had started in Mount Isa, and I joined this and in due time became secretary. I also joined the Queensland Succulent Society and the New South Wales Cactus Society, the latter because of its very good magazine, though I did manage to attend a few meetings when I was in Sydney. The Queensland Society couldn't call itself a cactus society, because after the problems after the introduction of the prickly pear the government had forbidden the keeping of cacti, though the small growing plants that were the main collectors' items would never become pests. The rule hadn't been enforced for years, and country people had even been encouraged to keep one or two prickly pears on their property, so the Cactoblastus [*prickly-pear eating moth introduced from Argentina*] would not die out. Members of the society bought and sold among themselves, but cactus plants could not be sold in shops. I very much enjoyed going to meetings and visiting private collections when I had the opportunity and made quite a few friends, eventually also joining the Bromeliad and the Rose Societies.

Gabriele and her cacti collection

Donald Kerr by then already lived in Cairns, and he once took me to an orchid society meeting, and also around various nurseries, and I also visited private collections in Townsville. Once when John and I were on holiday in Townsville we stayed not far from Ross River (the one Ross River fever is named after) and I visited a serious collector who went in for all kinds of oddbods, which I have never seen since. He also had a lot of insect eating plants. Strangely enough, orchids were fairly easily grown in Mount Isa, mainly because there was no problem with fungus diseases and few insect problems. I had quite a varied collection, and when I was secretary I used to do the buying for the Club. I had trouble once when I picked up three cartons of Phalaenopsis (moth orchids) from the railway station and came home by taxi. I had to leave one carton by the gate while I carried the other two, and by the time I came back about a minute later the contents of the third box had already been killed by the heat. We got quite cold winters, with winters going down to the low forties (Fahrenheit) but since day temperatures went up quite high even in winter the plants seemed to take it, though we had one exceptional winter when temperatures went down to 36 degrees F. a couple of times and I lost quite a few Phalaenopsis.

Later, when we were leaving Mount Isa I had to take my plants of course, and I discovered that it would be cheaper to sent them by plane, at a special back-loading rate, than it would by train or road transport. It was lucky I decided on this, as by the time we left the entire road and rail services were held up by wet weather for ages, and I probably would have lost the lot. Some friends from the Society helped me by packing up my collection (twenty-three cartons in all) and these were delivered to my door in King Street (Clontarf) just a day after I arrived.

Dusty was still with us of course when we moved to the town side. His end was sad. One day I came home and found him standing looking very uncomfortable. It seemed he must have been run over. We had no vet in Mount Isa so I phoned one in Townsville who sent me a prescription for penicillin just in case. However he got worse and was obviously in bad pain, not able to eat or drink or urinate, so eventually John asked a friend to shoot him for us. The friend did a bit of an autopsy and said his bladder had been completely torn, so even if we had a vet it wouldn't have done much good. By that time our neighbors were the Smiths, a son of the man who owned the picture show, and they had golden Labradors. Next time they had pups, they gave us the runt of the litter, which Lesley named Biddy, and she was with us until we left Mount Isa, when I gave her to a family of animal lovers with seven children.

When Rayna was eleven or so we bought her a bike. Eventually she learnt to ride well enough to go to school on it. Though being one of the youngest, she never had any problem about being near the top of the class and passed scholarship at thirteen, though she failed geography.

I took both children on a holiday to Brisbane, where I took Rayna to a professional guidance officer. The trouble then was that one had to take Latin and French for an Arts matriculation, and two Maths plus physics and chemistry for a science one, and it was impossible to fit in all these subjects into one course, so children had to decide at this early age whether to take arts or science subjects in secondary school. The man after testing Rayna said that she seemed to be equally good at both, but that science would offer more employment prospects, Arts only leading to school teaching or being a librarian. Rayna said she didn't want to be either of these and chose to do science, which turned out a mistake, as her memory wasn't terribly good, and in a science course it was a matter of memorizing more than intelligence, at least in the undergraduate course. Mrs. Dent was sending Marian and Mina to boarding school in Charters Towers, but I didn't like what I had heard of the schools in the area. Mount Isa at this time had the first two years but no senior high school, so I enrolled Rayna to go to the Brisbane Girls' Grammar School from Junior on. I had toyed with the idea of St. Peter's, this being then the only school teaching German, or even the Glennie School in Toowoomba, but the Grammar school was much cheaper and had then as now a very good academic reputation.

There was little racism in Mount Isa at the time, and certainly not in the school. We had lots of people from European countries in the place; at one time about thirty-six different nationalities, if I remember rightly. One of the largest groups was the Finns, many of whom couldn't speak English and worked under an English-speaking Finnish foreman. There was a Finnish girl in Rayna's class and I remember being very shocked when, after the periodical visit from the Dental Clinic she came home with a slip showing she needed some fillings. Her father said he wasn't going to spend his money on her teeth and sent her to have all her teeth out, at sixteen. There were also many Dutch people in the town, including Mrs. van der Hoek, whose daughter Tanya was at school with

Lesley, and who later lived near us in Redcliffe. We had a Dutch family across the road from us, the mother terribly house-proud and the two girls hardly ever coming out to play, having to help mum with the housework. Everything, including ceilings, had to be washed at least once a week and I, never having been interested in housework, found this ridiculous. It was always John who was the house-proud one in our family. When we first got married he had to show me everything, including how to hold and use a broom, and the first time I did washing in the old-fashioned way with a boiler, I stuffed everything in, including whites, coloureds, and even woollen socks, which emerged a slimy mess. I remember Rayna once telling her father, when she was about twelve: "Dad, you would have made somebody a good wife." Talking of boilers, Mrs. Dent had a wood boiler in her yard when I first knew her, and Mr. Dent used to bring in long pieces of wood from the bush. One day, she fell over the wood, cut her leg, and developed an ulcer, which didn't improve after being treated with all kinds of recent wonder drugs. Eventually their old bush friend, Rupert MacCulloch, brought her a tube of Goanna oil and this she used in desperation, and the ulcer disappeared in a few days. Later she bought a very expensive washing machine that started off by chasing her all over the laundry. When finally it was immobilized, it started giving her electric shocks. Mr. Dent told her she was just imagining things until one day he put his hand into it and got a shock himself, when he got the electrician immediately. It turned out the machine wasn't earthed [*grounded*] and it was a wonder she hadn't been electrocuted.

Lesley was still at the Mine School when we moved to the Townside, and either walked or got a doubler from Rayna to and from school. From an early age Lesley hankered after a pony, but we could never afford to let her have one. In Joan Street we couldn't have kept it in our allotment, and we didn't think it was safe to let her keep it, as most town horses were running wild along the river and were caught when required. At her age she really wouldn't have been safe walking alone along the riverbank for hours. Lesley too was bright, and I remember she once tried to help an older friend with her homework and then came to me and said: "I have been explaining this in words of one syllable for nearly an hour, and then said, 'Now do you understand?' and the girl just said 'No.' How's that possible?" This girl belonged to an assorted family of about six children, all from different fathers, the mother being good-hearted but without any moral sense and a congenital liar, with whom Lesley became very friendly, much to the worry of John.

I was delighted to find that Lesley had a talent for art and could draw quite well at an early age, having all my life felt sad about having no such talents. Lesley was particularly good at drawing horses and several times won money prizes sending in work in the Sunday Mail. I took her to the vocational guidance people, too, and though they told me that of many children with talent in art only very few ever ended up making a living with it, I think I may have encouraged Lesley to choose the Arts course in high school. *[This, again, was a mistake. Lesley had a real aptitude for science and could have had a very successful career with a science degree.]*

When Rayna was fifteen she went off to the Grammar School. I remember John and I saying that this was the beginning of losing the children and that we would have to get used to it and let them live their own lives. We took her to the aerodrome, where of course other parents also were saying good-bye to their children. I had never been nervous of flying myself, having done lots of it since I was quite young, but every time one of the children went off I got rather worried and didn't really relax till I found they had arrived safely. I had bought an educational insurance policy for Rayna when she was a baby but even then we had creeping inflation, and instead of paying for all her secondary schooling it paid for less than one term's expenses. Actually neither she nor Lesley had to pay fees at the University, because they each got a Government scholarship, and also got a subsidy for the airfares, as the government paid for train fares three times a year and we only had to pay the difference.

I felt rather lost after Rayna had left and considered taking a job, seeing she was certain to go to university. However, I did not want to leave Lesley alone after school, which cut out any shop jobs. Eventually I heard about, applied for, and got, the job of kitchen maid at Boyd's Hotel. This paid £9 per week, the second cook getting £10 and the first cook £11. Hours seemed to fit in very well. I worked from 6:30 a.m. to 1:30 p.m., and then again from 5:30 p.m. to 7:30 p.m. This meant that John could take Lesley to school in the morning on the way to work, and I would be home in the afternoons, then he would be back home when I had to go out again. The work was both easy and heavy, mainly washing pots and pans (there was a pantry maid who washed china and cutlery), doing the vegetables, and washing the floor.

There was no running hot water and I used to have to heat my own in an enormous soup pot, trying to find a place on the stoves that wouldn't be needed by the cook. If she did need the place she just would push my container to one side and I would have to wash up with cold water. Only bar soap was provided, so I used to buy my own detergent. On the two days I was off, Sunday and Monday, the second cook would do my work, and on the pantry maid's day off I would do her job. The main interest in the job was the number of odd characters I met, people I previously would have hardly believed could exist. To start at the top, Mr. Boyd, then an old man, had owned the next-door paper shop with his wife and apparently been a philanderer. Of him it used to be said that if he didn't like a girl employed in the shop he would sack her, and if he did like one, his wife would sack her. His son, Marshall, after having failed an apprenticeship as electrician at M.I.M., also helped with the hotel, and failing his apprenticeship did not stop him from doing electrical jobs around the hotel. Both the old man and his son were miserly. The storeroom was kept locked and opened for the cook just once a day under strict supervision. There was a hotel-size toaster in it, but she was not allowed to use this and had to make toast on top of the stove. Also she was instructed not to be extravagant with eggs or tinned fruit. We used to get potatoes (and other vegetables) by train from Brisbane, the potatoes in bags which had to be folded and kept and were eventually returned, bringing two pence each. I remember one wet day when everybody was tramping mud into the kitchen I put a bag down as a doormat, only to have Marshal say: "Mrs. Scott, don't you know these bags cost money?" Mr. Boyd used to fly into tantrums and swear at people or sack them for practically nothing. He was always polite to me, probably because he knew that I did not really depend on the job and would leave it if he did the wrong thing. When I first started, we had a very nice and efficient woman as first cook, Vi Topping. Unlike most cooks I later met, she was good-tempered and easy to get on with. I got my meals at the hotel as part of my remuneration, and during two years, though sausages figured on the menus at least twice a day, never once ate one. The staff got their breakfast after the guests had finished, and I always had a nice piece of steak plus toast and butter, the steak underdone as I like it, and specially grilled for me. The cooks' hours were half an hour earlier than mine, and they had to cook three kinds of meals for breakfast, apart from porridge and the toast. Then two entrees for lunch, plus generally some cold meat and salad, and three kinds of sweets, another two entrees and three kinds of hot main dishes and different sweets for dinner. All this for an unspecified number of guests plus a staff of about twenty people, and of course the meals always had to be ready at exactly the correct time. Vi never had any trouble with this, she generally had the sweets done not long after breakfast and used to have time for a bit of a rest in her room before lunch.

She too had the afternoon off, but had to come down once to put in the roasts and roast vegetables. Unfortunately she decided to leave only a few weeks after I had started, and the second cook was promoted to her job. She, like I, was a local woman who didn't live in the hotel, and she managed all right though she wasn't quite up to Vi's standard nor was she as easy to get on with.

There was a terrific turnover in the hotel employees during the two years I worked there. More than two hundred people came and went just among the kitchen staff and waitresses, and goodness knows how many among the barmaids. There was never any problem of getting new people, as housing was practically unobtainable in Mount Isa, and a room went with a hotel job. We had four people in the kitchen, and there were three waitresses. The head waitress stayed for a long time and was very good at her job, though totally uneducated. Generally the office girl would type the menus, but one time when she was sick this woman wrote them by hand and I still remember two particularly funny mistakes, for "Oxtail entrée" she wrote "Oxtail entry", and for "Pea soup with snippets", "Pee and sip it". Mr. Boyd used to take any good-looking girls out of the dining room and put them in the Bar, even though some were only seventeen or so, and I saw some of them in tears at what they had to see and hear.

After the first two cooks, others came and went, some staying a while, others only lasting a day or two. We had one man who was supposed to be a proper chef and who was terribly dirty. He dissolved some burnt sugar in water and kept this to darken gravies, leaving it sitting out all night. In the morning the dish would have cockroaches drowned in it, so he just strained them out and kept on using the stuff. He also used to lose his temper and throw food on the floor, then pick it up and use it. I did not have any meals at the hotel while he was there.

Another male cook had been a shearers' cook. He lasted exactly two days and then didn't turn up and was found drowned in about six inches of water in the river next day, having got blind drunk. One woman cook only lasted one day and then just didn't come back, another was not really a professional cook and used to work terribly long hours to get all the work done. She told Mr. Boyd that it was impossible to do it all in eight hours and she wanted money for overtime, and promptly got sacked. I was offered a cook's job several times, but always declined, as I felt all the extra work and responsibility was more than the little extra pay was worth. Among the waitresses I remember two rather nicely spoken young girls who came from Adelaide, I think. We had a housekeeper at that time, and one morning when these girls didn't turn up for work, she went to their room to find they hadn't been there all night. The police were eventually informed, and the girls were found in the blacks' camp down the river prostituting themselves for drinks. One was eighteen, the other seventeen. These girls were eventually sentenced to a few months jail mainly to get them off the drink, and then returned to their families down South.

Another waitress was not remarkable in herself but only for her past history. She had been a normal married woman and suddenly got very sick, with all her hair falling out. It turned out that she had thallium poisoning, and in fact while she was in Mount Isa her husband was in a southern jail serving a long sentence for attempted murder. Another girl seemed unremarkable at the time. She went out with a succession of boyfriends, including several local policemen. A couple of years later there was the famous Jorgensen case. Jorgensen was a young man who died in a police cell and showed all the signs of having been beaten to death. Some local policemen were accused of this, and the girl was brought up as a witness and swore that she had spent the night with the chief accused, who was then acquitted. Everyone thought that the policeman was guilty as charged, and it seemed impossible that a girl who spent her nights with so many different men should be able to recall two years later just who she had been with on one particular night two years earlier.

Talking about Blacks' camps, we had many Aborigines in Mount Isa who were completely accepted, had good jobs at the Mines, lived in Mines House and as far as I know were not discriminated against. However, once they were allowed to "get drunk like a white man'" as one of them put it, there were lots who lived in hovels and spent any money they got on grog. [*There was rampant alcoholism in the town, but Aborigines, like Native Americans, seem particularly to have no tolerance whatever for alcohol, and it destroyed many lives in the Aborigine community.*]

Unfortunately John was very unhappy about his wife working as kitchen maid in a pub. He had joined the bowling club, where there was a lot of social drinking. He would go there on Sunday morning, drink all morning, then, if picked for a game, go back after lunch and drink some more. I particularly hated Christmas, which Mount Isa spoilt for me forever, and Anzac Day, which was just another excuse for heavy drinking. ("The day to enjoy the freedom we fought for"). Drinking was one of the reasons I disliked Mount Isa so much, and I never drove a car all the time we were there.

After two years, when I was in my early forties, I became pregnant again. This was very early in the piece and the doctor sent away a sample for a toad test, but I gave notice immediately, having no doubts myself. Unfortunately, or maybe not at that age, I had a miscarriage during the week I had to work till the notice took effect. That was the end of my job at Boyd's, which I had found interesting. One reason I was glad to have had this job is that I had always worried about how I would manage if anything happened to John, and I now knew I would be able to support myself and the children if I had to, though I was sorry that it was so difficult for John. I still knew very few people; not drinking was one reason, and of course I had no talents so I could not join the theatre group or the Arts Society, nor was I religious enough to join a church group. I decided I would do some university subjects by correspondence and started off the easy way with German I, II and III, for which of course I got high marks. Before this I had taken an evening class in Senior English, which I enjoyed very much. However, after that I could not see any other subjects I would like and that could be done by correspondence. About that time I had another holiday in Brisbane, and spoke to Mr. Muir, who was now City Librarian, and he said, "Why don't you do the Library exams?" I told him we had no library in Mount Isa and he said: "You will, one of these days." I followed his advice and had actually passed the first exam, the Prelim by the time Mount Isa Library was built, and the North Western Regional Library Service formed. Mr. Muir, who was a very nice man but unfortunately even then had the cancer that killed him not long afterwards, recommended one of his Brisbane librarians, Berenice Culhane, who became the first Regional Librarian. I applied for the job of Mount Isa librarian when it was advertised, and was actually appointed, but decided to stand down when it turned out that there was a young married woman in the town who also had qualifications, and in addition had really worked as librarian. I asked however to be considered if an assistant was required, and within a couple of months got the job of assistant librarian. This time John didn't mind at all, and was even proud of me. He had by that time been promoted first to Assistant Clerk of Works, and then, when his superior got sick and left, to Clerk of Works, a job which gave him much more interesting work. By that time M.I.M. was giving out a lot of work to contractors, presumably in another try to make the town develop.

The library was an air-conditioned building, with proper electric air-conditioning, which was marvellous. There was one small work/cum tearoom for all the staff, local and regional, a small office for the Regional Librarian, and outside the back door a shed, not air conditioned, where the regional staff packed and unpacked exchanges to the branches. The system worked as follows: all shires taking part paid a precept which was based on their population figures (Aborigines were not counted in those days) and had a representative on the board, though the very small shires with maybe 100 or less people were represented by someone from the larger towns. The Library Board met I think every six months, and the Regional Librarian, and the Clerk of the Board, who was the Mount Isa Shire Clerk, had to submit reports. There was an annual government subsidy. Every year it was decided how much money would be required for salaries, books, and other expenses, and the precept worked out from that. Mount Isa at that time had over 15,000 people, whereas the largest of the other places, Hughenden and Cloncurry only had about two thousand, Julia Creek, Richmond about a thousand each and the rest a lot less, down to fifty in the whole shire for Croydon. This meant that Mount Isa actually carried the whole system financially, as well as providing the accommodation for the Regional staff. Each shire provided its own room or building and local librarian (part-time) and was stocked with books from headquarters, the book stock being regularly changed; we used to aim at having a complete turnover every year, maybe a bit more in the very small places, a bit less in the larger ones. Cartons of books were returned by rail (or road, or even plane) from the branches, put back on the Mount Isa shelves, and other books picked from these to send away. Some books we had in more than one copy, so one could stay in Mount Isa all the time, while the other circulated. Minor book repairs, as well as processing of new books, were done in the workroom, but major repairs sent to Brisbane, which was quite expensive. There were never any problems in Berenice's time, as we all got on very well together, but later on there were sometimes problems of divided authority, for example the local librarian would resent having the regional librarian taking up room in "her" building and taking books off "her" shelves.

During my early days in the library I joined Mensa. Actually I sent for away for the test, just because I like doing quizzes and tests. I passed and was asked if I wanted to do the supervised test, which I did and passed with higher marks than before. Mensa is supposed to be a society for people with high I.Q., but is chiefly for underachievers, people who though intelligent have uninteresting jobs. Very few University lecturers would bother, as they get enough stimulation at work. Unfortunately at that time there were only three members in Queensland, all in the southeast corner. I did manage to attend one meeting while I was in Brisbane, and was invited to visit the sugar mill in Nambour the next day, where one member worked. This was interesting and it seemed to be efficiently run, but very noisy. I went to only one meeting in Sydney, as they seemed to have pub crawls there, but I enjoyed the meetings in Melbourne, which were held at a member's house. It was particularly nice to find people could argue about all kinds of things volubly and excitedly without ever getting bad tempered. The magazine was a dead loss; it seemed to be full of letters and articles trying to give a definition of intelligence, and three dimensional chess problems. One day I had a member visit the Mount Isa library. He worked for Rio Tinto and was on his way to Bougainville where the copper mine was about to get started. He was a Personnel officer and said he was going up to persuade the local inhabitants to become fringe dwellers and work at the Mines, rather than living their normal tropical paradise life-style, and that he felt rather bad about it. I resigned from Mensa when I left Mount Isa.

Mount Isa had grown quite a lot since we had arrived in 1950; there must have been about 13,000 people there by then. When we first came there had only been one doctor in town. He worked at the Town hospital and had a clinic on the Mine Side once a week. He had been a navy doctor and was very good, but had absolutely no bedside manner, in fact was very rude to his patients. I remember once at the Mine Clinic a woman came with a small girl with a very bad cough and quite sick. He gave one look and said, "Just a cold, take her away." As they went out of the door the girl had an attack of coughing and he shouted, "Come back here", gave her a proper examination and found she had double pneumonia. By the time we left Mount Isa there were several doctors on the Townside in private practice, as well as one in charge at the hospital, and a full-time Mines doctor. After the Community Store closed the business centre of the town developed and many more people built their own houses on the Townside, so that there were houses far beyond ours and all the way into the town centre when we left. There were still the two areas of Mines houses, though South End, including our old house, eventually disappeared in an open-cut.

I remember one interesting case while we were living there. This was just at a time when a lot of publicity was given to a mixed-up baby case in which both sets of parents wanted the same child and had a long court case. (It must have been terrible for the child they did not want.) We had a mixed baby case right in Mount Isa, which came to light when the two families came to live as neighbors on the Mine Side. One family was Finnish, with parents and other children all blue eyed and flaxen haired, while the ten-year-old girl was brown eyed with dark curly hair. The other family shared this child's colouring, but had a girl of the same age who was blond and blue eyed. The mothers discovered that they had been in hospital the same time and the babies had been born within minutes of each other. Blood tests weren't asked for, as both parents decided they were perfectly happy with the child they had, and they would just go on as before, but make sure they kept in close touch so they could see both children.

Going back to racism, when I first came to Australia the Aborigines were "under the Act", which meant they didn't have the vote, were not counted in census figures, and had no civil rights. They were paid much less than a white for the same work, and didn't really own their wages. I remember being told of one man on the Atherton Tableland who got badly injured at work in a timber mill and got worker's compensation. He lived like a white man, but had to get permission, with some difficulty, to use some of his compensation money to buy furniture. Also on his death his possessions would revert to the Government and he couldn't leave them to his children. All this seemed terrible to me, but at least there was no alcohol problem as Aborigines were not allowed to drink and anyone selling or giving them drink was liable to heavy fines. Once they got their civil rights many did start to drink heavily, seeing whites doing this all around them, particularly in the North and West. I remember once when I was working late and alone in Mount Isa Library there was a family of blacks laying on the grass outside drinking, and one man stood up and shouted, "I am a black man, I am." I was quite scared to pass them going home. Berenice who after her marriage lived in a Mines House had a coloured family move in next door. She said she had no racial prejudices, but then found these people to be very undesirable neighbors, relieving themselves all over their yard, running around naked, and swearing most horribly. Also they used to get crowds of relatives staying and camping all over their yard. I suppose one can understand people not wanting to have such neighbors. Once when I was in Camooweal I was sitting on the Shire Chairman's verandah when a sweet little Aboriginal boy about three came in. He apparently had made a pet of the child, who climbed in his lap. He started to play the old game about pointing at his nose, mouth, etc., to be named, and then suddenly said, "What colour am I?" The boy said, "White". "And what colour are you?" "Black" was the reply. The boy was then given some lollies. I was very shocked at the time.

All this time of course Rayna was a boarder at Grammar, coming home for most holidays. She seemed to enjoy the school and made friends. One thing I liked about Grammar was that the girls were trusted much more than in the Church schools, where letters were censored and girls never let out alone. I remember one case in Charters Towers where a local girl, a day pupil, had taken some boarders' letters and posted them. It was this girl who got expelled, of course, not the boarders, who were much more profitable. At Grammar letters were not censored, and the girls were allowed to go into the city on Saturday mornings to shop. Rayna got in a bit of trouble early on when a Prefect saw her eating some pasties she had bought in Adelaide Street. Also she once got told off because she went to a Church of England service on Sunday instead of Presbyterian (just to see what it was like). She put on quite a lot of weight at first, because of the starchy diet. Once she told me that she never realized what study was until she went away. She could always do well enough in Mount Isa without much effort, but said she had to work at Grammar even to be close to the top dozen. I was in Brisbane a couple of times while she was at school and stayed at the new Country Women's Association Club, just across the road from the school, and Rayna could come and have dinner with me and visit after school. I paid for her to have tennis coaching the first term, and was going to continue to do so, but Rayna told me the coach (Gar Moon, a former Davis Cup player) had given her a message to tell me not to waste my money, she would never be any good at it. She told me about another girl who started at the same time and had never played in her life, but who without any extra coaching was good enough after the first term to get into a school team.

Meantime John's boss at work left and returned to Western Australia. The man who took his place had never liked him and was not keen on his appointees. Furthermore John's unshakeable honesty once again went against him. One of the large contractors at M.I.M. was Les Thiess, the future mate of Bjelke-Petersen, and he tried to bribe John to let him get away with some shoddy work. John refused to do so and Thiess went to Mr. Redpath and asked that John be taken off his jobs. Redpath couldn't actually demote John, but got over the problem by abolishing the post of Clerk of Works and dividing the work John had been doing among three young engineers, one of whom was the husband of our then Mount Isa librarian.

John was given a job as Senior Foreman in the Transport Department, which entailed working roster shift, one week each of day shift, afternoon shift and night shift. John hated this as his biological clock never had time to adjust and he could never get a proper sleep during the day. Also we saw less of each other, as unless he was on dayshift, he would be working while I was home and vice versa. Les Thiess once told John that he wouldn't dream of ever giving a job to any of the people who accepted his bribes, but that any time John wanted a good job with him he would give him one.

Shortly after the young engineers who replaced John started on the supervising of a high tower the company was building. John told me early on that it would collapse, which it promptly did shortly after completion. The husband of our librarian was the engineer supervising this job, and he was sacked, so after they left Mount Isa I was offered the job of librarian. During the previous months I had made up what I lacked in practical experience, so I accepted the job. Berenice, the Regional Librarian, was living at the M.I.M. staff barracks, as were the town's school teachers, and she met and married another young engineer. There was a whole group of them at the time going about together, and one of them, White, later became managing director. He was rather a hard type, of course, and Jim Murrie, Berenice's husband wasn't really the type to get on in a company like M.I.M. Berenice was instrumental in founding a Forum Club in Mount Isa, and persuaded me to join. This was a Club to encourage women to take more part in public life, getting to know meeting procedure and learning public speaking. I was very nervous at first, but soon became used to standing up and making either a prepared or an extempore speech, though I never liked formal things like giving a vote of thanks. This turned out very useful later on when I was Regional Librarian and was asked to give talks to such bodies as the Marie Kruttschnitt Club or the C.W.A.

In the meantime Rayna had finished her secondary education and finished the state Senior exam with two A's and six B's. This was regarded as a reasonable pass and she had no trouble getting a Commonwealth Scholarship, which gave her free tuition at University, and a place at St. Lucia University. She could not get the living allowance, as with both of us working our income was too high. She told me later that this was quite unfair, as some really wealthy girls got the living allowance because their parents, who maybe owned sheep stations, were able to write off income for various reasons. There was also a M.I.M. scholarship, which however she did not get, as there was a local boy, Paul Pollard, who had got two A's and five B's. Paul had a father who was very ambitious for him and kept sitting with him and helping him do his homework. Proud father bought him a car, and he went to Townville University, I think, but failed the first year, after which Rayna was given a bursary by M.I.M. She was also given a holiday job in the health lab during the summer vacations, which she didn't enjoy very much, because she wasn't given enough to do. The lab chiefly tested for lead poisoning by drawing a sample, making a slide, and checking for abnormal blood cells. There were quite a lot of positives. She told me she was given work she could finish in an hour and told to make it last the whole day, but to look busy at all times, which was pretty hard.

Rayna also told me that when the new students first arrived at St. Lucia during Orientation week, there were three distinct groups, one of State School graduates, one of the expensive private schools, such as Somerville House, and one of Grammar school pupils. She stayed the first year at Milton House, a fairly cheap students' hostel, after that she and some other girls she knew rented a house between them from a teacher who was going overseas for a year or two. Actually with her various grants and the holiday job she cost us very little for her university education.

In the meantime Jim Murrie had decided to leave and get a job in Woolongong, N.S.W. His father was very high up in Port Pirie smelters, which owned this company, perhaps the reason he got interested in the job. I was offered the Regional Librarian's job, but I refused as I felt I had not as yet enough practical experience, and also I very much enjoyed the job as local librarian. So the job was advertised, and Mr. Muir again asked to recommend someone. The girl he recommended had impressed him, having come to the service with only Junior standard schooling and done first matriculation, then Prelim while working. She was bright all right, but not dedicated to the job as Berenice had been, and in fact practically ruined the system during the year she was in the job. Just in the nick of time she married one of M.I.M.'s junior executives with a very good future ahead of him, a real catch, and resigned to become a full-time socialite. Again I was offered the job, and this time I accepted just in case the next person should be somebody like her, though I still regretted giving up the work with the public. I was asked if I would be prepared to complete the library course, and said I would and in fact did so, doing two units every year and completing registration in the third. I even managed to get a 'Merit' for one subject, and seeing the failure rate was thirty percent, and in some subjects 50% I hadn't done too badly. Strangely enough the subject I did most work for and which interested me most, the history of books and printing, I passed with just over the minimum marks, and got the Merit for something I hadn't bothered with all that much. My main trouble was studying about reference books, as we had few in Mount Isa, and though I took off a fortnight to study those at the State Library I was at a disadvantage there. I remember one of the questions in the final exam was about the future of computers in library practice, and I said I didn't think much of it. Little did I know, speaking from hindsight. Another popular question was about censorship, which librarians were supposed to be totally against. I remember a letter in a Library Journal which said: "If a librarian removed every book that some borrower objected to, she would be left with nothing on her shelves (this was in a children's library) except little tales about Janet and John going for a picnic with their parents, and the worst thing that happened would be that they forgot the salt." I quoted this myself later, when a mother in Cloncurry complained that the library was indoctrinating her small child with Communist propaganda, because we had a picture book about a little boy in a Chinese collective farm who took a very large pumpkin to a meeting.

We had not intended to send Lesley to boarding school, as by then we had quite a large and good high school in Mount Isa, but Rayna told me that, since we had sent her, it was our duty to give Lesley the same opportunity. Accordingly I wrote off to Grammar, only to be told they were booked out several years ahead. They suggested Ipswich Grammar as an alternative, and this is where Lesley eventually went. It was a good school and there must have been lots of bright girls in her class, as five of them later won state Open Scholarships, of which there were only about twenty given each year. Lesley made one very good friend, Eva, who took her home to a small country town on the N.S.W. border, and also came up to our place to visit. Lesley passed Senior with one A, I think two B's and the rest C's, and also got a Commonwealth Scholarship. It is interesting that in those days the Government had to use inducements to fill university places, whereas these days many thousands of pupils with very good results miss out. Of course at that time only about 10% of children starting school finished Grade 12, and only a third of these went on to university. Nowadays neither Rayna nor Lesley would have made university with the kind of passes they got.

Lesley actually had no idea what she wanted to do. I certainly didn't want to push her into anything. She had always said she wanted to be a vet, but we had told her that we could not afford to keep her at university for five years, and in any case she had taken the wrong subjects at school. I suggested that she didn't have to go to university if she didn't want to, but she said she couldn't stand the alternatives such as working in an office. So eventually she did go, staying at Women's College in St. Lucia. I thought she would probably eventually want to move into a house or flat as Rayna had done, but she stayed at the College, taking Psychology as her major in an Arts Course.

After Lesley went to boarding school I used to walk to work, unless John was home to take me, and during the hot weather take a taxi home. Occasionally on his days off John would pick me up, and I remember once as he did a right hand turn at the Post Office the wheel came off our car. He just had it serviced, and apparently the screws hadn't been tightened enough. No damage done, but driving in Mount Isa was certainly nerve-wracking, half the drivers were drunk, and the other half reckless.

Mount Isa street in 1962. Photo by Ken Hodges. Gabriele was a notable figure in Mount Isa, walking home reading a book or a newspaper.

A Hungarian who had fought in the German army during the war owned one of the local garages, and he was quite annoyed that he could not join in the Anzac Day festivities. He was a near neighbor of ours, and always very friendly, but once, on visiting his house, I saw lots of swastikas everywhere, and caricatures of ugly Jews with big noses along the walls.

Our neighbors, the Smiths who had given us Biddy, sold their place to people called Corcoran, who had two small boys. She was a domestic science teacher, and he something in the M.I.M. office. I used to feel sorry for the elder boy, as the younger was Mummy's pet. He would tease his elder brother, knocking down his projects, etc., and then, if he got so much as a cross word would run in howling to his mother, who promptly came out and punished the elder boy. I heard this boy once saying to his father: "Dad, if Mum died, would you get married again?" Actually it was the father who died suddenly of a heart attack in his forties.

Our dog, Biddy, was very lazy and inclined to be fat. She had several lots of puppies to a black Labrador with some of the offspring being either black or golden, and I never had any trouble disposing of the pups. When Lesley was home she got a certain amount of exercise, but later, with Lesley away and both of us working, she spent much time just lying around and acting like an old dog. As I already said, when we were leaving Mount Isa I gave her to a family with seven children, who took her about and played with her constantly, and she lost excess weight and became like a young dog again.

I had planted a Poinciana tree on the footpath at the corner of our allotment, and this grew into a large and beautiful tree, but never flowered till the year we left Mount Isa, when it had just a few branches with flowers. Mr. Smith had planted one outside his footpath, which stayed quite small, but flowered profusely every year. A caterpillar was introduced into Mount Isa about five years before we left, which would denude the Poinciana of all leaves in a matter of a day or two. The local Flickman *[pest exterminator]* lived just across the road and he used to inject our tree with some insecticide, which killed all the caterpillars and saved the leaves. Unfortunately this poison also killed the local birds, so that when the caterpillar season began and all Poinciana trees in Mt. Isa were injected there would be lots of dead and dying birds about the place.

When we got sewerage we had to get rid of the grapevine, which clogged up the system with its roots, so now we got all the westerly sun. We ended up getting an evaporative air-conditioning system for the whole house. This was reasonably effective, keeping the inside temperature down to about twenty degrees below the outside one. It did not help on the rare occasions when we had humid heat, as it worked with water running through a straw box, and a fan blowing air through it evaporating the water and cooling the air, so in humid weather all it did was increase the humidity. This is why this system is not used on the coast, but it was cheap to run, and at least enabled us to sleep a bit better. We also had a solar hot water system.

After I was appointed Regional Librarian, liking a peaceful life myself, I tended to take the line of least resistance and not act as the big boss over the local librarian, as long as she worked well and under the rules of the system. Staff came and went, usually to get married. Some of my assistants I remember were Noleen B., who had been a waitress at the Mines and had little education, but was a good and reliable worker. A New Zealand girl who had an Arts degree was asked if she could type and said no, but give her three weeks and she would learn. The job being largely clerical, typing was of course essential. I myself had been given my first typewriter at age fifteen, as my handwriting was so terrible, and encouraged to go to evening classes at a commercial college. I did this for one term, learning the touch system, and was told I would have to return for another term or two to develop speed. I stopped going, however, and as a result never got over being a terrible typist. I could type accurately enough when it came to such things as catalogue cards, which of course had to be perfect, but when I started typing as fast as I could think, I kept making typing errors, being fundamentally untidy. Linley, the New Zealand girl, had no lessons but taught herself and became a perfect typist in a matter of weeks.

Finally there was Janet Goodall, who came from Mossman North of Cairns, and was married to a man working for M.I.M. She was one of the brightest and most efficient persons I have ever met and a tower of strength to me, also getting on well with everybody else in the place. During a holiday we visited her parents (her father and husband were Masons, as was John), and were taken for a day on Cape Tribulation, where at that time the locals were hoping for a road to be cut through to Cooktown. We crossed the river by vehicular ferry and had practically all the population of Mossman and Port Douglas there, with drag races along the beach, food stalls and masses of drink. We were shown the famous bouncing beach, which is a black mass of rock. If one picks up one of the smaller rounded black stones and throws it on the rock it bounces like a rubber ball. I would have enjoyed the day more if everybody hadn't drunk so much. I still don't know how Mr. Goodall managed to get us back to Mossman, as the roads were really just bush tracks.

At that time we were staying at a guesthouse in Port Douglas, and John said he would love to buy a block there for us to retire on, which idea didn't appeal to me at all. However, Port Douglas was a lovely place and probably more so then before the developers discovered it. I remember visiting a nice and expensive restaurant on top of a hill with beautiful views and having my first taste of avocado made into a rather nice entree dish, and beautiful reef fish.

As for the local staff, we had Beverley Rice, who had worked in one of the Brisbane libraries, and with whom I still keep in touch. After she left to get married we had a local girl without any qualifications (it was very hard then to get qualified staff in places like Mount Isa) and she turned out to be pretty terrible. She used to swear right in front of all the borrowers and when I took her aside and said it didn't sound well, she said that this was just a part of her ordinary speech and in any case I had no authority over her. She used to gossip in a spiteful way about whomever was away at the time. I said nothing for quite a while, but eventually found out that I wasn't the only person to dislike her and that her own assistants, whom she herself had appointed, equally detested her. All things pass, and eventually she too got married. After her came the only fully qualified librarian we ever had for the job, she was appointed after answering an ad. She seemed all right at first, and was certainly efficient, but perhaps naturally, resented me more than anyone had ever done. During her time plans were made to extend the library, and she insisted that as local librarian she should be consulted, and not I. I don't believe that her ideas were successful later on, but nothing was done during my time. Eventually this girl too left, this time to become a nun.

We had a Junior in the library too, one of the Goodwin children from Devoncourt St., who had been just a toddler when we left there, who was employed under the condition that her father would pick her up and take her home when she had to work at night, as she was only sixteen. She turned out quite well, and she too eventually left to become a nun. All the Catholic staff thought this hilarious as her reading consisted entirely of light romances, even when, after first applying she was sent a list of recommended reading of a religious nature. Strangely enough she stuck to her guns, whereas another local girl, who started as probationer with her, and whom they all thought much more likely to succeed, left after only a few months.

Then we had Carole, another local girl who stayed quite a while. She had an unhappy home life. Her mother, who was a cleaner at M.I.M., didn't like her, and her father, who had been a good-looking and intelligent man, turned out to have inherited Huntington's Syndrome, a terrible condition that leads to complete physical and mental disintegration, and is inherited, not like hemophilia on the sex chromosomes, but equally by sons and daughters, with a fifty-fifty chance. Unfortunately it doesn't show itself until the person is middle aged, by which time children would already have been produced. Carole eventually went overseas. She had made friends with a Swiss family, who had returned to Europe and invited her, and she stayed with them and worked there until new Swiss regulations stopped foreigners from having jobs. She then went on to Italy where she worked, first as nanny to a couple of very spoiled little boys, and then in a very high class dress shop that worked out of an old palace. She eventually came back to Mount Isa, but in spite of speaking several languages fluently by then could not get an office job at M.I.M. and for a while worked as waitress. She married a Swiss man and used to send me Christmas cards cum letters for many years, living in Egypt for some time, eventually returning to Australia, her marriage having ended. She had a little boy, which I thought very reckless of her, as people with the chance of having Huntington Syndrome should really not reproduce, and one year suddenly she stopped writing, her last letter having been very peculiar, so I fear the worst.

Sometime during that period we had the famous strike in Mount Isa, which was really a lockout to start with. John, being on the staff, was not directly involved, but spent some of his working time sitting on top of a hill with field glasses watching for non-existing saboteurs. I bought him a small radio to make this less boring. By that time we had not only a local ABC transmitter, but also a local commercial radio station, though Mount Isa still didn't have television when we left in 1971.

Both Rayna and Lesley worked for a while when they finished at St. Lucia, and then got married, Rayna in Canada. Lesley's wedding was in Brisbane and John's mother and brother came over for the event. This was in January, and everybody including me, warned John about travelling by car during that part of the year. However he insisted and we had no trouble getting down. One day a trip to the Gold Coast was arranged, and John's mother was in our car. By that time the Gold Coast had become very developed, with high-rise buildings and lots of people and cars. Mrs. Dalziel didn't like it at all and said to us: "Let's get out of here, it is just like a typical Yankee rat-race." I had never liked the Gold Coast, even when it was just beaches and meager second growth. The actual wedding was at a Methodist Chapel at the university, and the reception at the Bellevue Hotel, even then a bit run-down, and later demolished by a Bjelke-Peterson mate in spite of being listed by the National Trust. It was a small affair; I think Lesley didn't want us to have to spend too much.

On the way home the inevitable happened. We managed to keep ahead of the wet-season rain all the way to Townsville, but from there all the roads were closed, and we ended up having to go home by train and having to get the RACQ to put the car on the train for us. One thing I still remember from the wedding is Mrs. Dalziel speaking of Lesley and saying, "Such a gentle girl" and my replying, "I wouldn't exactly say that."

The first time Rayna came over to visit with Alison and David, then about two and nine months, I went to Sydney and met her at the airport. She came out carrying a very heavy David, with an airhostess carrying Alison. I had intended for us to stay at the CWA Club but found that they would not take small children. They suggested the seaside home in Manly, but this was too far and we went to a King's Cross Hotel. David promptly got a very bad case of chickenpox, which effectively stopped all our plans and we ended up once again with Mrs. Kerr coming to the rescue and putting us up in her place in Payne Street. Alison had left her stuffed toy on the plane, and Rayna had worried as she always took it to bed, but she never seemed to miss it. Every time we thought David was getting better, he developed another crop of chickenpox and was very irritable with them. He used to wake up about 4:30 a.m. and start making a lot of noise, so I got in the habit of putting him in his stroller and walking about the hilly streets with him till I thought everybody else would be awake. David was a noisy baby and I remember Alison coming to her mother, and, sounding rather peeved, saying: "Mummy, Jonathan is louding." (We called him as Jonathan before he was born and he was called that until he got old enough to choose, when he said he preferred David, the name he was given at birth.) We eventually went up to Mount Isa, expecting Alison to get sick any day and wondering whether this would affect her trip home. However she did the right thing and waited till she arrived in U.S., and then got a rather mild case of chickenpox.

A year or so later Lesley, who was then living in Warwick, asked me to come and babysit Jack while she went to hospital to have her second child. I came about a week before the event, and while I did not think much of the town, the good roads and the nice countryside impressed me when John took us for drives. On one trip we saw a large black snake crossing the road and Jack got quite excited and kept demanding "Another 'nake'." We assured him that he couldn't see another one, but just then we did see a second one also on the road.

Lesley had another caesarean, this time a planned one. I did not have a lot to do, apart from cooking, as she had a woman coming in to do the housework. Her neighbor was a widow with two small boys, who was working as secretary to a local solicitor; he encouraged her to become a solicitor herself. She asked my advice, and I said that I was sure she would be able to manage this. She eventually became a partner and later sole owner of the practice, but years later I read in the paper that she had embezzled nearly half a million from trust funds and got sent to jail, as well as being debarred.

As Berenice had done, I made it a point to visit each library once a year. TAA (Australian Airlines) had offered the Board free travel for the Regional Librarian for such visits or for book-buying trips. I used to go down to the towns along the railway line, Cloncurry, Julia Creek, Richmond and Hughenden, then another time would go up to the Gulf country, where we had libraries at Normanton, Burketown, Croydon, and later at Georgetown, and another time down to Boulia, and later to Dajarra. A separate trip to Camooweal was easier, as it was only 112 miles from Mount Isa.

During my first visit I found a very good middle-aged woman, who was popular with the local people, working as librarian in Cloncurry. The library was well run and well used. She stayed there right through my time. In Julia Creek we had a very active board member, Mrs. Cooney, who was one of the few women I knew who thought like a man. Generally women in public positions tend to concentrate on the woman's point of view, but she always saw the general picture. However, the males in the Council still gave her jobs like Library, and Health, and not on the Works Committee or things like that. Her stepdaughter had been sent to a snobby Catholic girls' school in Brisbane, and emerged completely useless. She got a job at the local paper shop, but got sacked after a week because she couldn't give correct change. Mrs. Cooney always was a tower of strength to me, both on the board and when I visited Julia Creek. In Hughenden, the largest town after Mount Isa, things seemed quite hopeless at first. The library had no librarian, a couple of junior girls from the council were sent to open the library at official hours, and sat there reading love comics and chatting to their boyfriends, with no one ever using the library. I talked to the Shire Clerk, who was not an easy man to get on with, and suggested he appoint a proper part-time librarian, someone interested and popular with the people. After some delay, because one of the girls at the library was the daughter of the shire chairman, my advice was taken and another middle-aged woman, Edna C. appointed. She certainly succeeded in getting people to use the library, which became very popular and well used, but she had certain failings that I overlooked because having the library used was my first priority. She never kept daily statistics but just dreamt up some figures at the end of the months, the books were kept not in correct order but as she wanted them, and she would tell lies about things, as for instance saying a book had been lost when actually she just did not want to give it back into the regional system because she thought people still wanted it. When I left Mount Isa my successor could not put up with these things and asked the shire clerk to sack and replace Mrs. C., whereupon Hughenden pulled out of the Regional scheme and went it alone.

In Boulia a young girl from the Council acted as librarian. However, she was really interested in the job, and the library was quite well used. She was the daughter of the manager of Marian Downs, and invited me out to the Station, which was in the red soil area and had plenty of water, so there was a really nice garden. The Miller's asked me to come back and to bring my husband, and a year or two later phoned to say that after a heavy rain that the Channel country was in flower. John and I drove down, and Mr. Miller took us to the Diamantina. [*The **Diamantina River** is a river in central west Queensland and the far north of South*

Australia. Wikipedia] We drove through miles of wild flowers, just as colourful as one sees in Western Australia. This was the first time John had seen this.

Going to the Gulf places was quite an adventure. TAA had two flights a week to the Gulf, and then on to Cairns, then stopping along the way at several stations, and also on Mornington Island and Domabee, then both Mission Stations. The population of Burketown and Croydon was predominantly Aborigines, also a lot of them were in Normanton, the majority of the school children in all these places anyway. The teacher at Normanton who was our librarian said that during the first year or two at school the black children appeared to be somewhat brighter than the white ones. However, by the age of ten, or even earlier if they were very bright, they had the attitude: "What do I want an education for? I'm only going to be a station black." Mrs. Belcher in Mornington tried several times to get bright young boys and girls to accept scholarships to Thornburgh or Blackheath College, hoping they would become leaders for their people, but in each case they got too homesick and insisted on coming back. I had a problem too, in providing books for the schools in the places where nearly all the children were Aborigines. Our books just weren't relevant for these children, being written for the typical suburban/city child. Much that is commonplace in these books was complete fantasy for these children, and in fact the most popular books were a series that gave lives of children in different parts of the world like India, Kenya, etc., or nature books.

Drink was a problem even before it was officially permitted. There were always unscrupulous whites who would buy cheap alcohol for the Aborigines, and cheat them when handling their money. I was asked by a station black once to buy him some lemonade when I went to town. He gave me £20 and was very surprised when I gave him his change of about £18.

When I first came to Burketown I stayed at the hotel, but didn't get any sleep, as the bar stayed open all night. Next day I mentioned this to the local librarian, and she suggested that they open the local CWA place, which had a small bedroom for countrywomen, and I did use it afterwards. The local Aborigines were often very beautiful, having an admixture of Malay and Chinese. There was a huge old general store in the town that had been a Burns Phillips store and had stock right back from the early days of the 20th century, such as steel corsets. I bought an old German made pendulum kitchen clock, which John loved, and I am sorry we didn't take it when we left Mount Isa. Later this store was demolished, and a more modern one built. I was told that amongst the things thrown out were biscuit tins sixty years old with all the contents fallen into dust, and lots of old things which probably now would be valued by collectors. An interesting man lived in Burketown called Barramundi Joe. He was a Czech and used to go out in his quite small boat, most of the deck space being taken up by a huge refrigerator, and not come in again till he had filled this with barramundi which he then put on the plane, and sold profitably down South. On a visit to Melbourne he married a city girl who came up and lived on the boat with him, even after she had a baby. The child was kept in a lifejacket and taught to swim as soon as possible. After this woman had a second child she stayed ashore which is where I met her.

In Normanton we had a good librarian, a most unusual thing for such a place. She was a local woman who was also a schoolteacher and did the library work more for the love of it. (The library only opened four hours a week.) She encouraged the schoolchildren to use the library too. Croydon was a problem. The people in the Gulf Country all tend to drink a lot, and in fact just about the only person over fifteen who did not drink in Normanton was the Shire Clerk, who had diabetes, but in Croydon even the Shire Clerk was an alcoholic. I used to stay at the hotel, which went right back to the gold-mining days when there were fifty hotels in the place and several thousand people. The hotel was beautiful inside with magnificent old staircases and lots of wood paneling. Another Croydon hotel had been taken to Normanton and re-erected, this was the two-story Great Northern in which I used to stay as well. We used to send about four hundred books to Croydon, half of them children's books, but hardly need have bothered as quite often I found that the lot we sent the year before had not even been taken out of the cartons. Of course there were only a few station people who would read anyhow. Later I had an agreement with the schoolteacher to send the children's books directly to him, as in those days there were no school libraries in the area, so they at least got used. I also offered this service to Mornington Island and sent books there regularly, but was refused by the mission people on Doomadgee, who said that the Bible was all the reading necessary. Mr. Belcher, the Missionary of Mornington, encouraged the Aborigines to be proud of their heritage and practice their old skills, music, painting, dances, etc., but in Doomadgee that sort of thing was called heathen and severely discouraged. It is interesting that nowadays both communities seem to have the same problems of drinking and fighting.

There was no problem about getting as far as Croydon as the plane schedule fitted in very well. However, it was always difficult to get back from Croydon to Normanton. I never went on the famous gulf train, as it would have meant sitting six days in Croydon. The Shire chairman, who ran the store and petrol bowser used to ask locals or travellers who were going to Normanton and known to be reliable, to give me a lift. This way I met a nice young Canadian couple, who were having a working honeymoon around the world and complaining that they hadn't seen any kangaroos. I asked them to stay with us when they got to Mount Isa, which they did. By then they had been on a station and were delighted with all the wildlife they had seen. The girl was a schoolteacher and told me that one of her pupils once brought a *Time* magazine to school and she said, "Put it in the garbage, that is the only place for it."

Another year I got a lift from two Australian girls also having a holiday, and asked them to stay with us as well. During their stay the river came over the bridge just when one of the girls had to catch a plane home. The other girl drove her to the aerodrome, with the river just at bridge level. Halfway we couldn't cross a creek in her little Morris Minor and a man with a large lorry offered to take her the rest of the way. We went back to find the bridge about ten inches under water. The girl tried to cross, but stalled halfway. I got out and tried to push, with a crowd of men standing on the other side watching. Eventually a couple of them took pity on us and came to help pushing and we got safely across. An hour later, three feet of water were over the bridge.

After some years Georgetown in the Gulf country also asked to join our Regional system. Actually Georgetown is much closer to Cairns than to Mount Isa, but there was no regional service based in Cairns. Georgetown was always a nuisance for us, costing a lot of money for transport of book cartons, which then mostly wouldn't be used. There were only a few local women who wanted to read and they wanted chiefly light romances. On the other hand Georgetown was an interesting place to visit. It was the starting point for people going to mine agates in Forsyth, and a local woman who had a shop had a very nice collection of them. She also sold agate rock to unsuspecting tourists, knowing by feel whether they were going to be any good, and only selling those that weren't much. An elderly woman had the contract of meeting the plane and taking freight and passengers to the town. She turned out to be a very keen Scrabble player and introduced me to the game. The old hotel had burnt down and the first time I came up I had to board privately, but the next year a new hotel had finally been built, and this was an oasis in a desert, being built like a modern motel, air-conditioned and all, with very nice meals as well. The owner called it Whenaroo, because, after the fire having rebuilt the bar and then run out of money, people kept on asking him "When are you going to finish this pub?"

One year a Mount Isa woman offered to take me to the Gulf towns in her car, which also was quite an interesting experience. We took the opportunity to go up and have a look at Karumba, and ate some of the best prawns I have ever had, straight off the trawlers. Ansett (Airlines) had a lodge in Karumba and used to fly Sydney people up for a couple of days' bush holiday. Unfortunately, even though the place was mosquito proofed, the sandflies could get through the netting.

Later still, John and I used take our holidays so that he could take me in our car, with my holidays starting after we had left Georgetown, when we would go on to Cairns, and maybe return home via Townsville. The actual holiday part of the trip would take us back to places like Port Douglas, Daintree, Mount Spec, the Atherton Tableland and Green Island.

Apart from the annual visits to the libraries, there were also book-buying trips. Berenice had just gone to Brisbane, but I asked the Board if I could go on and include Sydney and Melbourne, which had many more and more varied bookstores, including warehouses selling "remainders" where one could pick up good books very cheaply. I got the plane trip free, of course, and used to stay at the CWA Clubs in Brisbane and Sydney but at the YWCA in Melbourne, which was very plain, but central and clean. All the rest of the year I had to depend on booklists and reviews, so this was my only chance of really seeing what was available. It was quite a tiring business, standing up all day and looking along all the shelves. During the weekend I could go to the Botanic Garden or the Zoo.

One time the plane from Melbourne left late and I missed my connection in Brisbane and had to spend the night at a motel near the airport, very flash, but terribly noisy. This reminds me of another time when I was visiting the Cloncurry library. The TAA agent was supposed to pick me up at his office, but forgot and went straight to the aeroplane. When the plane had left he finally came to the office, to find me sitting on the doorstep. He offered to put me up at a hotel, but seeing I had a free trip and in any case was anxious to get home I asked if there was not some other way. It turned out that a mixed train was going to Mount Isa, taking all night for the trip. I took this, and had the tedious journey enlivened by a very tall and very drunk Aborigine coming into my compartment and saying very politely: "Madam, can I have you for five quid?" I just said, "Don't be silly," and next time the conductor came he put me in a women-only first-class compartment. He later brought in a young Aboriginal girl whom this black had also annoyed and who was really terrified of him. All the Aborigines left the train at the next station, and a family of railway fettlers who were returning to The Isa after a holiday joined me. The train got in very early, just on daylight, and it took me quite a while to get a taxi to take me home.

Back to Mount Isa Library, and a few words about the cleaners. The Council employed a very good woman to clean council and library buildings. However one day she found somebody's miscarriage in the public toilets in the park, with all the resulting mess to be cleaned up, and promptly gave notice. At that time a Labour Council had just been elected, and the cleaner's job was given to a Mr. W., a good Labour supporter who was completely hopeless. He used to come and give a few perfunctory flicks with a duster and sweep the floor, but never wash it. The floor was covered in fairly pale blue plastic tiles and these became a dark brown while this man was there. I complained about this several times, but even when the Labour Council went out after the next election the new lot wasn't game to sack him, in case they got accused of discriminating against him because he was a Labour man. Eventually I got desperate, and one time when the Council was holding a public meeting in the library I came in the night before and cleaned about one square yard of floor, to show the original colour. This finally worked and we got rid of this man.

Once I was fully qualified, my award wages went up a great deal. I did not really like this, as it meant less money would be available for book buying, but during succeeding years the Library Board kept voting me increases. I took to going to work in the weekends, if John was on day shift, particularly when we had to do exchanges as I then could do them in the library instead of in the hot shed. One thing I really didn't like was the keeping of statistics and the petty cash. One time I made a mistake with adding this up and was twenty cents short, so put in twenty cents of my own money. When the auditor came he told me off, having found my original mistake, and said it was just as bad to be over, than under. After that I handed this job over to one of my assistants, as I really didn't think it worth wasting a lot of time over. Next year the same auditor came again, and after checking the books said: "Well, it's right, but only just." I asked what he meant and he said "It's not a penny over or under."

In the meantime Rayna had finished university and been told she was not Honors material. I feel she may have done better in post-graduate work, when intelligence started to be more important than memorizing. However, she took a job as assistant to some researcher and occasionally baby-sat this man's children. She told me they were bright and in the Argonauts' Club, but that by that time it was getting much harder to earn points or blue certificates. One time her boss talked of buying a copy of an old botany book with a lot of plates, cutting it up and using the plates as wall pictures. To save the book she bought it herself, paying £25, which was then a very large amount. She still came home for holidays, as did Lesley who was finishing at Ipswich Grammar. Rayna once brought home a Chinese friend, a very bright girl doing medicine. I remember her telling me that her grandmother had told her fortune and said that she would never marry and die young. She has now been married for many years and is still very much alive. Also she offered to cook a Chinese meal, and much to my surprise did not cook rice properly but had it emerge a sticky mess instead of the dry, every grain separate way it ought to be.

Our time in Mount Isa came to an end in 1970. John had had high blood pressure for quite a while, and was told by his private doctor that he wouldn't live to retire at sixty-five if he didn't give up shift work, and he finally resigned. Ironically, after telling him that there was nothing else, when he resigned they asked him would he consider staying if they took him off roster-shift. However, he had made up his mind and so we sold the house and moved to King Street in Clontarf, just north of Brisbane, where we had bought a house some years earlier. I had to stay a couple of months until the Board had appointed my successor, and I then mentioned the difficulties of divided authority in the same building, with the result that the job of Mount Isa librarian was abolished and the Regional Librarian put in charge of this library, which worked out much better. I was sorry to give up this work, but happy to leave Mount Isa.

[*Mount Isa is a mining town in the northwest of Queensland, 900 km from the coast and 400 k south of the Gulf of Carpentaria. It is in an arid semi desert area with an average rainfall of 18" and an average high temperature of 89 degrees F. (32degrees C.) The mines produce lead, copper, silver and zinc. For all the years the family was in Mount Isa, fumes from the smoke stack would regularly blanket the town in choking sulphur dioxide gas. The short stack that was in place in 1950 was eventually replaced with a taller one, which reduced but did not eliminate the "fumes". A creek heavily and visibly polluted with toxic runoff ran though a section of the town; it was called Lead Creek. We were told to stay away from it, but other children certainly played in and near it. Mount Isa Mines is currently (2014) the highest atmospheric emitter of sulphur dioxide, lead and several other metals in Australia. There is widespread contamination of soils with lead, copper, and other metals in and around Mount Isa, and these contaminants derive from both historic and ongoing smelter emissions and fugitive dust from Mount Isa Mines. Queensland Health reported in 2008 that the average blood lead concentration for children (1–4 years old) in Mount Isa was more than twice that in urban areas. Recent medical research has documented likely adverse health effects at these levels. The current mining owner has denied responsibility and stated that the town has naturally high levels of lead in the soil.*

However, a more recent study led by Macquarie University environmental engineers showed conclusively that the ingested lead originated from smelted ore and not surface deposits. The same situation also exists in Broken Hill, site of another large mining company.]

AROUND THE WORLD IN FORTY DAYS

[Maxwell John Scott died of melanoma in 1991. Previously the Berlin government had written to Gabriele several times offering her and a companion an expenses-paid week in Berlin, including airfare. This was the "weider gutmachen" programme, for Berlin Jews forced to emigrate during the Nazi regime. Gabriele refused the offer while John was alive, because he had absolutely no interest in going to Germany. He was from that Scottish tradition that believed personal past history, particularly painful memories, should be forgotten; it was a precept to which he adhered throughout his life. In the same spirit he urged Gabriele to throw away all her personal papers from Germany, and in fact she probably did so, though her excellent memory undoubtedly helped in subsequent restitution claims. After his death Gabriele accepted the Berlin government offer, and in 1992 she and Lesley set off from Australia to fly to Berlin. She was eighty-one and not particularly well, suffering from (rheumatoid) arthritis and heart related ailments. Still, she had a wonderful trip to Berlin. The programme representatives were extraordinarily kind and accommodating. Her cousin Hilde, daughter of Max Grumach, who had

never before returned to Berlin, came to see her, and Lesley (as Gabriele's companion), Wendell, Rayna and David were there at the same time. This return to Berlin was profoundly meaningful for Gabriele, who had always retained a deep affection for the city and country that had rejected her.]

The trip to Europe was unexpectedly pleasant. I consigned my large suitcase right through to Amsterdam and the wheelchair service that I requested was available for the whole trip. I stopped in Sydney and then in Melbourne, where Lesley joined me. The KLM plane we took from there was completely booked out in Economy, and when they discovered that I had not been assigned the aisle seat I needed, they put both Lesley and me in the Business section. This meant much more comfortable seats, though of course we still got economy class food.

Travelling at a height at which the outside temperature was often -50°C it got rather cold in the plane, and I had to ask for extra blankets. We were over clouds until we left Pakistan, then the weather cleared and we had a marvellous view over some very high mountains in Persia, including many mountains high enough to show up well even traveling at our height, a blend of brown rock and white snow looking at times like modern art at its best. I particularly noticed Mt. Elburz just north of Teheran, a volcano shaped rather like Fujiyama, but with a plume of smoke coming from its crater.

After arriving in Amsterdam and retrieving our luggage we took a taxi to the Victoria Hotel. The driver took us on what amounted to a guided tour through some of the old and interesting parts of Amsterdam, giving a running commentary, which I felt was worth the extra twenty guilders he charged us. We were getting a free overnight stay at the Victoria Hotel, but though it was supposed to be a four star hotel its wallpaper was peeling and the plaster was cracked. It was hot and humid, and the window in my room could not be opened (because of security, we were told), though there was a fan and a small ventilator at the window. This hotel is just across a square from the railway station, a chief hangout for drug addicts and pickpockets. There was plenty of staff, but at least some of them seemed to have dealt with too many tourists. Also the hotel had no restaurant and served only breakfast. We went round the corner and down a street that had cafes and restaurants, and within five minutes Lesley found a man with his hand in her handbag, just about to steal her purse. She said, "What do you think you are doing," or words to that effect, and he just said, "What are you talking about?" and went on. After that she decided to buy a bag with a zip across the top and a shoulder strap. We had a quick look at the square between hotel and railway and found a fruit stall where we bought some very nice nectarines.

We got up early next morning. To my surprise I didn't seem to have any jet lag, and I had a really good breakfast. It was buffet style and had everything from cereal to eggs, hams, sausages, cheeses, all kinds of nice bread rolls, fruit, cake and even plates of puddings, and such things as smoked eel, herrings, and mackerel. We left our luggage in the reception hall and went for a walk first to a canal, which had lots of flower stalls along it. Since this was Holland the flowers were very nice, and we particularly admired one man's dried flower arrangements, which were quite works of art. Lesley talked about buying some flowers to take to Berlin, but I reminded her of our already far too copious luggage.

Lesley bought a new bag with a zipper. Unfortunately on the trip to the airport, which we did on a train with all of our luggage, Lesley discovered that her purse was no longer in the new handbag. It didn't have a lot of money in it, but it did have credit cars, driver's license and her address book. I thought at first that she just had not looked properly, but the purse had really disappeared. (The zip on the new bag had not been quite closed). We had about an hour before our plane was due to leave so went to the KLM desk, told them what had happened and that the credit card at least would have to be cancelled. The people were very helpful and a young man took us to a post office and helped Lesley to phone Australia, then told us to wait while he got an electric cart on which he whisked us through all formalities with luggage, passport, and security. He got us to our plane within ten minutes of departure but not before we had been called for over the loudspeakers.

At Tegel Airport in Berlin, Rayna, Wendell, David (my grandson) and also Hilde Grumach, my cousin from France whom I had not seen for almost sixty years, were waiting for us. David had been in Berlin for a fortnight, but everyone else had arrived on the same day, we being the last to arrive. We needed two taxis to fit in our entire luggage and us.

The Spreehotel in East Berlin was quite large and certainly more pleasant than the Victoria. I had been given a "suite" with a small living room as well as bedroom, probably because of my disabled status, and had a very nice view over the Spree River. The hotel shared with most I stayed at the failing of having the bedside lamps attached to the wall too far to be any use for reading, and like all German and Dutch hotels, a single thick quilt instead of a sheet and blanket, no matter how hot the weather. I took the cover off and used it like a top sheet. Also, the Spreehotel, which had been used by East German officials and important people when they visited Berlin during the days of the DDR, had a very old fashioned lift *[elevator]*. There were two doors, the inner one had to be closed by hand, and there was no way of holding the outside doors open when they started to close. Even if the lift was on the ground floor the doors might close and the lift start moving if someone upstairs pressed the button. We jumped in and out of it very quickly, expecting to be cut in half by closing doors, and we were all frightened of it. *[This hotel has since been converted into an embassy.]*

The underground station near the hotel had not yet been connected to the West Berlin U-bahn (Underground), though it was handy enough to the main museums, the old churches and the university, and actually not far from where my grandfather used to live and our firm was located. All that part had been destroyed during the war, and where our firm had been was now a public park.

David had suggested a restaurant specializing in German food for dinner. Unfortunately, owing to the uncompleted junction of transport between East and West we had quite a job getting there, having to change trains about five times, each time having to go up and down stairs. There are no escalators in the German underground. By the time we finally got there we were tired and none of us was crazy about the

German food, which generally was heavy and stodgy with enormous helpings. However, I did have a list of foods I wished to try once again after all those years, and actually managed during the next seventeen days to get many of them, such things as boiled eel in dill sauce; Rote Grütze, a kind of red jelly made from real fruit juices, mainly red currants and raspberries; and even venison, which however was a bit disappointing. I could not see any Speckgans which is gooseflesh cooked and eaten like ham; this is apparently only sold in winter. Also we were told that hares had become very rare since the war, rabbits had bred up again but hares had not. I also drank a typical Berlin beverage called Weisse beer with raspberry syrup, which I remembered from my childhood, when children were given this on visits to beer gardens with their parents because it has very little alcohol, and I found I still liked it.

The following morning we met at 7:30 a.m. in the breakfast room, where once again we found a rich and varied buffet style breakfast. David had made an appointment for us at the Town Hall (Rotes Rathaus) to discuss the programme for our stay. There a very pleasant young woman handed me money for the airfare and spending money while in Berlin, and welcomed us. She then said that we could choose two shows or concerts we wanted to visit, for which they would supply tickets, and showed us a list of what was available during our stay. This being the middle of summer some of the theatres and concert halls were already in recess, and of course we had to choose something that was of interest to all of us. They included David in the free tickets as well. We were advised to choose a new stage performance, highly acclaimed, of *The Blue Angel* in a theatre off the Ku'damm, and I suggested the Comic Opera, which is in East Berlin, with a performance of Johann Strauss' *Night in Venice.* I love the music, though the original story was very silly even for an operetta. They also arranged a bus trip through Berlin for the following morning.

We spent the rest of that day walking around the old part of Berlin, visiting the Aegyptian Museum (which contains the famous bust of Nefertiti), and the castle in Charlottenburg (Schloss Charlottenburg), which is now a museum and contains a collection of china from the Prussian Porcelain manufacture started by the Huguenots, with examples from early days to the present.

Both Hilde and I had been brought up in West Berlin and didn't really know the Eastern parts very well, but I recognized some of the buildings such as the Nicolai church which we used to pass on visits to grandfather, and which went right back to before Berlin became one city, about 800 years. However, apparently some of these buildings, including this church, had been damaged or destroyed during the war and later restored. I did remember the unique paving of the street as soon as I saw it. On the middle of each footpath was a strip of flat concrete slabs about 15" across arranged in a diagonal pattern, on either side of this a strip of small stones set in soil or sand, in the cracks of which we used to anchor our spinning tops to start them. It was also always a challenge to walk on the central slabs without stepping on any cracks, because they were so small. Another thing both Hilde and I remembered were the two big shoe-stores called Stiller and Leiser, both meaning "quieter" in German.

That evening we went back to West Berlin to see the stage production of *The Blue Angel*, which was very good. We took a taxi, as usual. The taxi drivers in the daytime were often Turks - there are about 125,000 of them in Berlin. There were also lots of Rumanian gypsies who had come into Germany after the fall of the DDR, and we often saw young women holding undernourished looking babies begging in the streets.

Next morning we went on the bus trip in a minibus with a driver and a very nice and knowledgeable young woman to do the guided tour bit. We went through lots of parts of Berlin quite unknown to me, working class streets in East Berlin as well as the main street, Unter den Linden, which had been restored or kept up. Surprisingly there were many buildings still with bullet holes from the fighting at the end of the war. The former no-man's land between the Western and Eastern posts on the wall was full of stalls selling souvenirs, including small pieces of the wall. It was still disputed territory, potentially very valuable real estate, but with nearby houses occupied by squatters who didn't want to leave. The guide took us the place where I was born, though I knew that the actual building was destroyed in the war. Bayrischer Platz was still there, but much wilder and with big trees, whereas in my childhood it consisted of shaven lawns with flowerbeds. Where our apartment block had been was now a huge office building.

Eventually, we asked to be left off at the Kurfürstendamm. We went down a couple of blocks past the ruins of the Gedächtniskirche to the KaDeWe (Kaufhaus des Westens, or Department Store of the West), which was still where it used to be and is now the largest department store in Europe. I had been told not to miss looking at the food department, which is enormous and full of odd and interesting things, but didn't have nearly enough time there.

The following day we had to go to the official luncheon at an upstairs restaurant near the town hall. We shared this occasion with a couple from Israel and were hosted by another very pleasant young woman. She actually mentioned the Hitler era, and said that she disagreed with the silence on the subject and that the memory of happenings ought to be kept alive as a warning. We each were given a package containing a booklet of pictures of Berlin, generally showing the same streets, houses, and churches, first as they were before the war and as they are now. After seeing them I was no longer surprised that I remembered so little of the place, it certainly had changed a lot in the past half-century.

That evening we had our second show visit, this time to the operetta *Night in Venice.* This was a wonderful production, with the story rewritten to make it somewhat less stupid. All the cast looked their parts, acted well, and sang very well. One of the highlights was a mime artist who performed right through the overture in front to the curtain and also at intervals during the show; he was Harlequin and there was also a Columbine, but the man was really outstanding. Once again Hilde and I went home by taxi. I complimented the driver on his English and he told us he was a university student driving taxis at night to pay for his studies.

Rayna and Lesley wanted to visit the Jewish cemetery and see the graves of my maternal grandparents and my mother. The Weissensee Jewish cemetery was never vandalized. Apparently before the war the Nazis left it so that they could use it as proof for foreign visitors that stories about persecution of Jews were not true, and then during the war they were too busy with other things to dismantle it. It was very overgrown and wild; there were a couple of people cleaning weeds from paths, but most of the graves were quite overgrown, mostly with ivy, which was in the process of taking over the entire place. There were many large trees, and I believe that it is a favourite place for birdwatchers in Berlin. One of the two birch trees that I had planted on either side of my mother's gravestone was still alive. *[It has since died. A small bird accompanied us part of the way along the path, flying ahead until we caught up and then flying on.]*

Wendell had ordered a hire car from Sunday morning, and we were to leave for Bavaria early on Monday morning, with Hilde and David also returning home on that day. I would have liked to locate my father's grave in the forest cemetery he was buried in; not being Jewish by religion he could not be buried with my mother in Weissensee. David and Wendell wanted us to go to Potsdam, which they had visited two years previously. As David was staying in Stieglitz, on the way exactly, so we picked him up there and drove by the tall iron fence of the Botanic Garden in Dahlem, unfortunately with not enough time to visit this. I remembered the fence well, as I used to pass it daily during my early days at school. We had a look at the Dahlem university, which used to be called the Free University while the city was divided, and then drove to

Potsdam along a very pleasant road passing by some of the lakes that are a feature of the surroundings of Berlin, as is the Grunewald, a pine tree forest. The area has very sandy soil; asparagus grows very well for that reason. We did not have time to visit Sanssouci palace, which Frederick the Great built in imitation of Versailles on a much smaller scale, pure Rococo with rather nice parks. We did visit another castle with a very beautiful park (Glienicke), where the wheel chair we had hired through our hotel finally came into its own, though I always felt silly being pushed around. We drove around Potsdam for a while, and eventually returned to Berlin through Zehlendorf, the outer suburb where I was told the forest cemetery was located. Unfortunately we arrived there too late, as the office closed on Sunday afternoons, so we just had to go in and look around. The place was very beautiful, the forest containing mainly of large birch trees. There were benches on the wider roads and lots of beautifully kept graves, as well as many neglected ones. We saw several people actually working on their relatives' graves, but there were also others with a little tag, which apparently was a sign that care of the grave had been paid for and was carried out by the staff. After a while Hilde and I sat down on a shady bench. We watched some interesting birds, including a group of tree creepers, and saw one lot of earnest bird watchers with binoculars. Eventually the family returned but said that they had been unable to find any section of the cemetery with graves dated prior to 1945, so it might have been the wrong place. However, it was very peaceful and beautiful and certainly worth visiting. By that time it was late afternoon, so David guided us to a restaurant much visited by students, and we had one of my better meals in

Germany. I fulfilled a longtime dream and ordered boiled eel in dill sauce, which was quite as delicious as I remembered it.

I had thought that a week in Berlin would be too long, but actually we could have done with at least two more days. I would have loved to walk through the Tiergarten, the Botanic Gardens, the Zoo, and some of the nice lake country around Berlin. However, we had a lot more to do in the ten days that we had left in Germany.

Wendell had been studying the maps, so we managed to get on the Autobahn that was going to take us to Bavaria. Wendell had estimated about eight hours for the trip, which was on the Autobahn (freeway) nearly all the way. Our Opel travelled about ninety miles per hour so we kept out of the fast lane, on which we saw Mercedes and Porsche cars whizzing by so fast it was almost as if we were standing still. The pollution was very bad and continued that way until we went way past Munich and into the tourist area. Every little place we passed had some kind of industry; this was all country that previously had been East Germany, so factories were highly polluting, as were the old East German cars. At one place we struck some roadwork and what appeared to be a major traffic jam loomed up ahead. In the nick of time Wendell managed to leave the freeway, and we traveled the next twenty miles or so on country roads through Thuringia, also in former East Germany. This was an area quite off the beaten tourist track, but even so the landscape looked neat and tidy and the houses had window boxes and gardens.

Unlike Australians, the Germans do not appear to litter at all, and this general tidiness is a feature of all places we saw in Germany. We returned to the freeway ahead of the traffic jam and had no further problems. However, it was getting late and we didn't have time to go on an alternative scenic road, which probably would have been a lot nicer, but also a lot slower. Bypassing Munich we went right on to the Tegernsee and after asking at a garage Wendell managed to find our inn, though I shall never understand how he did it. There are four main little tourist towns scattered around the Tegern Lake, full of chalet-type buildings with magnificent window boxes, and lots of tourist shops. Our inn had been recommended to us, and the owner did all the cooking, her son and daughter-in-law assisting as waiters. The son was a champion skier and had a cupboard full of trophies in the lobby, and the whole place was full of attractive prints on the walls. The son told us that he really was a builder and would like to stop running the place as a guesthouse, but kept it up just to give his mother an interest.

The next day we spent looking at the town Tegernsee and other places round the lake. Lesley was pleased to see that Bavarians did not mow their laws, but let the grass (and wildflowers) grow - no doubt using it for hay at the end of summer. It is really quite remarkable just how much unspoiled countryside there still is in both Europe and U.S., considering they have fifty to 100 times the population we have per square mile. Once you get away from the big cities and freeways, things haven't changed much since I saw them sixty years or so ago.

That evening TV predicted a change in the weather, and in fact we had cool weather with showers and some afternoon thunder for the rest of our stay. We had planned the next day to go up the Zugspitze, Germany's highest mountain at just under 3000 metres, but decided to call in first at Mittenwald, one of the smaller and prettier towns in the Bavarian Alps. By the time we had a look at this town it was getting rather too late to attempt the Zugspitze, and it was rather cloudy too, so we decided to go up another mountain, the Karwendel, which is 300 metres lower than Zugspitze but has a cable railway starting right at Mittenwald, taking you to the top in just four minutes. At the last minute Lesley decided she couldn't brave the funicular rail and would stay in Mittenwald, which was a pity. The cable cars departed at regular intervals, but one had to queue to get onto them, and the number of passengers was fixed, so if one missed one had to wait for the next car. They turned out to have only one seat right at the end, which the attendant gave to me. Everybody else stood, and it was rather like being in a crowded lift. Actually the day did not turn out too bad. Clouds came and went but rain held off, and because the summer had been cooler than normal the flowers were still out and we saw quite a number of the alpines, including the "alp-rose", a dwarf rhododendron, and gentians, as well as colourful patches of many other flowers. I only went up the track a little way and then sat and looked at the view. On the terrace of the station building, one overlooked a snowfield where several children were playing and making a slippery slide, and I had a beautiful view right down the mountain and to several other high mountains round about. Apart from those who had come by car there were also hikers who had walked the whole way up, and in fact we saw several lots of hikers on the paths one could see from the cable car.

The next day was even cloudier, but we decided to go to Garmish-Partenkirchen and see what the weather was like when we got there. We went the shortest way, and decided to go up after all, as it appeared to clear up a little. Lesley had decided she would attempt the cable car. First we got into a conventional little railway carriage and in about half an hour reached the terminal, about 2600 meters up. By then it looked pretty clear and Lesley wanted to go out and look at the view, but we stopped her, thinking that we might miss the cable car that went the rest of the way to the top. This was a mistake, as the high part was completely in the clouds by the time we got there and it was snowing. There was a tourist shop and also a restaurant, both heated, and I sat there and had a cup of coffee while the family had a look around. However, as all they could see were other damp tourists, we decided to take the next car back down, and by the time we got to the railway the view there too had disappeared in the clouds. The railway has existed since the thirties and goes through nice forest country at first, and through a tunnel on the last kilometre. We went home a different and longer way, which took us into and out of Austria.

The farmhouses in Bavaria are not generally of the decorative chalet style of those in towns, but plain with white walls and brown roof. Mostly they had the stables built right onto the house, possibly so the animals could be reached in winter even if the place was snowed in, and invariably they had a ripe and smelly manure heap near the front door.

The cattle were mainly small animals looking rather like Jerseys, though near the Austrian order we also saw some Swiss type cattle, a brighter brown and with much larger udders. We had originally decided that we would not go to the famous castles of the mad King Louis of Bavaria, which were quite a long way from Tegernsee, but found that we had time after all, when we returned from the Zugspitze. One of the castles is the model for the fairytale castle of Disneyland fame. We saw both these from the outside and some distance only, as being Sunday as well as summer holiday time, cars were parked on both sides of the road and we knew we would not have a chance to find parking within a distance I could have walked.

I saw an interesting notice in one of the woodland areas we passed through, to say that baits had been put out for foxes, not to kill them, but to immunize them against rabies, and asking people not to touch them.

I had forgotten a lot of German during the fifty-five years I hadn't spoken it. I could generally understand people, unless they spoke very fast or in dialect, but could not think of the right words when I had to speak myself. However, my pronunciation had remained German, so I had to explain to people that I had been born and brought up in Germany, but left when I was young.

We were lucky to leave Bavaria when we did, as on arrival in Amsterdam we saw on television that that region had had extremely severe thunderstorms just after we left, with many buildings damaged and several people killed.

We had decided not to bother about the larger cities on the road, as two days were not really long enough to see everything, so our first proper stop was at Nördlingen, one of many picturesque medieval walled towns along the Romantic Way. A feature of this city is a town hall that on one side has an outside staircase that is a remnant a much older building. This town had a very bad time during the Thirty Years War, being sacked by the Swedes and then decimated by plague.

The Germans on the whole seemed pretty prosperous, and of course there were also many foreign tourists, but we saw many shops selling expensive clothes or children's toys, including some lovely dolls priced from 350 to about 1200 dollars. We were booked in the Red Cockerel Hotel in Rothenburg for the night, the building going back to 1338 AD, though it wasn't a hotel then. This was not only the cheapest, but also one of the nicest hotels we stayed at, right in the old part of the city with a good, though expensive, restaurant and for once even a bedside light properly positioned right over the bed. We stayed in the town till about 11:30 a.m. next morning, so we had a chance to see it early before all the tourist buses arrived. Both Dinkelsbühl and Rothenburg escaped destruction during the Thirty Years War (1618-1648). Dinkelsbühl was spared when all the children came out and begged for their parents' lives, and Rothenburg because of the famous Master Drink, the then major of the town, who lived in the Red Cockerel house. When the town surrendered to the Austrian general Tilley, he offered him a very large beaker of wine. Tilley promised to spare the town if the major could drink it all in one gulp, and the major did so. Both these events are re-enacted every year in those towns, but fortunately not at the time when we were there. I met the mother of the present owner of the Red Cockerel in Rothenburg, who told me that it had been in her family for several generations, each making improvements and additions.

After leaving Rothenburg we stopped at a few more places famous for churches or castles, and went for quite a while along a nice scenic road along the Tauber, eventually rejoining a freeway that brought us to Wiesbaden in the late afternoon. This town had grown and changed a lot since seventy years ago, when my grandparents had a house there. Then it was a small and very pretty spa, now it is quite a large town with even some industry. Our hotel was right in the centre of the town, not far from the railway station. The next morning we returned on the freeway to Frankfurt Airport, where Wendell handed back the hire car. I did my only buying in a duty-free shop there, getting a large bottle of 4711 Eau de Cologne for $20, as against $26 which a quite small bottle had cost me in Australia. We then saw Rayna and Wendell go off to U.S. and then went back with KLM to Amsterdam. This time we got a taxi driver who went straight to the hotel. We arrived about lunchtime and decided to catch a bus to the Rijksmuseum. However, when this arrived the driver had run out of bus tickets to sell. We had got into conversation with a very nice young black woman from Jamaica, who explained this to us in very good English, but when we thought we would have to wait for the next bus she said she had a book of tickets and would pay for us. When Lesley tried to pay her back in the bus she refused to take the money. I quite enjoyed the museum, but after walking through it for some time we went on to the van Gogh museum, which was only about a block away and which we actually both liked better.

Next morning we went to the Floriade, the large flower show (on 268 acres) which is held only every ten years and this time was near The Hague, about an hour's drive from Amsterdam by bus. The area of the Floriade had previously been wasteland and the trees and shrubs were not very old or big, but there were some very nice displays of lilies, roses, and so on, and a magnificent large area of water garden with multicoloured water lilies. Around it were various national gardens including Indonesian, Japanese, German, and French. There were also large areas and pavilions devoted to commercial exhibits dealing with marketing, plant pests and diseases, which we skipped. We had of course missed the time of the tulips and other bulbs, but I enjoyed the visit. We had a quite reasonable meal in a restaurant with different national foods in different areas. Lesley had wanted to see dikes, and we read that the raised structure on which the monorail traveled was actually a dike. We returned to Amsterdam by bus and next morning took another taxi back to the airport.

Again we were lucky enough to be put into the business class portion of the plane. We traveled most of the way above the clouds, but were lucky enough to strike a patch of clear weather just as we passed over Greenland, and saw some remarkable views of snowy mountains and sea with icebergs. We arrived in Chicago airport at the quite civilized hour of 5:30 p.m. and we had only about another hour's trip to Columbus, where Wendell and Rayna were waiting. Wendell decided to show us some nice country taking a side road instead of the freeway, and it was certainly very pretty. We even saw three young deer coming out to graze on a meadow.

This was of course the first time I had been in America and I was pleasantly surprised at how pretty Ohio is. Delaware itself is a nice country town with a university and seems quite prosperous, and Ohio is not a bit what I expected from the Middle West. All the grass was green and there were lots of beautiful trees, maples, beeches and many others not familiar to me. I had expected something like our inland Australia, flat brown country with wheat fields and everything looking brown and bare. Actually though there had been rain recently, it was still dry and had been for some time.

One of our first excursions was to a Highbanks Park in Columbus, one of about thirty parks in this city, which is half the area size of Brisbane. I think it became the capital city for much the same reason as our Canberra; the two large cities, Cleveland and Cincinnati did not want to see the other get this honour, and also both were on the edges of the state, whereas Columbus was right in the middle. Highbanks Park had a tourist centre where volunteers gave tourists information about flora and fauna. It also doubled as a tourist shop and sold books on American plants, animals, and geology. There was a large bird feeder just outside a window, and there we saw not only cardinals but also chickadees (similar to the English tom tits), American blue jays and even a woodpecker and a couple of humming birds, the smallest bird of in north-eastern U.S. and the only humming bird in that region. There were also lots of grey squirrels and chipmunks under the feeder eating the seeds spilled by the birds.

One thing I found disappointing in America was the coffee, which quite often was bad, and never really good. Also one never got real cream to put in it, but only a kind of top milk, with about 10% fat. This, of course, might be for health reasons, but it certainly did not improve the coffee. Also unlike the rich cream cakes that one got in Europe, American cafes and restaurants went in for sweet pastries, things like bagels, blueberry muffins, and so on, which did not tempt me at all; maybe it was just as well, because by the time I arrived in Ohio my health wasn't the best and I got breathless even when doing nothing much at all. Rayna took me to a local clinic. I told the doctor my symptoms and that I would be back home in little over a fortnight and did not want to incur a lot of medical expenses. After taking chest x-rays he diagnosed congestive heart failure, said the breathing difficulties were because I had a lot of fluid in the lungs, prescribed a diuretic, and told me to eat two bananas per day to make up the loss of potassium. This, and a new lot of nitroglycerine tablets kept me going till I got back home.

My daughters were not too happy about my travelling from Ohio to San Francisco on my own with a stop in Chicago. Rayna phoned Continental Airlines and told them I was old, disabled, and had a heart condition, and after a bit of conversation found that I could actually transfer to a direct flight by paying a mere $18 more. After that Lesley decided she was would try too, so we went to Columbus airport and actually managed to get the direct flights for both of us. Lesley was leaving early to join her husband John in California.

I phoned my cousin Lilli in Florida, and her brother Fred, who now lives in Cleveland, Ohio. We arranged to visit him as soon as Lesley had gone, at the Cleveland Museum. We had lunch at the museum cafeteria, then saw Fred's flat, which had wonderful views over the city and Lake Erie. Fred, whom I had not seen since he was about nineteen, was remarkably fit even though he had had bypass surgery and several heart attacks, and was still playing tennis regularly. He spoke English with much more of an accent than I do, and remembered a lot of Berlin expressions and jokes that I had long forgotten. David said that while he was in Berlin, where everybody tries to forget about the Nazi period, he constantly referred to it, which would have embarrassed me no end. One he remembered was Fred asking in a restaurant whether they had juice, and when they told him they didn't have any he said, "Well, of course you have no Jews, you killed them all." However, David said no one seemed to take offense.

It had been decided that we would stay for the night at a place called Honeyrun Inn, which is in the Amish country on the way back to Columbus, and that Fred and his friend Jean would also come and spend the night. It is typical for Fred that when he first phoned there and asked the cost he said, "I want a room for the night, I don't want to buy the place." Honeyrun lies in fairly deep forest and is very nicely designed to blend in the landscape, with every one of the sixty-four rooms decorated in a different way. Mine had wild ducks as motif. There were bird feeders outside all the windows, but with so many we did not get the concentration of varied birdlife I saw in Columbus. Fred and Jean were staying at an annex built into a hillside and overlooking a slope of wildflowers, and Jean had brought a bottle of champagne to watch the sun go down behind the trees.

Next morning we called in at a very interesting place called Quailcrest Farm, which we would never have found on our own. This is on the edge of the Amish country. The Amish belong to a pacifist religious sect that left Germany in the 19th century, and they still live more or less their original lifestyle. They dress in old-fashioned black or blue clothes, the men don't cut their beards, and they don't use electricity or cars. They have become a tourist attraction, and are famous for their beautiful handmade furniture and quilts. In Honeyrun they had a weekly newsletter that had an article on the "Employee of the Week", in this case an Amish cook who had worked there for eight years and had seven children, of whom four still lived at home. She gave gardening and quilting as her hobbies, though with family and working full time I don't know when she had time for hobbies. Anyhow, Quailcrest Farm started off being just a farm, but over the years grew into a tourist attraction, beautifully landscaped and with three shops, one for garden supplies, and one for Amish crafts (cheaper than nearly anywhere else). They also had a herb festival every year. After leaving there we went to a very popular Amish restaurant, visited by the Amish themselves as well as tourists. The food was rather heavy and German in style and the service was very slow. When we came out at 2 p.m. there was still a queue of people waiting to get in. In the parking area there were some horses and buggies as well as cars, and we saw one young woman with about a dozen children in her buggy (possibly not all hers). Remarkably the young people seem to stick to their parents' ways and religion, though these days the boys ride bikes, and many of the adults I saw had buttons on their clothes. Originally they used hooks and eyes only, regarding buttons as symbols of militarism. Having large families is of course a problem since farmland is limited, and children may have to move away. Some men work in furniture shops, unmarried women work in local restaurants, and there has recently been other colonies started somewhere in Mexico or Canada, I believe.

Shopping in America seemed more fun than in Australia. The supermarkets generally are much brighter, the aisles wider and the shelving not up so high. Also in Delaware there was a Farmers' Market every Saturday, which was very popular. Farmers and their wives had stalls in some hall where they sold fruit, vegetables and flowers mainly. Everybody had to wait outside a gate till 10:30 when it opened and there was a rush of buyers all wanting to get the best bargains.

One day during my stay we visited Wendell at his university, and met most of his colleagues in the zoology department, all of whom, including Wendell, went to work, even though it was officially holiday time. They were talking about the general insecurity among academics -- even those with tenure could not be sure of their jobs, as some universities just closed down some of departments and so made them redundant. We also went to the Delaware Public Library, which was in a new building and very attractive, and so far not crowded. On the last day Wendell took me to another small national park or sanctuary, noted for its lakes and waterfowl, but for some reason the birds had moved out and we saw nothing except one wooden decoy duck. However, it was a very nice spot.

While I was in Delaware we went to the American equivalent of the Floriade, called Ameriflora, which this year was held at Columbus. It was not quite as large as the Dutch show but very nice indeed, and had the advantage of being in one of the city parks with a lot of magnificent large trees. There were wheelchairs for hire there too, even motorized ones. Some of the events had already ended; there had been a display of international gardens earlier, and also a great display of orchids by a Hawaiian nursery that I had missed, though I saw photos Rayna had taken on earlier visits and also an orchid calendar this nursery had handed out. There was one very large glass house with sections for cool mountain plants, hot dry plants and the usual tropical moist part, which once again had lots of plants that are quite commonly grown in Queensland, so not the novelty they were for people from cooler climates. I very much enjoyed this show and tried to remember the names of some of my childhood favourites I had not seen for years. One large display was of Australian plants; a nursery was trying to popularize these in America, and they had a large display of trees, shrubs and groundcovers, which seemed to attract quite a bit of interest. They employed a young Australian who was on a working holiday and we had quite a long chat. My daughter bought a small Eucalypt tree (snow gum), which was supposedly frost resistant, but did not survive a really cold winter, and she was toying with buying a Lilly-pilly as well. There were a couple of very nice rose gardens, many lilies and lots of Rudbeckias

(Black-eyed Susan) which are of course natives of U.S., though not the Golden Glow which is most commonly seen in Australia.

My plane to Denver left Columbus just after 7 a.m. I consigned my, by now, rather full suitcase through to San Francisco and only put what I needed on the trip in the carry-on bag. As it happened we got to Denver in plenty of time for me to have caught the earlier plane, and I was offered a seat, but decided that, as John and Lesley were expecting me on the later one, I might as well sit in Denver airport instead of the San Francisco one. This meant waiting three and a half hours, but the seats were comfortable, as always in airports, and I had plenty to read. Also, as I have mentioned already, Americans generally are very friendly and particularly when they hear you haven't an American accent tend to talk to you. I asked one woman to mind my bag while I had a look at the shops and bought a cup of coffee and a blueberry muffin, neither of which I enjoyed very much. Later on another (black) woman asked me to mind her bags while she went off somewhere, and when she got into her plane she said to me "God bless you." My plane left half an hour late and did not make up time on the trip. This was the first time I had actually sat in economy class, but I did not find it uncomfortable.

When I arrived in San Francisco John, who had a hire car, took us to the hotel his uncle had found for us, which was a small old-fashioned place with very nice staff and rooms, and within a block or two of the main city centre where all the good shops are. They had borrowed a wheelchair from a friend, but as the city is built on hills this didn't turn out to be all that helpful. Lesley stayed with me at the hotel. The breakfasts didn't start until 7:30 a.m. and were not as elaborate as in Europe, with bread and rolls, cereal, butter, jam and honey in little plastic containers, and a bowl of fresh fruit put out on a sideboard in the corridor of each floor. However, on the first morning John arrived very early and decided we better start straight away as he was taking us to a small national park called Muir Woods to see the redwood trees, and he wanted to beat the traffic and also the crowds there. We succeeded in both objects, going over the Golden Gate Bridge, which is red and rather striking, with lots of traffic was going into the city, but very little on the outward side.

Muir Woods was very quiet; the heavy shade allowed little undergrowth, so that there were no flowers to attract insects and insect-eating birds and also there are few seeds to attract other birds. After we left it, and had some breakfast, we drove to a beach where there were actually some people swimming, though it must have been very cold in the water, and we also saw several seals on rocks a bit further out. We went home a different way and this time stopped at a lookout point which overlooks the city and also Alcatraz, now is of course no longer a prison, but a tourist attraction.

My main impression of San Francisco, apart from the beauty of the city, which I appreciated even more when I had seen more of it later on, was the tremendous difference between rich and poor. There were luxury shops all round, limousines with uniformed chauffeurs, and then lots of derelict old and sick people living in the streets with all their belongings in a couple of plastic bags. Lesley told me that when Reagan was governor of California he had cut down on welfare and closed many homes for old and intellectually disabled who had nowhere else to go. She said there were 30,000 homeless living on the streets in the city and one could not possibly give money to them. However when one old chap we passed called after her, "Have a nice day" she rushed back to give him something. Apparently these people use the streets as toilets, having nowhere else, so every morning early all the streets are hosed down. Some of the people seemed to be really insane, but most were just old and pathetic. I have since seen that California has decided to cut down even more drastically on education, health and welfare spending.

On Wednesday morning John's brother picked us up and took us to his mother's house in Oakland. He had arrived early so that he could take us on a sightseeing trip through some of the places on the Northern side of the Bay. To get there we went over another very long bridge. We cruised through the university town of Berkeley and saw the parts where the student shops and restaurants were located, as well as some rather depressed looking "black" neighbourhoods. In Oakland we went around the parts that had been affected by the bushfires, including the house belonging to John's uncle, which was burnt to the ground and was about to be rebuilt. The neighbours' house had not been touched, but all they could save was the uncle's dog. The family was away on their boat for the weekend when the fire broke out. Houses in this area are extremely expensive and some are what you would call mansions, many have beautiful views and there are masses of trees about, hence the bushfires. John's mother at eighty-six was quite remarkably fit physically and mentally. I had met her just once when she came to Australia for

Lesley's wedding about twenty-seven years ago. Her house was not extra large but full of treasures, as she loved to go to antique sales. Once a year she had a sale herself, mainly to get ride of some of the things she liked least, and to make room for some more. She was also a keen gardener, though these days a gardener was doing most of the work. There was a small but very pretty front garden, and where we would have a backyard there was a walled in paved area with a swimming pool. Plants including citrus trees, climbers, shrubs and flowers were growing in large containers.

Next day Lesley and John were going back to Australia. As their plane did not leave till 8 p.m. I hoped that we might be able to visit the Golden Gate Park, which has a very good museum and a famous Arboretum. However, by the time John arrived it was getting too late for this, as with traffic we would have got there and then had to come straight back. I was not leaving until the next day, when there was a direct flight to Brisbane, so I booked a half-day trip on a tourist bus to have a guided tour through San Francisco. I picked a smallish bus and that was the right thing to do. Our driver/guide made me sit right up next to him so I had a wonderful view. San Francisco has an odd weather pattern. Even on fine days there is always a fog in the morning, which usually then disappears by midday. This was not really a nice day, the morning fog did not clear and it remained very cloudy. Passengers got picked up from and brought back to their hotels, and we then went back to Fisherman's Wharf where the office was and the trip started officially. I was very glad to have this trip, as we went to lots of places I would never have seen otherwise and the guide was very good at explaining and giving historical background. I was particularly interested in seeing lots of the West Australian pink and red flowering gums planted in the streets of residential areas, all in full bloom, also quite a few bottlebrush trees.

What makes San Francisco so attractive, apart from the harbour setting, is the fact that only one area is allowed to have high-rise buildings, and there are still lots of those gaily-painted terrace houses that were built after the earthquake of 1906. They are now far too expensive for the average family to afford, and most are bed and breakfast places. Of course we went through the old Chinatown, as well as other ethnic areas, and also to that lookout on the Golden Gate Bridge, which was a bit of a joke, as we could hardly see the closest span of the bridge, let alone Alcatraz or any other parts of the view.

The bus deposited me back at the hotel about lunch time and I went across the road to a very good Chinese restaurant, then back to my room to have a shower and rest for the afternoon, seeing I wasn't going to get much sleep the following night. Lesley's friend Bonnie had offered to take me to the airport after work, and we had no trouble with the traffic, as she knew all the side roads and shortcuts. She helped me to check in my suitcase and get my seat allocation, and we made arrangements to return a little later and pick up my wheelchair service. We then went down the hall to a very good restaurant, where we had dinner. Once I got into the wheelchair I said goodbye to Bonnie, who of course could not go through security and passport control. I complimented the man who pushed my wheelchair on his excellent (and educated) English, and he told me he had been a lawyer in his own country. I said I hoped he was going to get American qualification and he said that he was studying for this part-time.

The planes were full again, and of course there was nothing to see. We had to change planes again in Honolulu and had to wait another hour and a half at that airport. By that time it was midnight local time, but about 3 a.m. California time so I got rather tired. On the Brisbane plane I sat next to a couple who had just had a holiday in Honolulu, and who by coincidence, came also from Redcliffe Peninsula. I had run out of Panadol tablets and asked the air hostess whether she had any, she gave me the same thing under a different name, and ten minutes later came back and said they had decided to put me in business class till we got to Auckland. This was of course much more comfortable for me, as well as for the Redcliffe couple who had three seats to themselves for the rest of the night, and we actually got some sleep. In Auckland lots of people left the plane, but many others got on, so the plane was fuller than ever, but now it was daytime and it was only a few more hours to Brisbane. To my surprise the friends who had taken me to the airport when I left were there to take me home, and I got to my place about midday, spent the next couple of hours unpacking, and the rest of the day sleeping. In fact I slept a lot for about a week after I got back home.

In retrospect I am very glad I took this trip, though while I was actually travelling I often thought I was quite mad to go. I certainly do not plan to go overseas again.

[Gabriele died in June 1998 of a heart attack. When she felt the first symptoms during the night, she took some nitroglycerine pills, phoned the emergency services, unlocked her front door, and sat in her living room chair to wait for them. She was dead by the time they arrived. I was in the Los Angeles airport on my way to Australia. Thanks to the marvels of modern communications, I was paged for a phone call giving me the news. I arrived twenty hours later and went to the house, which was empty and very neat; she had got the cleaner in for the visit of my sister and me. Her open word puzzle book and her pencil were in her bed, the nitroglycerine pill bottle by the phone, and the paper envelope from the paddles the medics had used was on the living room floor near the chair. Outside the resident brown honeyeater sang in the bottlebrush tree.]

APPENDIX I

MAXWELL JOHN SCOTT

1908-1991

A Personal Remembrance

By Rayna Scott Patton

Of the people I have met in my lifetime, the person whom I am quite sure that I never fully understood was my father. He was deeply private man with an instinct for secrets and I am sure he took many to the grave.

My father was born in Belfast, Ireland on August 1st, 1908. There is no record of his birth; apparently a fire destroyed a number of birth records from the period. My father's parents were originally from Scotland, but probably lived a while in Ireland before setting off to Australia with their two-year-old son. Recently Lesley's husband John discovered passenger list records from the *Dorset*, which arrived in Sydney in November 1911. Listed are John Scott, Lizzie Scott, Bessie Scott and John Scott. I was told (by our mother, our father never discussed these things) that his mother, Elizabeth (Laird), came from a more distinguished family than her husband, perhaps related to the Earl of Houston? After the family arrived in Australia, John Scott set up a contracting business in Sydney. There were three more children, a girl called Mary, a son called William, and the youngest a girl called Violet. If it was truly our father's family on the *Dorset,* then the older child, called Elizabeth (Bessie) like her mother, must have died after the family arrived in Australia. Of all his siblings my father liked his sister Mary best, and disliked Violet.

For years I had an unfounded idea that my father attended Sydney Grammar, but a letter I wrote to the school revealed that to be untrue, so I assume he attended the local state school. Our mother said that he wanted to be an officer in the Royal Navy; it would have been a perfect career for him, but his father refused permission. I feel sure that his father was strict and often harsh with him. We can say this was Calvinist: "Spare the rod and spoil the child," but it was also in many cases normal child rearing for the period. As the eldest son he was told that he would have to carry on the contracting business, and that he could study architecture or be apprenticed as a carpenter. Feeling that he had relatively little artistic ability he chose the apprenticeship. He had three years of technical school, and was apprenticed to his father for five years, ending as a journeyman carpenter and joiner. He spoke with an educated accent and used correct grammar, not at all the stereotypical Australian cockney-based accent that was characteristic of working class Sydney at the time. He had a very neat handwriting, he enjoyed reading, and he was indisputably intelligent. He had excellent table manners, another sure sign that he came from a respectable family. He often said: "We Scotts have standards!" and I suspect that phrase accompanied him from his childhood and wasn't minted just for us. He was Presbyterian, and probably spent his share of time in church while he was growing up. He wanted me to be baptised Presbyterian and I was, but after a brief encounter with the Ann Street Presbyterian Church where they wanted him to contribute more time than he wanted to give, he lost interest. Still he wanted his children to attend Sunday school, an indication that he had also done so when he was young.

When Lesley and I checked 1940s Sydney phone books we found a John Scott, Builder, living in a working class suburb (Five Docks) of Sydney, and we even visited the house there, a single story brick that had been extensively "modernized" in the meantime. But that John Scott, according to the voter records, was married to "Alice", so either Dad's mother died and his father remarried (which could mean that some, or all, of his siblings might have had a different mother); or that his mother died after the children were born and his father remarried; or that this John Scott was someone unrelated to us. Australia, it turns out, is full of John Scotts.

My father was "handy", meaning that he used tools well and was good at making and fixing things. It was a skill that he valued, and when he said that someone wasn't handy it was reflection on that person's capacity to be useful. He was not in the least given to derogatory statements, but in this case he seemed to regret for the person that he lacked an important talent. Like my mother he was born left-handed and, like her, was forced to write with his right. In his case his writing was neat, while our mother's was practically illegible. However, he used tools in his left hand.

I am sure that my father was a thin good-looking child, who grew to be a good-looking man, with thick springy hair that he never lost and a skin reddened and hardened by constant exposure to the Queensland sun. He had rather slender bones for a man (his shoe size was a six). I inherited his bone structure, (and also his shoe size - I still have his slippers). I think that when he was very young he had sandy fair hair, fair skin, and unusual clear blue eyes, which I also inherited. As he grew up under the scorching Australian sun his eyes changed to a colour called officially hazel, a kind of greenish colour. Our son David inherited his blue eyes, and grandson David has them too. When he tried to grow a beard it was dark red, and his features were regular with that characteristic blunting that marked him indisputably as Scots-Irish. Sean Connolly has a more polished and very bald version of that look, and though I perhaps my father was never in Glasgow, when I was there the town seemed to hold his ghost, I caught so many glimpses of him.

What do we know about our father's life in those early years? Apparently he was a lifesaver on a Sydney beach (Manly?) for a while, which meant that he was a strong swimmer, though his skin took the first of many beatings that would lead skin cancers and eventually melanoma. He was certainly immersed in current boys' literature and absorbed to the core of his being the reigning British paradigms of the day. He grew up with a sure sense of decency, honour, and patriotism. That is how he was all the years that I knew him - honest and generous, a believer in the Empire and the Crown, with an unshakeable sense of fair play, and a stubborn pride. He was imbued with a code of behaviour that probably represented the best of the late Victorian age. He treated women with respect, he was not racist, he was staunchly pro-union, he stood for the National Anthem, and he never ever took advantage of anyone in his life, often to his own disadvantage. He could never have been a captain of industry.

My father's brother William, not being the eldest, apparently had a choice of careers and may have become an accountant. My father obediently apprenticed to his father and became a carpenter, but when he was twenty-one he left home. Presumably he felt resentful about his lack of work choices and had no intention of taking over his father's business. For several years he knocked about in Cape York, working as a stockman, (he had his own horse called Ned Kelly), and as a carpenter, builder, and prospector. When my mother arrived in Cooktown to begin collecting for the Field Museum in Chicago he offered to guide her. Less than a year later they were married.

During the seven or more years that he was in Cape York my father evidently stayed in contact with his family. When he wrote to his parents telling them he was planning to marry (a German-Jewish refugee), they shot back a scathing letter. Deeply angry, he went ahead with the wedding and wrote off his family forever. It was a measure of the man that having made up his mind he would never change it.

When he married my mother, my father took on more than he could have guessed at the time. No two people could have been more different in background or habits. My mother was highly intelligent, traumatized, neurotic, and profoundly and irredeemably untidy. This was an innate character trait reinforced by years of living with servants. My father had to show her how to hold a broom, and though she learned, she never had any real interest in it. Her wardrobe and drawers were a study in wild confusion, though which she would root whenever she was looking for something. Her untidiness affected even her professional life, as she admitted; she would collect a rare specimen, preserve it carefully, and then wrap it carelessly and throw it haphazardly into a box for mailing. My father by contrast was extremely neat. The garage where he kept his tools was always meticulous and his large wooden tool chest was highly organized, with every tool clean and its correct place. Over the years he took more and more responsibility for the housework, simply because he wanted to live in a reasonably neat house, while my mother spent most of her efforts in the garden. She was a wonderful gardener and her gardens were always notable, even when we were living in Mount Isa and growing anything was an effort. I never heard my father complain about my mother's housekeeping. He was proud of her intelligence and resigned to her failings, not the least of which was to nag relentlessly until he finally lost his temper, in which case she would burst into tears.

Of course every marriage requires compromise, and to do her justice, our mother made many too. She learned to cook plain Australian food, on which my father complimented her often, though in fact she would have preferred to reproduce the German and continental dishes of her youth. She lived for twenty years in a small outback-mining town where beer was the chief social lubricant and for much of the time she had few friends. She had a sincere lack of interest in money and not much skill in managing it. (When I was young I remember trailing after her into a Brisbane pawnshop where she pawned her wristwatch, yet again.) But everyone we knew was no better off than we, and usually worse off, since our father was a skilled carpenter and was paid well. Also he didn't drink in the pub after work, which is where a lot of paychecks went. Our father never wanted his wife to work; it was source of pride for him that he could provide for his family. When our mother did begin working after years in Mount Isa, it was a terrible blow to him, compounded by the fact that she applied for, and got, a job as kitchen maid in the local hotel. But sending me, and later Lesley, off to boarding school required money, and our mother wanted to prove to herself that she would work and keep a job. Later she worked as a library assistant shelving books in the new Mount Isa library. When she got a degree in library science and was eventually appointed director of the local, and then regional library system, our father was proud of her and glad that she at last had an interest that Mount Isa had previously not provided.

A year after they were married I was born. My father wanted to have a son, but as the first child he welcomed me. Shortly after I was born the war started, and though he waited several years in deference to my mother's pleas, he signed up in the Royal Air Force as soon as he was able. He certainly could have got a deferment, but I am sure that he very much wanted to serve. At the time of his enlistment in 1944, his height was five foot nine inches and he weighed 136 pounds. During the remainder of the war he served mostly in New Guinea. At his enlistment he told the only lie that I know of. In the enlistment papers he was required to give his father's name and address, so that his parents could be notified in case of his death. In the space for father's name he put "deceased." (Did he know his mother was dead, and his father in his mind was certainly dead to him?) In the space for Nationality he wrote "British", then, doubtless instructed by the clerk, crossed it out and wrote above "Irish".

We have a picture of my father with his unit in New Guinea. In the photo he is standing in the back row smiling slightly, looking, I think, happy. While he was in New Guinea he made a shell pendant for me out of mother of pearl, which I still have, as well as an inlaid wooden jewellery box for box for my mother.

RAAF, New Guinea, c. 1944. John Scott is in the back row, fifth from the left.

Before he enlisted, my mother got pregnant again. It was the boy he was hoping for, but the pregnancy ended in a late term miscarriage. In 1944, however, Lesley was born. My father might have been at least somewhat disappointed. He had previously decided that it would be irresponsible to have more than two children and so his chance of having a son was gone. He had a strong belief that the world was overpopulated, and as well he felt that he could not afford to give more than two children the opportunity of a decent education. Lesley feels that she suffered the repercussions of that disappointment. He was overly critical of her and I probably remained his favourite. However, if he had had a son I think he would have been just as hard on him as his father had been on him. Incidentally, after the birth of Roger my father wrote to me the only letter I ever received from him. He congratulated us on the birth and said as tactfully as he could that three children were more than enough in a crowded world. At that time the world population was about three billion.

After the Second World War ended our family embarked on an adventure in a caravan that Dad built on the back of a former Army truck. They took to the road, my mother to collect for the Field Museum and he to look for contracting work at cattle and sheep stations in the outback. This project did not last long. I got very thin and anemic and my mother's collecting and his work did not pay enough to make the venture worthwhile. Of course my father loved the bush, though my mother was a lot less keen on it. For years they took separate holidays, he to fish near the Gulf of Carpentaria and she to the coast and Brisbane. In the months we were travelling I remember once he took me to a waterhole at sunset to see a huge flock of black cockatoos come down to drink. Generally though he took neither Lesley nor me anyplace where we might be exposed to bad language or rough manners. If we had been boys I am sure it would have been different. This pattern continued after we moved to Mount Isa, and Lesley is still resentful that he did not take her to any of the interesting places that he found around there, and that she would have loved.

After we moved to Mount Isa my father quickly moved up the job ladder until he was Clerk of Works (building supervisor) for Mount Isa Mines. He took architecture correspondence courses and his designs were implemented at M.I.M. But then his boss died unexpectedly and the replacement person wanted his own people. My father was moved to a foreman's job that may have paid as much but required shift work, and that was much less responsible. Any chance of advancement was curtailed, as well as the opportunity to do interesting work. (After he lost the position of Clerk of Works, three young graduate engineers filled his job - portent of a worldwide trend.)

While they were still in Mount Isa our parents planned their retirement close to Brisbane, and with money they had saved they bought a house on a large double lot on the Redcliffe peninsula. It was entirely in character that they rented their newly purchased retirement house to a family with many kids who had no references, and to whom no one else would rent. The family repaid their generosity by completely trashing the place, down to holes in the walls and floors and filling the yard with junk. When my parents moved to Brisbane and saw the house my father said he thought that it was beyond repair. But he set to work, and over the next few years he fixed and rebuilt, dragged away the trash, built a "bush house" and dug gardens for my mother, who was at last given soil that fully repaid her efforts. The project of renovation was a real interest for him. During his years working in Mount Isa my father had had many skin cancers, all treated successfully with radioactive creams. He had planned to spend his retirement fishing in Moreton Bay, and bought a boat and outboard motor. But a doctor told him that even the reflected sunlight off the water was too much for his skin, and that he should give up the idea of fishing. He sold the boat, and after that spent his time working on the house, making furniture and occasionally going to local Masonic meetings. It was here that my father confronted another problem. Though he was brought up in Sydney he was quintessentially a man of the bush. He had a few good mates in his life, but he never did do well in hail-fellow-well-met situations. Besides, years of working in the noisy Mines environment had given him tinnitus, so that he could not hear in large groups, and was increasingly deaf in any case. Gradually his interest in gatherings of any size diminished and then petered out all together.

After a while our parents moved into a smaller, single floor, brick house in the same general area, (Margate), and again my father spent quite a lot of time fixing it up, and again he built a large bush house for our mother's orchids and cacti. And when all was done, and he had made what furniture he could, including a very nice grandfather clock that he built from a kit and that Lesley has now, he ran out of things to do. He lost an eye to a melanoma tumour, and his other eye was perhaps impaired by cataract; his hearing was bad, and I think he felt very isolated. On his doctor's orders he took long rambles around Redcliffe. I went on one of these once, and though I was initially impatient with his slow pace, at the end of the walk he was still going and I was tuckered out. In the afternoon a neighbour would come over and they would drink beer together. My father had never been a big drinker; the neighbour was a pleasant but stupid man, and those afternoons could not have provided much stimulation. He drank more than usual and was often irritable.

In contrast with my father, my mother, who had spent many years lonely and isolated in Mount Isa, found herself in Redcliffe surrounded by people who shared her interests. She joined the Orchid Society and the Cactus Society, and took multiple courses at the University of the Third Age (U3A). She won prizes at local and the Brisbane show for her intricate knitted lace and needlepoint. Everywhere she met interesting people and impressed them with her extraordinary memory and intelligence. She was honoured by the Queensland Museum and gave two lectures (without notes) to sizeable audiences on her collecting trips in Queensland fifty-five years before. She entered a memory research project at the University of Queensland and did so well on the test that she was invited back several times. She wrote to people all over the country whom she heard on the ABC, and many wrote back. My father was proud of her, as he always had been, but he had to have noticed her variety of interests and compared them with his own narrowing sphere. He told me more than once something he had been told many years earlier: "At the beginning of a marriage, the man walks ahead of the wife. During their middle years, they walk side by side. At the end of their life, the wife walks ahead and leads the husband."

And then our father got melanoma again, first on his big toe, (which hadn't seen the sun for at least sixty years) and then throughout his body. His doctor was fond him and told him the news sadly. Then he said, "I can order chemotherapy and radiation, and it will prolong your life, but it won't save it. You must decide what you want to do." It was entirely characteristic that my father decided against treatment. I came to Australia for several weeks during that summer of 1991. My father was not in pain, but he felt increasingly ill, and spent more and more time in bed. My mother would sit bedside his bed for hours, reading her book and holding his hand, and it seemed to comfort him. Eventually he went to the hospital, where he lapsed into semi-consciousness. It was at the hospital that for the first time I thought he was in pain. His doctor had promised him that he would not let him suffer, and I asked the nurse to give him morphine. She advised me that it would shorten his life, but with the doctor's approval gave him an injection. He fell into a deep sleep and never woke up. He died almost exactly three months after the diagnosis, just as the doctor had predicted. His death was, I thought, entirely characteristic of the man. None of those stages of denial and anger and grieving that we all read about; he died bravely, decently, and without a fuss.

Just before he died, I asked my father whether he ever thought about his family. I meant his family in Sydney, as he knew right away. Without hesitation he said: "*This* is my family." So he never forgave them. Perhaps I should have pushed him, but I didn't. Somehow I thought that it would be easy to find those lost relatives. I couldn't have been more wrong.

Lesley's husband John is a man who, more than most, likes a quest. He launched himself into the search to find out more about our father's family. He checked birth records in Belfast; he checked shipping manifests. He even paid a Sydney detective agency to check whatever it is detectives check. He found our father's wartime records, and found out that enlistment lie about his father. And that is all he found - beyond that, not a thing, until much later the passenger manifest from the *Dorset* showed up. Our mother went to Sydney during the war and said that at that time the family was still in the phone book. (Was it John Scott, Builder whom she saw? I think so.) After John had done his best and finally given up, my sister constructed a theory. She suggested that the Scotts adopted my father - either the child of a relative or someone else's child. Lots of children were adopted at that time in the early twentieth century and large numbers of them came to Australia. Perhaps he was ashamed of his murky beginnings? Perhaps his father was harsh and critical of him because he was an adopted child? Or perhaps none of this is true, which I believe, and which the record of the *Dorset* seems to suggest. Why would John Scott want an adopted child to take over the family business, after all? We simply don't know any of this, and as the years go on it seems as if we will never know, which is a shame and which leaves a void in our lives.

In the end I know that my father liked secrets. He never gossiped and would preserve a confidence forever. (He often told me, perfectly correctly, that I talk too much.) That inlaid jewellery box that he made in New Guinea for my mother had a carefully cut thin piece of wood at the bottom that could be lifted out so that a letter or a pound note could be hidden below invisibly. I am sure that my mother, who had no interest in keeping secrets at all, never used it to conceal anything. I found other little boxes with a false bottom. In the first Redcliffe (Clontarf) house he constructed a built-in bookcase with a certain board that when hit the right way would swing open revealing a space into which anything of value could be safely hidden. When they moved my parents took with them a sideboard into which apparently my father had built yet another hiding place. My mother showed it to Wendell, but he paid little attention and now can't remember where it was. Our son David has that sideboard now, and we still haven't been able to find any secret compartment in it, though I think it is there.

My father and my mother often said that they were glad they were born when they were, and that they didn't envy us the future. They lived long enough to see that my sister and I were the beneficiaries of an age of affluence, and that our lives have been more prosperous than theirs. We haven't experienced the Great Depression, or two World Wars, or the anti-Semitism that marred our mother's life. Still I know that our father wouldn't have wanted to live much longer, a witness to the coarsening of public life and culture, the widespread destruction of the bush he loved so much, and ever-greater erosion of the values that he believed in so deeply.

2015

APPENDIX II

Rudolf Rochocz, a long-term employee of Gebrüder Grumach, wrote twice to the Leo Baeck Center of Jewish History in New York, first in 1962 and again in 1971. Mr. Rochocz had immigrated to the United States, presumably before the war. The Center made an Internet record of these letters and we were able to obtain copies. Unfortunately Mr. Rochocz's handwriting was extremely difficult to read and the two letters repeat in some instances. Comparing the two, I have put them together, using mostly the second letter, which was longer and more structured, but including some sentences from the first in context. Dagmar Grote did the transcription of the two letters, and Dagmar Grote and Helmut Kremling did the translations. I am extremely grateful to both. R.

Leo Baeck handwritten note: "Very moving.......in its..........

Perhaps you can encourage him to write in greater detail about the firm Gebrüder Grumach."

Dear Madam Müehsam,

I believe that you will certainly find more about the firm of Gebr. Grumach, Pty. Ltd., Berlin in the Leo Baeck Institute.

I would like to submit to you documents about an honorary citizen of the city of Hohenberg, East Prussia, the founder of the firm "Brothers Grumach" (in) Berlin, my revered boss LOUIS GRUMACH. I was employed as a buyer for the firm until 1938 and saw the tragic ending....

The (wholesale/retail) textile business (of Gebr. Grumach) in Berlin was situated (on) Spandauer Ecke (on the corner of) Königstrasse at the town hall (Rotes Rathaus), opposite the world famous firm of N. Israel. Gebrüder Grumach had a well-known high-end retail business (on the first floor) and above this (were) four floors of a wholesale firm, perhaps the most notable German Enero building for textile clothing and accessories. Retailers were strictly protected and only people with wholesale licenses could purchase goods from the wholesale department. It was one of the few companies that protected legitimate individual businesses. There were 40,000 registered customers from all over Germany, but also customers from Russia, all the Balkans, and European (sic) countries came there to purchase goods. We had (a) direct connection to the main post office located right next door to us with an automated conveyor belt that enabled the sending of hundred of thousands of parcels that we franked and stamped. Along with Witt in Waiden, it was probably the largest mail order business in Germany. The giant catalogues with copper plate engravings, which were forwarded half yearly to 40,000 customers, were masterpieces, and approximately 350 employees dealt with the written orders and the customers who called there.

Louis Grumach along with his brother had opened a small textile store and while the brother stayed in the shop, Louis Grumach travelled. The constantly growing business was incorporated (A.G.) as a family business after the death of the brother. I was employed there as an apprentice, salesman, fitter, and finally buyer until 1938. When I was an apprentice in 1924 or a bit earlier, the "old one" paid his employees' wages in the cellar in gold. He often came through my department murmuring, " The 'dicke Fresser' (fat glutton) will bankrupt us, all he buys is worthless", and he was always dry and brusque, but he promoted me, and in all his dealings he was honest to the bone.

The old fellow agreed to turn over to me 100,000 marks for purchases, and after two years my department had accumulated more than half a million. And there were larger departments, like wool, tricots, stockings, and Grumach's well-known prime (?) goods.

On a lighter note, Louis Grumach loved to stand at the entrance of the wholesale business to greet the clients. Once when a man with a long beard and stooped posture entered, he greeted him, "How are you, young man? Fifty years ago I saw you playing marbles when I was on the road and visited your father..."

Our Director was the especially able Richard Neuhäuser, Doctor of National Economics, (who was) very much revered by us all. I am forwarding to you Richard Neuhäuser's (1928) lecture on customer service, with notations. If anybody is worthy of remaining in peoples' memory, it was this elegant, attractive man, whose abilities and honesty served as a model of a Jewish/German businessman. Director Neuhäuser

(Louis Grumach's son-in-law) lost his wife while she was young, and he had a daughter who often conducted archeological (sic) expeditions. She must still be alive, and I would give a lot to see that daughter again.

The collapse of the Jewish economy with the appearance of Hitler was also horribly apparent in our firm. Old Grumach died in 1933 in the little office at the business he occupied as Chairman of the Board. He was about ninety years old, a lean man about six foot tall. I enclose a photo....

Neuhäuser carried his leather chair into the kitchen on the lowest floor, where he sealed all the entrances and placed a warning outside, "Danger, Gas!" We found him the next morning.

Our Personnel Director was Eduard Lichtenfeld. He was married to a Christian and went abroad. He lived in England, survived the war and supposedly has a business on the Kurfürstendamm.

Director Fuld shot himself in his office.

After the death of the old redheaded buyer Liebert, and buyer Alexander, Richard Tauber took over the purchasing department. *[Tauber was the head accountant who blackmailed Richard Neuhäuser. He later became director of the company.]* This individual had a horrific effect on Lichtenfeld and Neuhäuser. He was well situated in the Party and a district leader (Gauleiter), and on the orders of Goebbels started the cleansing of non-Aryans. The climate became unbearable, former friends and lower employees displayed arrogance and made openly offensive remarks. One buyer, Emanuel Wolff returned after a prison stay with his hair shorn and his body emaciated. On November 1st, 1938 the doorman prohibited entrance to us; only pure Aryan employees had the right to work there. This Tauber fellow now supposedly has a store on the Hauptstrasse (Main St.) in Schöneberg.

It was a good education for one's life to grow from youngster to maturity in the firm Grumach, always in the environment of a business leadership that really wanted to serve its customers with quality and moderate margins of profit. Like Julius Berger, who produced German quality work, so Grumach had served only with quality, and (in the same way) most German Jews produced goods of first-rate quality.

Respectfully,
Rudolf Rochocz
2081 Joan Drive
San Leandro, CA

APPENDIX III

GABRIELE NEUHÄUSER

A (1997) biographical sketch by Dr. Steve Van Dyck, Senior Curator of Vertebrates, Queensland Museum.

Gabriele Neuhäuser (1911-), scientist, was born in Berlin, Germany the daughter of Richard Neuhäuser, businessman, and Meta, nee Grumach, both of Jewish descent. Determining at age six to be a zoologist, Gabriele abandoned dolls for books, and before the age of eight had realized the bio-geographical inconsistencies in the assemblage of animals (kangaroos, tigers, tapirs) in *The Swiss Family Robinson*. To adjust her appetite for books to the limits of her reading material, she tried reading books upside down. This technique slowed her down for about two weeks, after which the pages, whether attacked from the bottom or the top, were devoured at an equally voracious pace. By the age of ten she had refurbished her childhood nursery with aquaria in which she bred South American cichlids, and cages where she kept an assortment of finches and softbills, though she yearned in vain for unaffordable expensive Australian Zebra finches. Ironically, in sixteen years she would be in Muckadilla, Queensland, and later in Mount Isa, surrounded by flocks of the birds.

Following her early schooling in Berlin, Gabriele studied science at Freiburg University near the Black Forest. She embarked on a doctoral thesis in 1933, the topic of which was suggested by Dr. Hermann Pohle, Curator of Mammals at the Berlin Museum of Natural History, who had been approached by a delegation from the Turkish Ministry of Agriculture looking for solutions to rodent plagues in their country. The consequence of Pohle's insistence that she learn to shoot, skin, and preserve specimens before departing for Turkey was to be realized a few years later when self-preservation demanded her own speedy departure from Germany. By 1936 Gabriele had received her Doctorate for the *Muridae of Asia Minor*. In Turkey she acquired a saluki, presented to her as a mark of respect before she left the country, and a Great Horned Owl she could not bear to leave Turkey without. She could not possibly accommodate it, but she managed to find a good (big) home for it. By then both her parents had died, and she realized that the options [in Germany] for a 25-year old Jewish mammologist were painfully limited in the festering political climate of the day.

So having established herself as a competent museum collector and eminently capable of looking after herself in foreign lands, Gabriele Neuhäuser accepted a fortuitous offer from G.H.H. Tate of the American Museum of Natural History to collect mammals in northern Australia. Obtaining a "non-Aryan" passport and a two-year Australian visa, she sailed to Sydney on the P & O vessel *Narkunda* in June 1937. There Ellis Troughton of the Australian Museum received her with superficial cordiality which belied a deep professional jealousy, prompting him to write to Canberra and Brisbane in an attempt to have her requests for collecting permits rejected on account of her connection with Tate. This worked in Canberra, but failed with Heber Longman, Director of the

Queensland Museum, who assisted her in obtaining permits, offered to dispatch her material overseas (in exchange for some token specimens) and arranged for J. Edgar Young, an honorary collector, to accompany her to Cairns in the new Chevrolet utility truck she had purchased in Fortitude Valley [Brisbane] for £326.

Young, who never collected with Gabriele, introduced her to the North's leading naturalists, Frederick Parkhurst Dodd and Hugo Flecker, before leaving her in Cairns. From there she proceeded to collect (mostly alone) throughout the Atherton Tableland at Yungaburra, Lake Barrine, Evelyn, Mount Spurgeon, Mount Carbine, and Mount Malloy. Forever challenged by her innate distaste for killing animals, she found some comfort in rationalizing that she was collecting from isolated patches of Tableland rainforest destined for clearing. Later in 1938, accompanied by a nature-keen timber worker, Sid Liptrott, she left for Coen, then a frontier outpost. Determined to collect in the distant rainforest, she employed two Aborigines from a Mission, and sought help with packhorses from stockman and prospector, [Maxwell] John Scott. Scott, full of pity, admiration, or perhaps both, offered to accompany the intrepid 27 year-old to the edge of the Rocky Scrub, which they reached on horseback two and a half days later. Their tents could not be safely set up before they dispatched fourteen deathadders from the site. Forced out after two weeks due to lack of provisions, Gabriele left Coen to collect through Cloncurry, Malbon, Pentland, and Quamby.

The union of John Scott and Gabriel Neuhäuser six months later in the Cairns registry office began a marriage which would see them first in

Perth, in Brisbane where their two daughters were born, then Mount Isa. [Living in] Mount Isa between 1950 and 1970, Gabriele became [Mount Isa and Regional] librarian and husband John, Clerk of Works for Mount Isa Mines. They finally retired in Brisbane in 1970. In spite of overtures from G.H.H. Tate for Gabriele to supply [more] Australian specimens to the American Museum of Natural History [after the war], she realized after some collecting trips that this was no longer financially viable. Instead she devoted herself to raising her daughters, both of whom were later to graduate from the University of Queensland.

Gabriele Scott genuinely shrinks from words like "extraordinary", "brave hearted", "intrepid", and "courageous". She modestly dismisses the personal dangers she may have been in by responding that she was "quite plain" and was therefore not at much risk. However, in her day the isolated North was a place that cultivated and tolerated a full spectrum of eccentric behaviours. While she was in Coen, non-working Aborigines were still being rounded up, manacled, and marched in chain gangs to local Missions. There is no doubt that Gabriele is a remarkable woman, an outstanding collector, and a solitary figure in her time. Even by way of voucher specimens her efforts significantly enriched the Queensland Museum's mammal and bird collections. Many specimens bearing a "Neuhäuser" label are still the objects of current research, often being the only examples of that provenance available. Her life, reading like a movie script, homogeneously blended scholar, explorer and professional collector, [with] spouse, parent, and grandmother.